The Traveling Sketcher: *City*

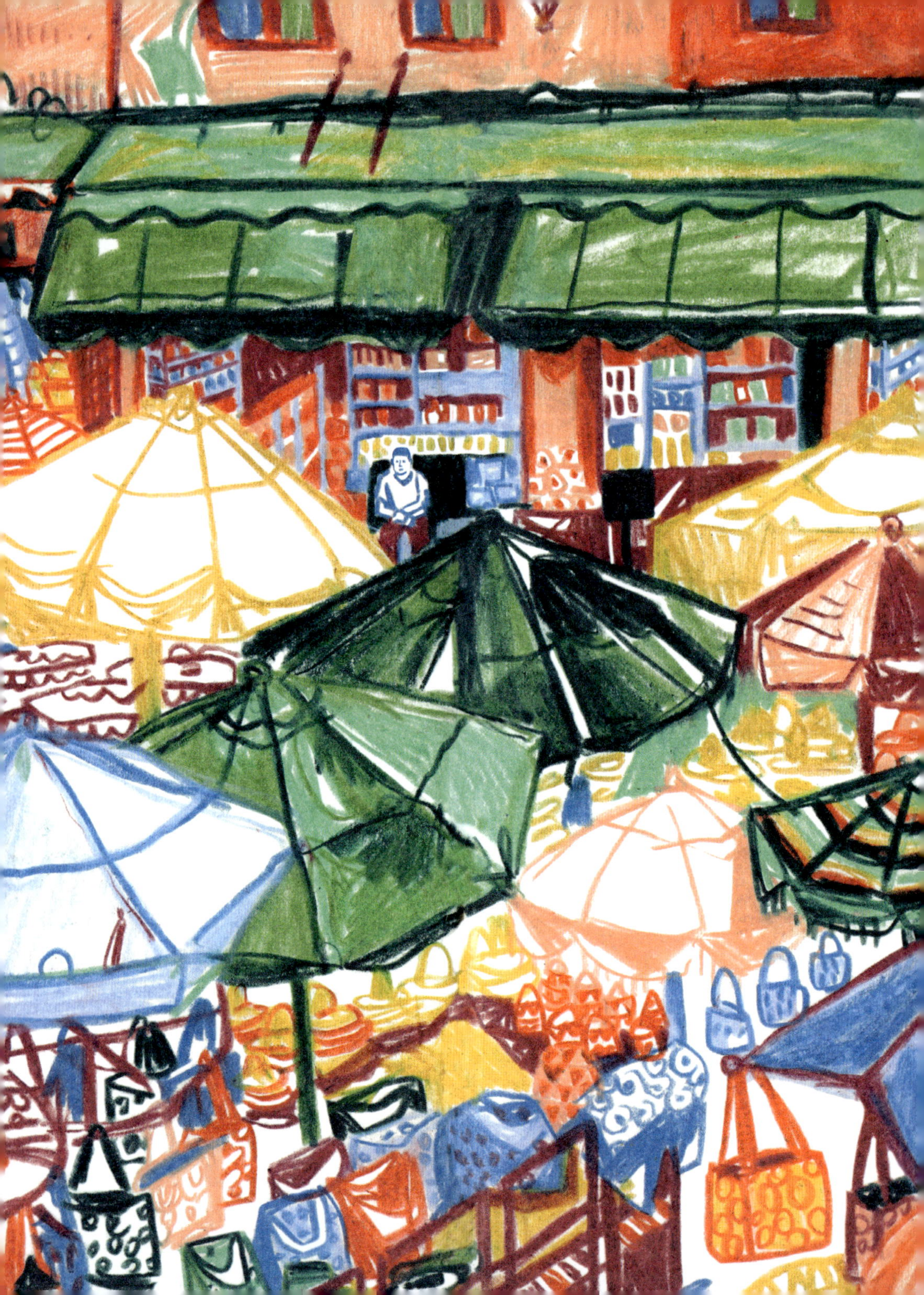

The Traveling Sketcher: *City*

LEARN TO DRAW YOUR TRAVEL MEMORIES

Alice Mawdsley

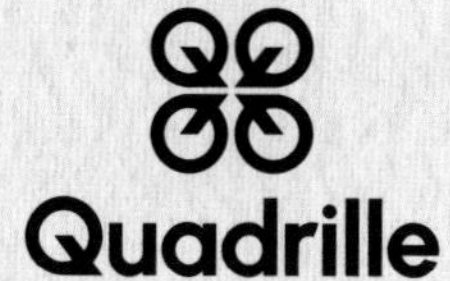

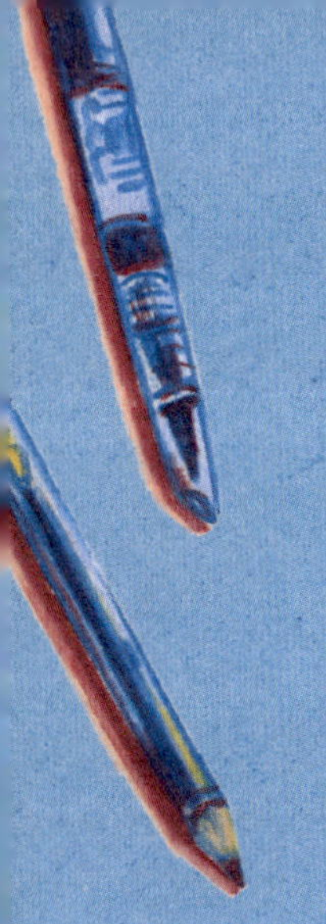

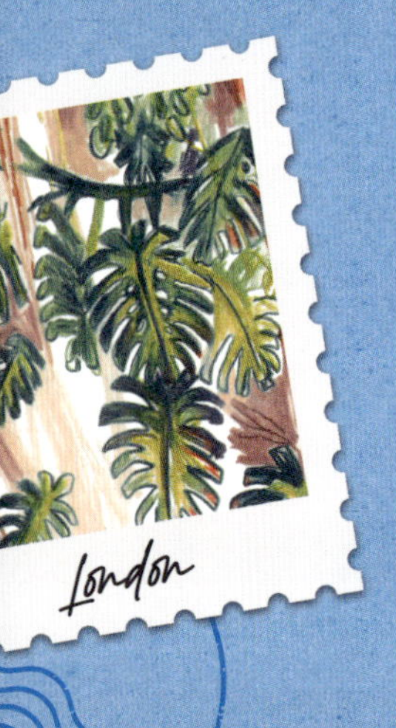
London

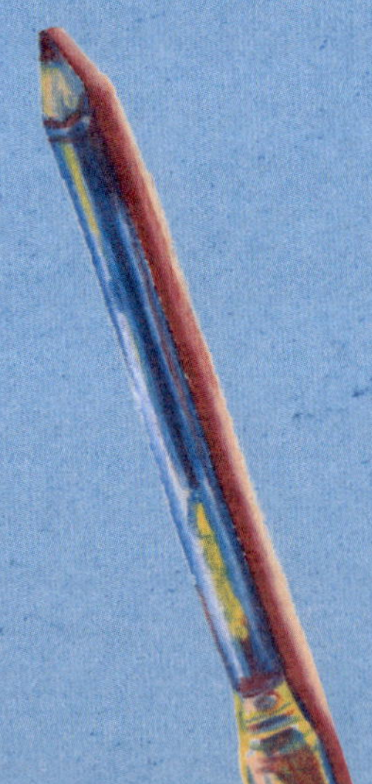

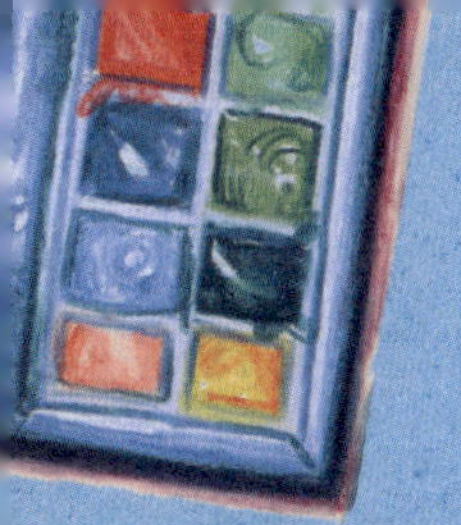

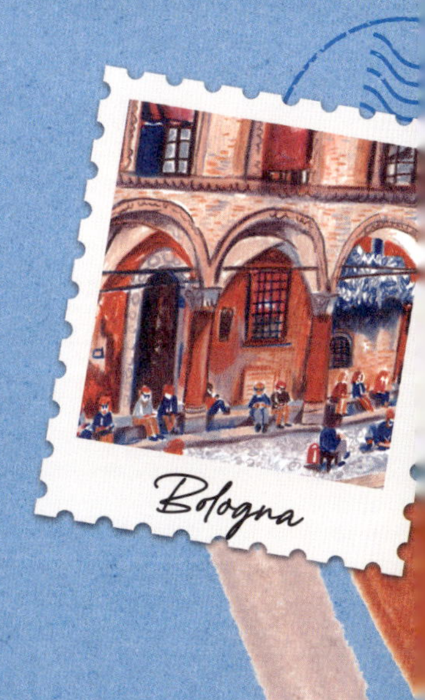
Bologna

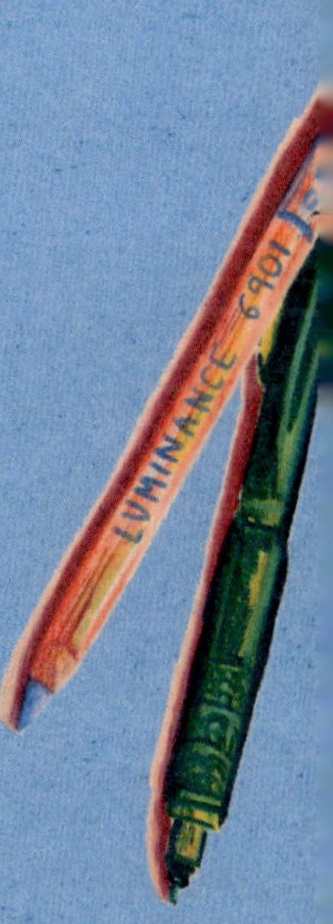
LUMINANCE 6901

hello and welcome

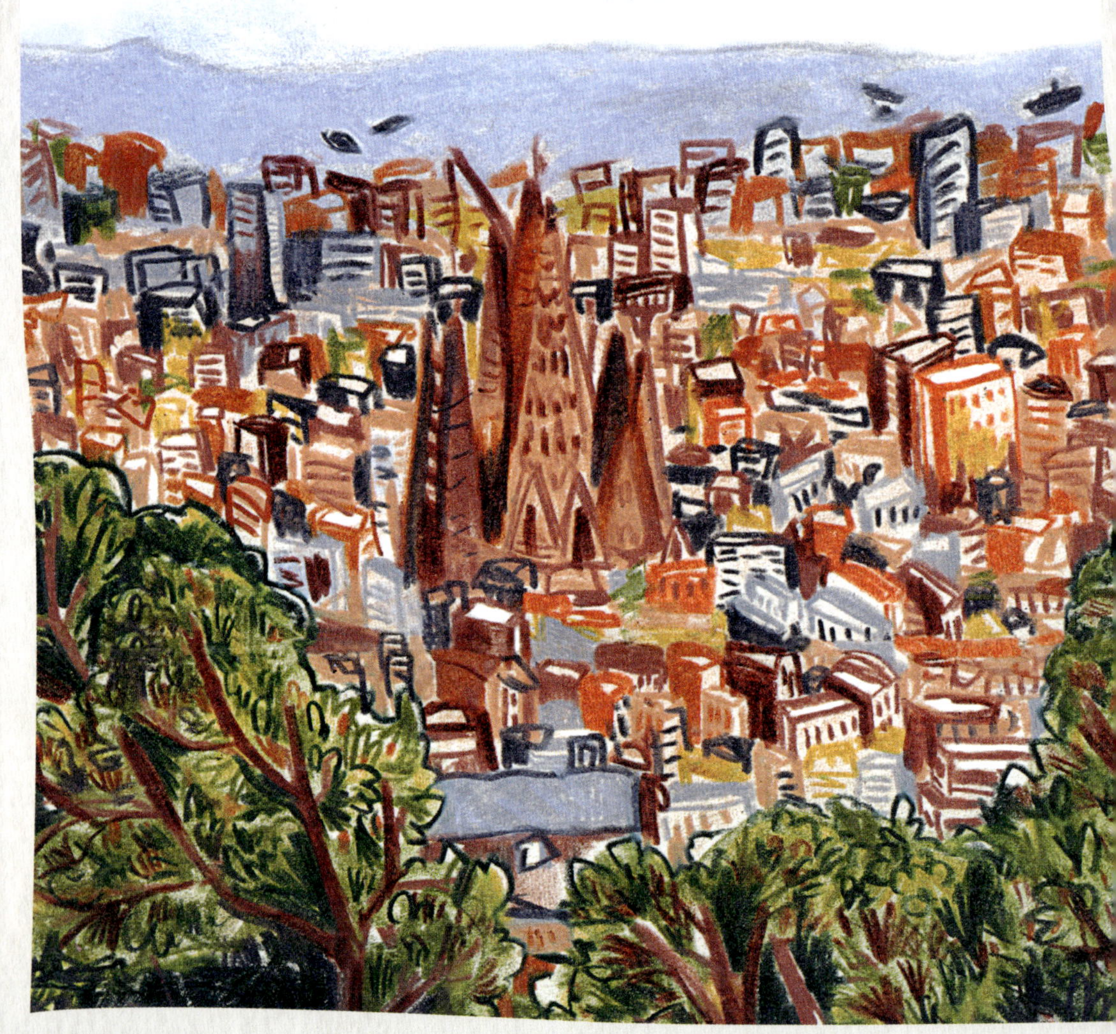

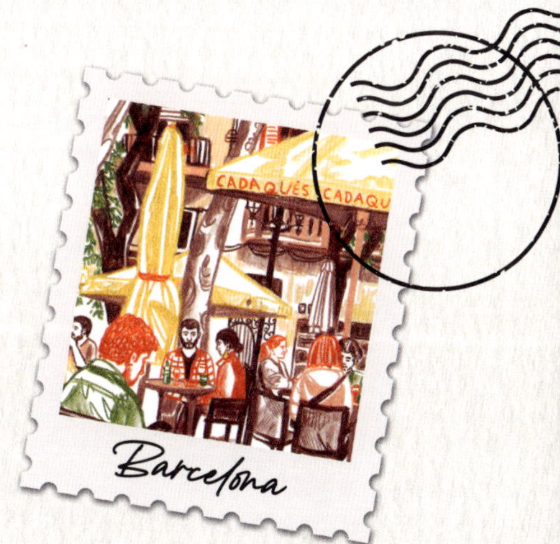

YOU ARE NOT A CAMERA

Drawing – 'a picture or diagram made with a pencil, pen or crayon'[1] – is a magical, universal language that allows you to communicate across language barriers. Drawing on location – leaving the confines of your desk and capturing 'live' images – is an even more enchanted act, which not only develops your art skills but also teaches you about the world around you.

Creativity has always played a big part in my life. Whether it was acting, playing music, photography, writing or creating art, I am so grateful to have been raised in a household that supported creativity. I was also fortunate enough to travel in Europe with my family as a child. My dad was the planner in the family, aiming to help us to learn and discover by experiencing life from a local's perspective on these trips.

These early experiences culminated in a degree in illustration at Falmouth University, by the sea in Cornwall, England. It was during this time that I found out about reportage illustration, and was immediately captivated. Reportage illustration is a combination of journalism and art, focused on human interactions and connection. It allows you to use illustration as a way of sharing events, places and people's stories to educate, inspire and help others.

The beauty in drawing on location is its openness. People are often curious about the act. It becomes a conversation starter, inviting others to look, connect and share their stories.

In a heavily digital society, there is a peaceful charm in spending time creating traditionally. Stepping away

[1] *Oxford English Dictionary*

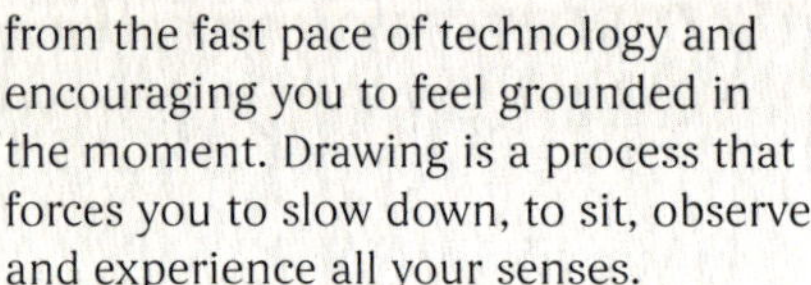

from the fast pace of technology and encouraging you to feel grounded in the moment. Drawing is a process that forces you to slow down, to sit, observe and experience all your senses.

Through illustration you are able to communicate much more than just the subject itself. Photography has a lens, which creates distance between you and the subject. When you bring out a camera, people will often change their behavior, with an awareness - and sometimes cynicism - to it. When you bring out a sketchbook there is a softness and curiosity.

You are not a camera. Your drawing is not intended to be a copy of the location; it is a recreation of your experiences and thoughts, and an artistic representation of the essence of your surroundings. Drawings capture events as they unfold, layers of time coming together in a world that is constantly moving and changing. Every mark tells a story: the heat of the day, energy of the location, the season it was drawn. There is beauty in the intimacy and spontaneity of drawing that can't be replicated with a camera.

For me, illustration is about much more than just creating. It is the thing that keeps me going.

As a traveling illustrator living with rare and chronic health conditions that cause pain and fatigue - including MCAS, POTS and HMS - illustration has become more than a profession. I went through a traumatic five-year journey to reach a diagnosis, and even now, I continue to face challenges every day. Amid everything, drawing has become my way of staying grounded and present.

It has been a constant that has helped me see the positives in life, giving me strength, connection and a way to keep moving forward.

I know how scary, isolating and exhausting it can be to live with rare conditions. Through my illustration projects, I always look for ways to share unheard voices, to support, educate and inspire. I never want anyone to feel defined by their diagnosis.

This is why I am so passionate about sharing illustration with others. Through my own drawing experiences, I have seen how it connects us, shifts our perspective and helps us find beauty in the smallest moments. By sharing my own experiences and teaching, I hope to encourage more people to get out and be creative. I would love to inspire others to see the power in art and to continue doing the things they enjoy, no matter what obstacles they find themselves facing. So next time you are traveling, debating whether to bring out your sketchbook or not, do it!

I am so excited to be sharing all the tips I have picked up across my city travels. Through this book you will learn the fundamentals of illustration, from color theory to composition. The main chapters dive into different subjects you are likely to come across in a city, such as people, architecture and nature.

It is such a beautiful skill to be able to capture the world around you in your sketchbook; to use your artistic eye and own travel experiences to share a new perspective on everyday life. I hope this book inspires you and gives you the confidence to go out and capture the beauty of city life.

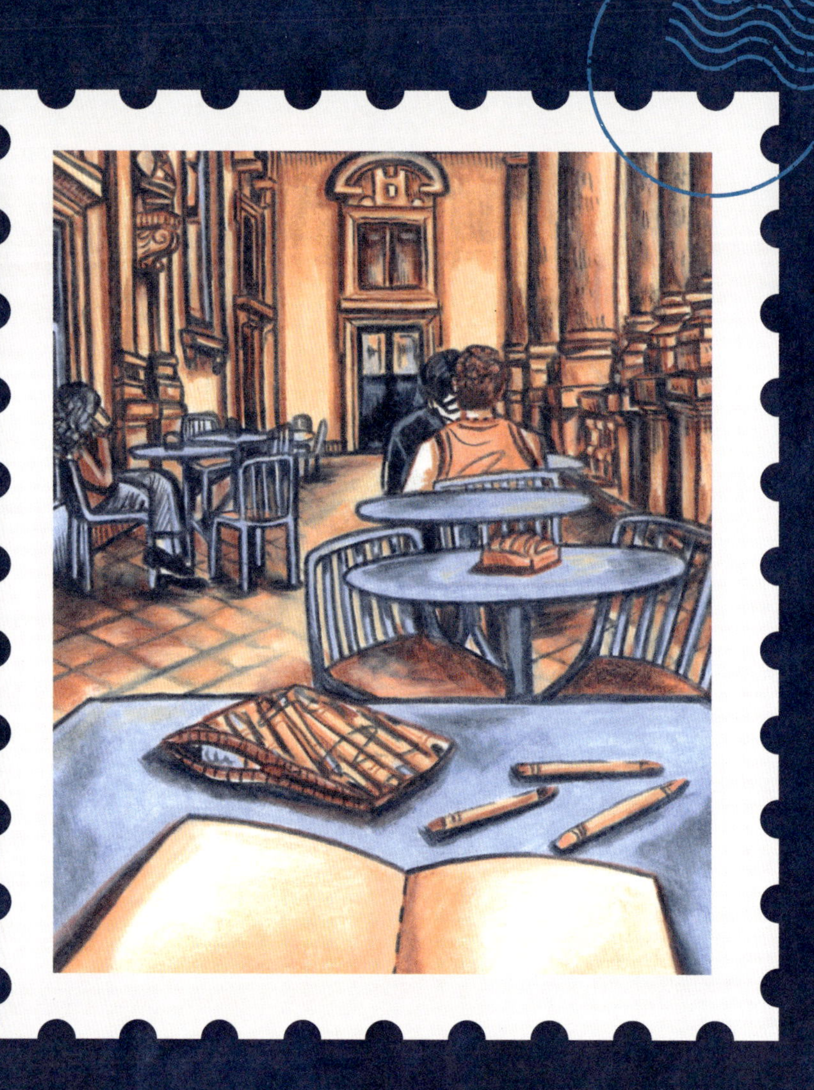

CHAPTER ONE

Introduction *to* Location Drawing

HOW TO DRAW ON LOCATION

Drawing on location is more than simply putting pencil to paper – it's about slowing down, engaging all your senses and creating illustrations that tell a story. To craft a drawing that truly immerses the viewer in the place, there are a few things you need to consider before even setting foot outside.

In this section, I will guide you through everything you need to begin: starting a sketchbook, finding inspiration, developing your style, choosing the right materials, selecting drawing spots, and feeling confident and comfortable on location.

HOW TO START A SKETCHBOOK

When you have just got a new sketchbook, with every page perfectly untouched, an overwhelming feeling can often creep in as you stare at the blank page. The pressure of needing to create the 'perfect' first illustration.

For the best creative outcomes, you need to release yourself from that pressure. Your sketchbook is your own safe space for experimentation and exploration as you find your artistic voice. Each drawing is a step in the right direction.

When you are creating in a space of comfort and openness rather than restraint and worry, you will see the positive difference in your illustrations.

Here are a few tips to build your confidence, find your style and get inspired when starting a sketchbook.

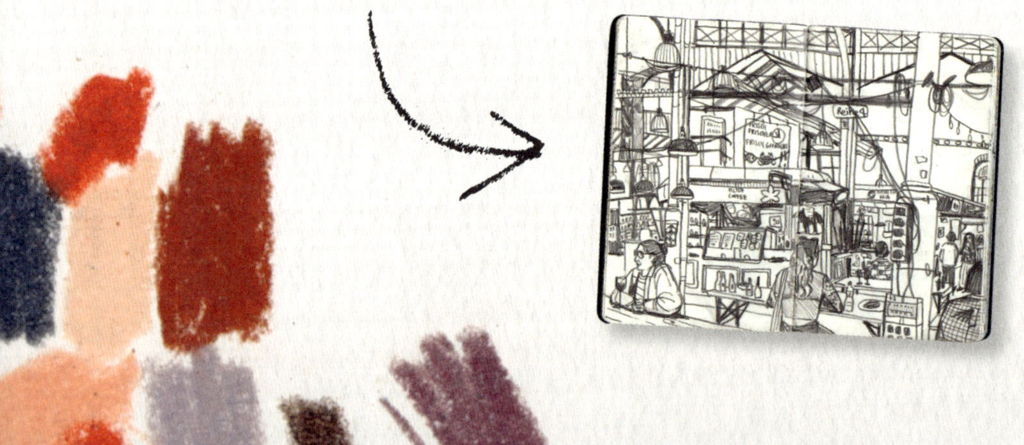

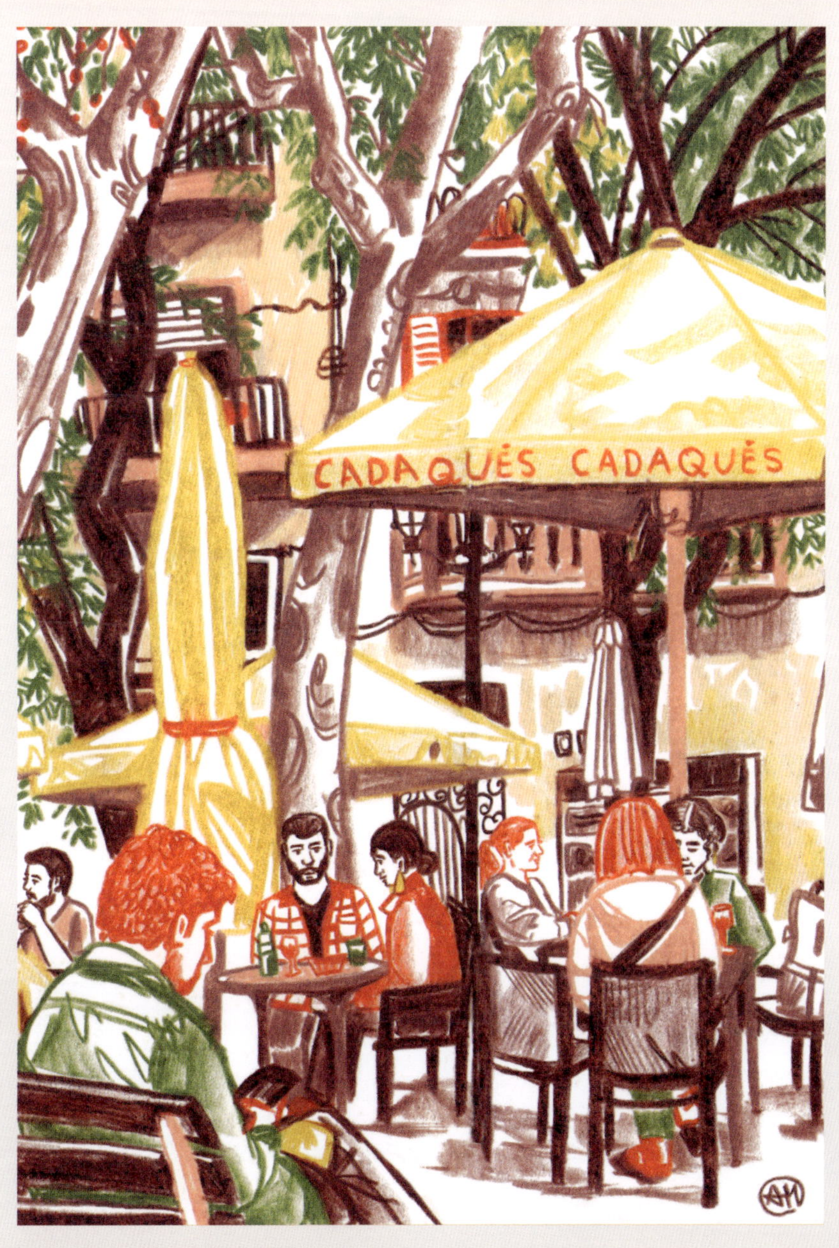
CADAQUÉS CADAQUÉS

Tip 1

TIMED DRAWINGS

Timed drawings help get rid of the pressure of creating the 'perfect' illustration. For that short time, you are solely focused on the lines you are drawing, lost in the process rather than outside factors. These timed sketches teach you how to simplify scenes quickly and translate the world into art.

It is important to spend most of your time staring at the subject rather than at the paper. You need to be observing, analyzing and learning, rather than guessing from memory.

Drawing involves muscle memory. For example, if figure drawing is something you want to improve on, the more you watch and draw people, the better you will be at proportions and creating a balanced figure. You build up a bank of poses and how people interact with their environment. So, when you are in a busy scene with lots of movement, you can continue the drawing even when the person leaves, as you have gained this confidence in the fundamentals of the figure.

Try these quick exercises

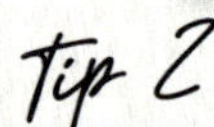

1. **60-second poses**: Sit in a location where people will be walking past, such as a café, park or market, and sketch a new person every minute. Continue this for 5–10 minutes. Focus on the gesture and posture, not details.
2. **Composition thumbnails**: Choose a location that interests you and create three compositional thumbnails (small line sketches within a rectangle). Spend two minutes on each, varying the angle, perspective or framing to capture different narratives of the same scene.
3. **Objects and shadows**: Pick three objects near you. Do a one-minute sketch of each of them to capture the basic shadow pattern and shape.

Tip 2

LINE DRAWINGS

If I am in a busy location or don't have much time, I will reach for my handy graphite pencil – a Blackwing 3B pencil (see page 20). Using just a single pencil means you focus on the lines and shapes of the subject, rather than adding the extra concern of a color palette.

Line drawings are great to develop your understanding of negative space, balance and proportion (see pages 44–48). They can also strengthen your own visual language.

When drawing, I rarely use an eraser. I follow my intuitive marks that help steer the drawing in a direction that stays true to my visual language. The point of this exercise is to develop confidence in your mark-making (see page 31). Focus on a single strong line, rather than lots of sketchy lines.

The way you hold the pencil and guide it across the paper is the foundation of your distinct style. Everyone has a unique way of drawing, even if the differences are subtle.

Line drawings don't have to be limited to graphite pencils. You could use a wet medium such as a brush pen, leaving no room for changes or second-guessing. Or you could use a single-colored pencil, which is another thing I like to do.

Try these quick exercises

1. **Continuous lines**: Draw a nearby object or person in one continuous line. Don't lift the pencil off the paper. For a challenge, try drawing an entire scene. Concentrate on the main shapes and structure without adding shading.

2. **Pen/ink drawing**: Use a brush pen or paintbrush and ink to do a line drawing of a street corner. You won't be able to erase your marks, so this will strengthen your drawing confidence.

3. **Opposite-hand drawing**: Use your non-dominant hand to sketch a figure or building. Let your intuition and loose marks guide you.

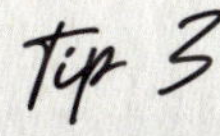

PRE-PREP YOUR PAPER

If the blank page is overwhelming, you can pre-prep your page with a simple watercolor or gouache wash, so you have a base to work with on location. Then you can draw on top with pencils, pens, inks or more watercolors and gouache.

Another option is to create a collaged background. Collect things from your trip, such as receipts or magazine snippets, and collage these together on the page.

WHERE TO FIND INSPIRATION

Inspiration is truly everywhere. For me, everyday life is mainly what inspires my illustrations. I take my sketchbook with me wherever I go to sketch daily moments, interactions and color palettes; anything that catches my attention. These become references for future projects and help define the direction of my work.

My biggest tip for finding inspiration is to go on a 'creative walk'. Bring your sketchbook and a few materials and stroll until something grabs your eye to draw or note down.

You don't have to travel far. You can walk around your local area and maybe come across a café, bookstore or a park with people sitting and relaxing. Sketch quick composition thumbnails of the scene and jot down the color palettes you like. This task forces you to slow down, truly analyze and appreciate your surroundings.

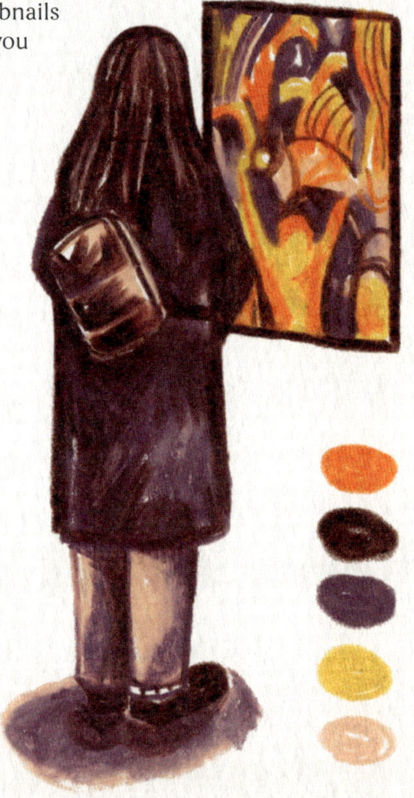

Bookstores are also great sources of inspiration. You will often find me browsing covers, looking through children's books or magazines and analyzing the layout, style and color palettes. Food packaging is another great source of design and color inspiration.

I take photos of anything I like and then reflect on why I found it interesting. Was it the font, colors or subject? Reflecting on why something appeals to you is a big part in discovering what you like.

For other great places to open your mind, visit galleries and exhibitions. When using other artwork for inspiration, remember it is to spark your own creativity and not to be copied. Be true to your own voice but use these as ways of discovering new subjects, formats, techniques and colors.

HOW TO FIND YOUR STYLE

Your style is your artistic voice, created by combining your art process, subjects you illustrate and the way you see the world. As you continue learning, experimenting and getting inspired, your art will start to evolve with you.

If you are stuck in finding your style, try answering these questions to reflect on your own creative practice and help give you direction:

1. **What do you enjoy drawing?**
2. **What do you not like drawing/avoid drawing?**
3. **What do you want to improve on?**
4. **What formats do you like? Posters, comics, books, etc.**
5. **Are there any colors you like using?**
6. **Are there any colors you don't like using?**
7. **Which artists inspire you?**
8. **Where would you like to see your work?**
9. **What do you want to say with your illustrations?**
10. **What is your favorite piece you have created?**

One of the biggest tips for finding your style is to continue creating. Make a lot of art. Explore what inspires you, what resonates with you and note what you didn't enjoy. Even the challenges and pieces that don't go as planned are great in helping you navigate what work feels the most *you*.

Push your boundaries. Continue challenging your creativity. Create for the pure enjoyment of it. When you truly enjoy it, your own artistic voice will come through and you will realize you have already found your style.

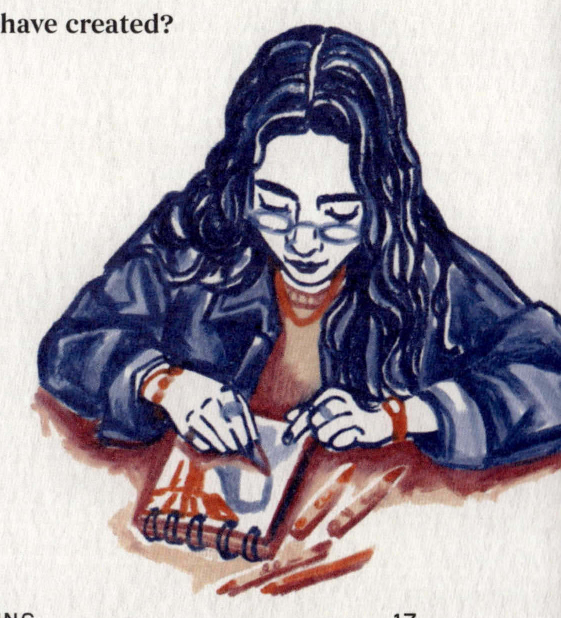

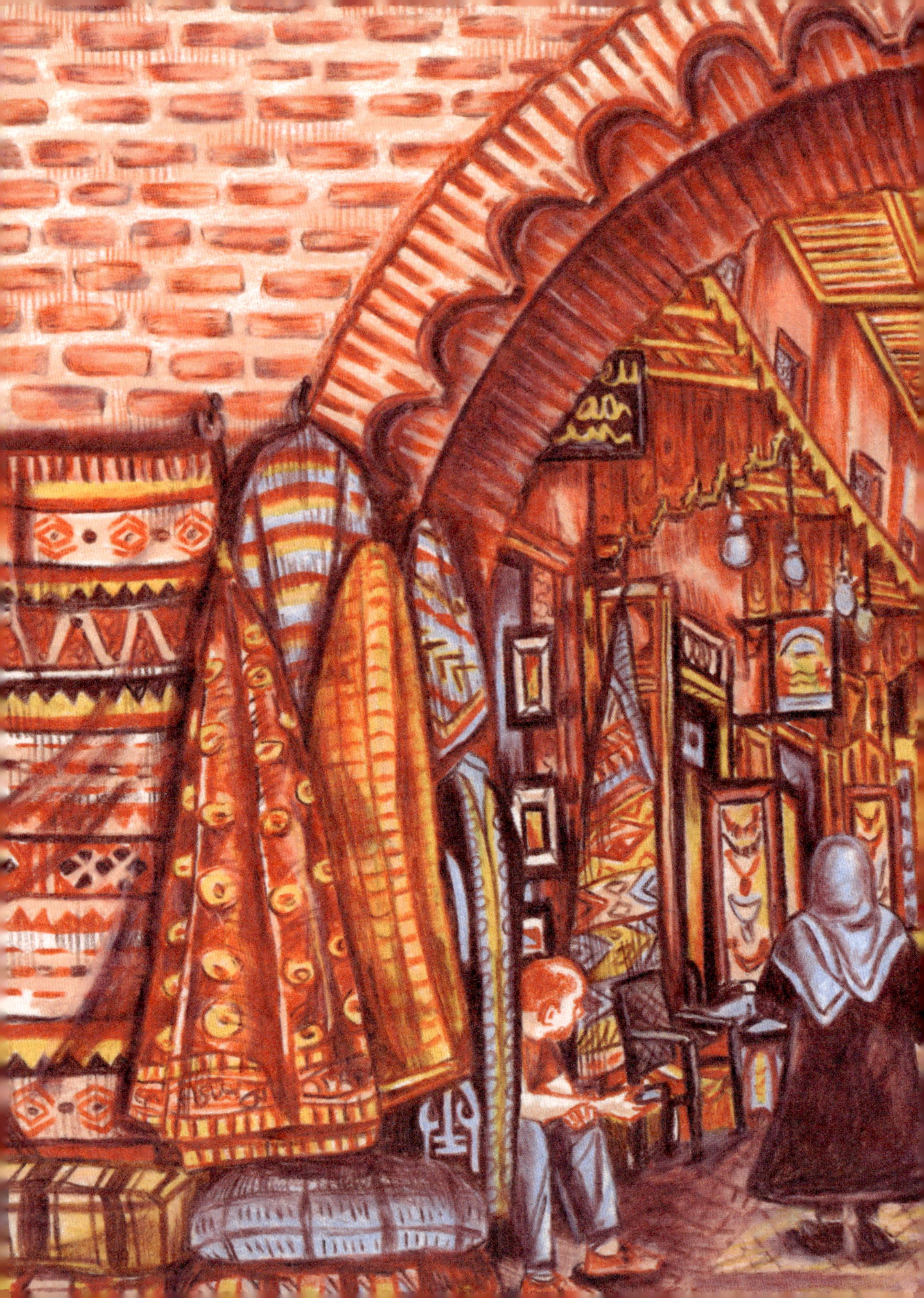

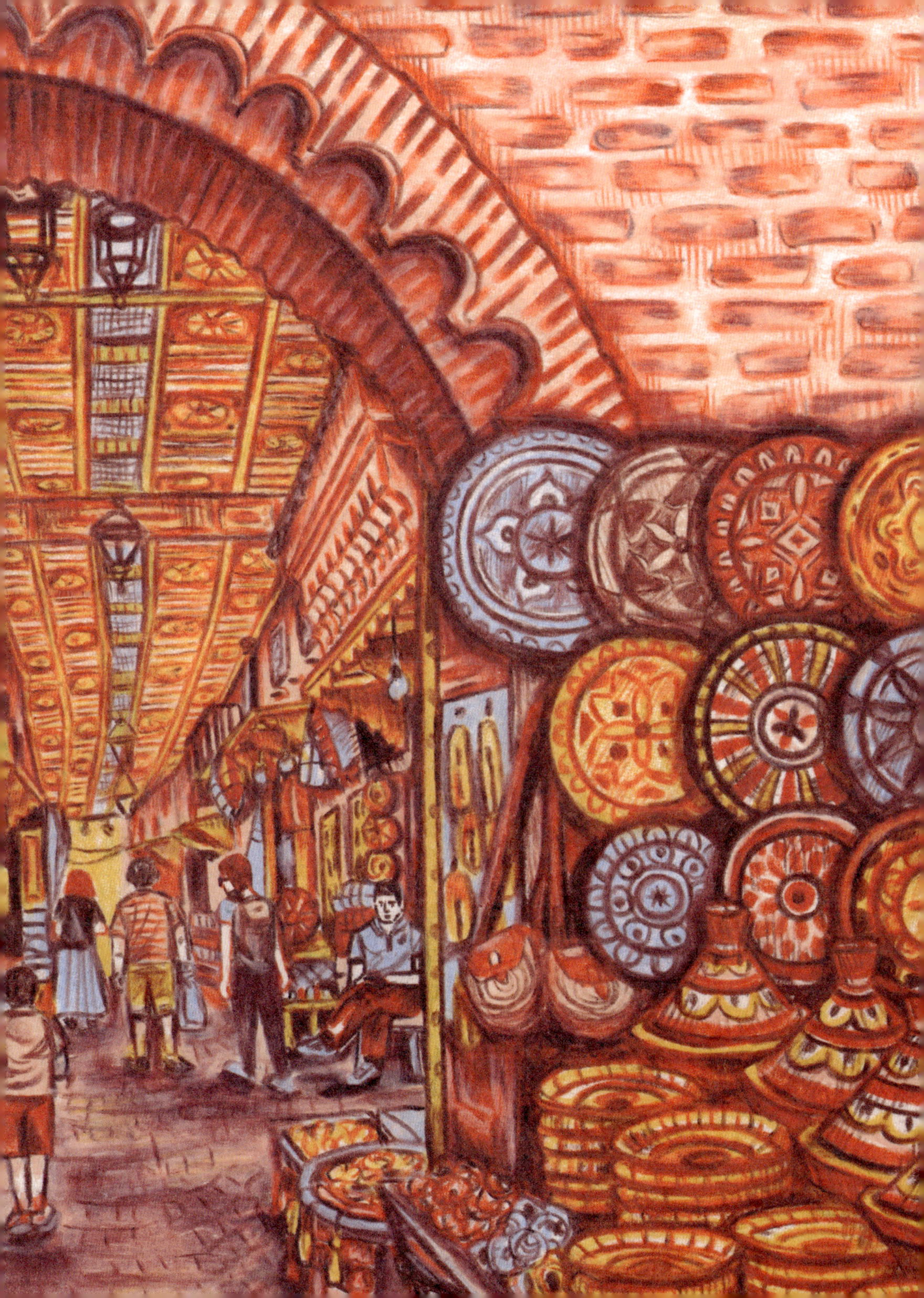

ART EQUIPMENT

WHAT MATERIALS DO I USE?

When drawing on location I like to keep to a minimal kit of materials. My sketching bag includes three main things: a sketchbook, colored pencils and graphite pencils. This makes my studio easily portable and shows how accessible drawing on location can be – all you need are a few materials to create beautiful art.

I firmly believe that you do not need the most expensive tools to produce great work. However, having experimented with a lot of different brands, there are some pieces of equipment where I feel the quality and price are worth it.

Materials in my drawing bag

- **Sketchbook**: Moleskine Art Collection 5 in x 8.25 in
- **Pencil case**
- **Colored pencils**: Caran d'Ache Luminance Pencils
- **Graphite pencils**: Blackwing Matte (4B) and Pearl (3B) Pencils
- **Eraser and sharpener**
- **Brush pen**: Pentel Colour Brush Pen in black

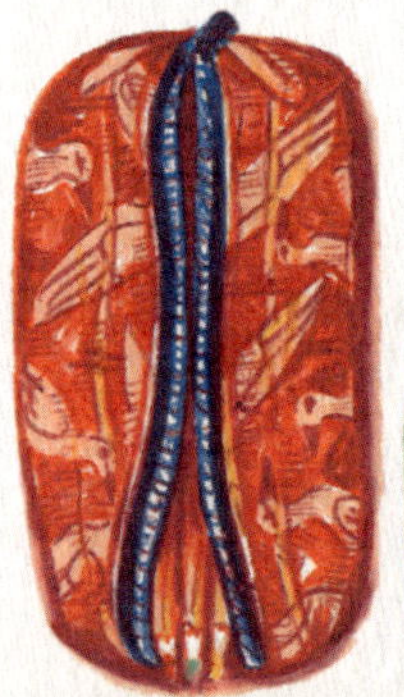

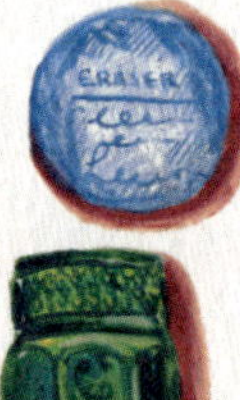

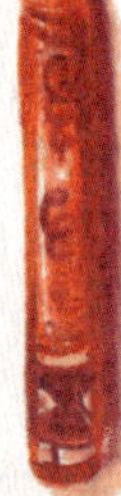

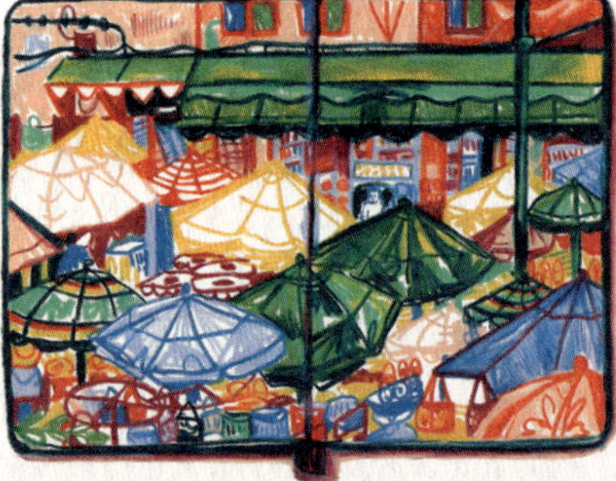

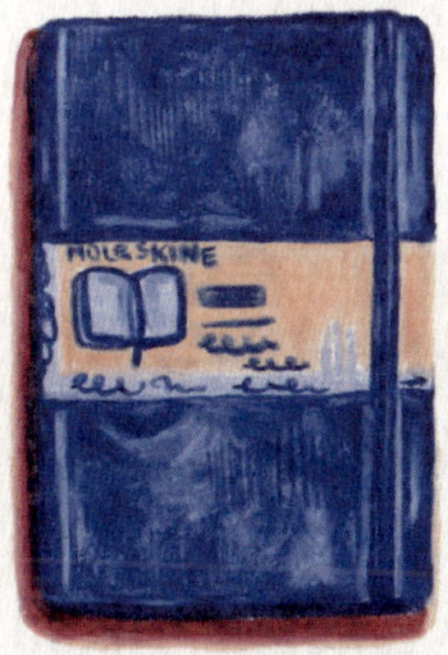

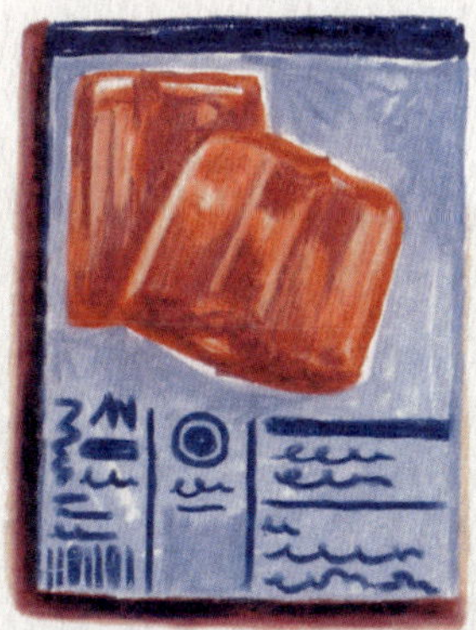

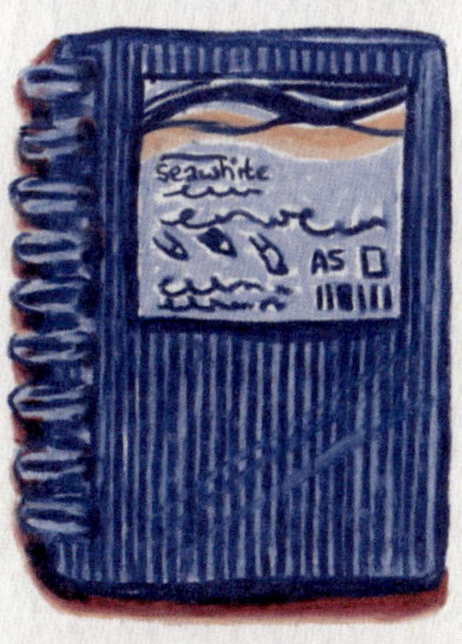

SKETCHBOOKS

There are a few things to think about when picking a sketchbook.

1 **Size:** What size do you feel comfortable drawing on? Small and contained or large and expressive?

2 **Format:** What would best fit your subject? Square, landscape or portrait format?

3 **Paper weight:** For paper thickness, GSM (grams per square meter) is the unit of measurement used. The higher the GSM, the thicker the paper and the more medium you can layer on it. For pencils I would go for 160 GSM and for wet mediums look for 300 GSM.

4 **Texture/tooth:** When choosing paper, consider your medium. You can use hot-pressed or cold-pressed paper. The main difference is its texture, or tooth.

Hot-pressed paper has a lower tooth and is smooth – perfect for dry media like pencil, charcoal and pastel. Cold-pressed paper is more textured, making it great for layering wet media like watercolor, gouache or ink.

5 **Binding:**

- → **Spiral-bound:** A good choice if you want a sketchbook that lays completely flat.
- → **Hardback:** The most durable option, perfect for keeping all your work together.
- → **Sketching pads:** Great if you want to easily tear out pages.

6 **Covers:** You can get soft or hard covers. Hard covers are more durable and better for protecting work, while a soft cover is flexible and lightweight, if you want to easily transport your sketchbook.

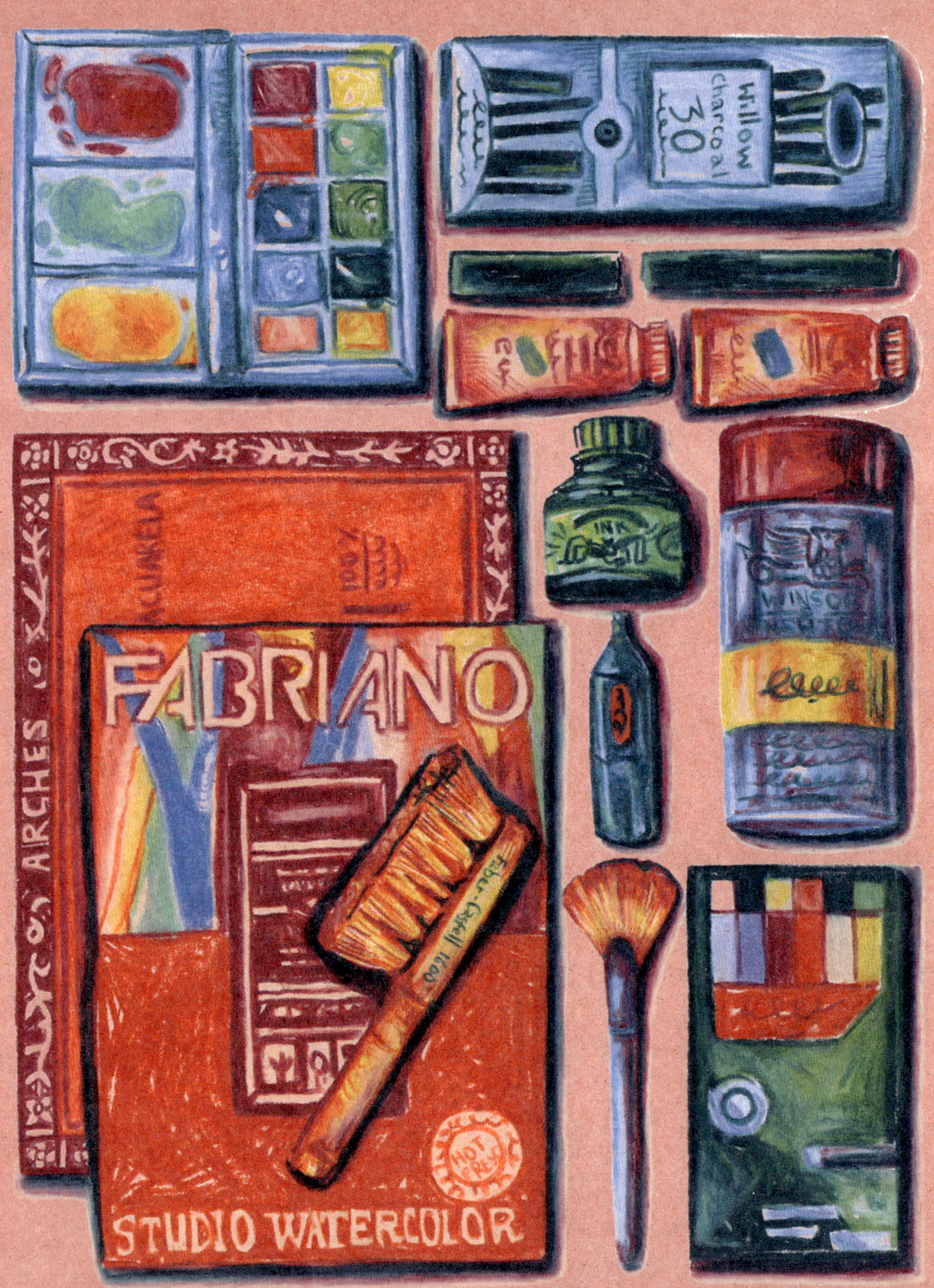
Willow charcoal 30
ARCHES
FABRIANO
STUDIO WATERCOLOR

PENCILS

The next important consideration, alongside deciding on your sketching surface, is choosing your pencils. For my location drawings I focus on colored or graphite pencils. I am always amazed by the versatility of pencils. The more I continue experimenting with this medium, the more I discover how many different textures and styles can be created to produce engaging and beautiful illustrations.

Colored pencils
Having spent years experimenting with a variety of different colored pencil brands, I have discovered that Caran d'Ache Luminance pencils are my favorite. These pencils are made with a highly pigmented wax blend, which results in very vibrant, saturated and creamy colors that are perfect for layering and blending.

If you were to go for a different brand that has a harder lead, such as an oil-based pencil from Faber-Castell, you won't achieve the same smoothness when blending.

Other notable brands to try include Derwent Coloursoft and Faber-Castell Polychromos.

Graphite pencil scale
For graphite pencils, I predominantly use Blackwing pencils. These come with a useful eraser on the end and the lead has a lovely softness that allows you to create strong tonal contrast in your drawing. Other brands I like are Derwent and Faber-Castell.

When choosing graphite pencils, you need to think about the hardness of the lead. Graphite pencils are graded on a number scale, which indicates the ratio between clay and graphite within the pencil core. The scale includes 24 grades going from 10H to 12B, with HB being the midpoint. These numbers are important to know, as they tell us the softness and hardness of the lead, which will influence the thickness and darkness of the pencil lines.

H (Hard) *– Pencils marked 'H' have a harder lead, so they contain a larger amount of clay than graphite. This means the pencil lines will be finer and lighter. The scale starts from H and goes to 10H, with a higher number indicating a harder lead.*

B (Black) *– Pencils marked 'B' have softer leads, as they contain less clay than graphite. This results in thicker and darker lines. The scale goes from B to 12B, with a higher number corresponding to a softer lead quality.*

When drawing with graphite pencils, I always use 'B' marked pencils, ranging from a 2B to 4B, depending on how dark I want the line to be. The higher the number, the greater the tonal contrast and the darker you can make the marks. I always stick with 'B' pencils as I prefer the softness and feel of the pencil on the paper.

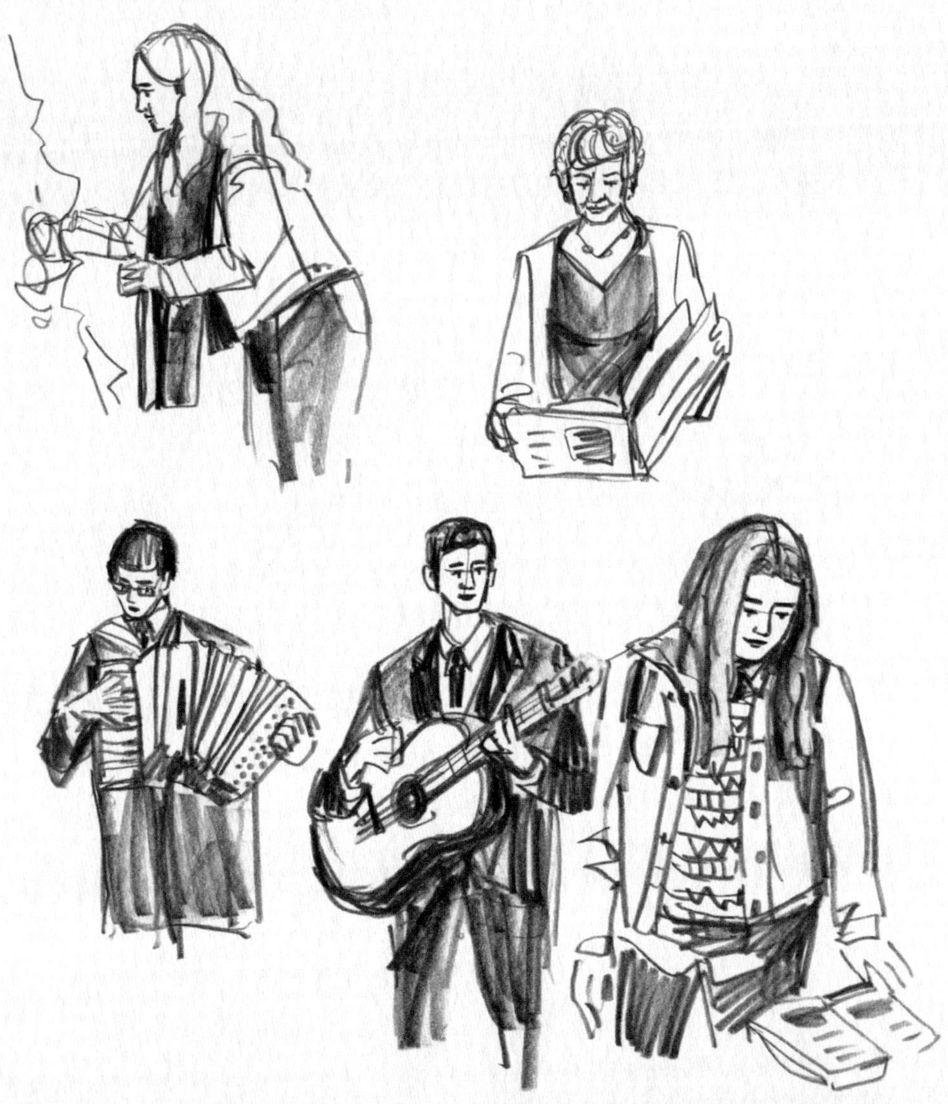

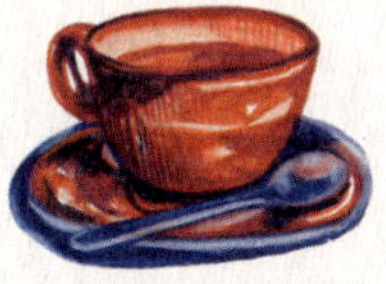

HOW TO CHOOSE WHAT TO DRAW ON LOCATION

When traveling, deciding where to draw can often be the biggest challenge. You are in a new location, may have limited time, and don't know how to capture the essence of the city.

Start by writing a list of subjects you enjoy drawing. If you enjoy capturing nature, you could go to a park, and if you enjoy drawing people, then a market or café scene would be perfect.

You could also draw points of cultural and historical interest. City maps are a great tool for finding these locations, though they will probably be popular, so make sure to plan and be prepared before you start drawing. If you aren't comfortable sketching in crowds, try to pick the quietest time to visit.

I personally love going to squares. You get a sense of community and an insight into everyday life, while often in a quieter location to help you feel more comfortable.

The essence of the city is usually seen in these smaller moments. My biggest tip for choosing locations is simply to bring your sketchbook with you everywhere. Stroll around the city. Walk until you find a moment that captures your attention and start drawing.

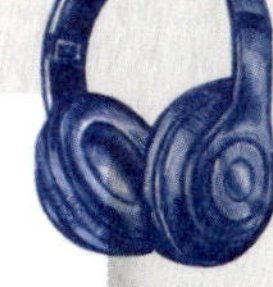

Extra things to think about on location

Below are a few added extras you could bring on your next drawing trip. They aren't essential, but can make your drawing experience more comfortable.

- **Biodegradable wet wipes:** Great for wiping dirt away and cleaning hands covered in pencil shavings.
- **Portable chair:** So you always have a place to sit.
- **Water and snacks:** Keep your energy up and stay hydrated during longer drawing sessions.
- **Portable charger:** Always useful if you end up staying out longer than planned, especially in unfamiliar places where you may need to access maps or contact someone.

HOW TO FEEL COMFORTABLE ON LOCATION

Drawing on location isn't just about drawing. It also involves researching locations, knowing how to draw in changing environments and, most importantly, learning how to be confident creating in public. I am going to take you through my tips so that you can shift your focus from worrying about those around you to the beauty of creating and being in the moment.

1 Start With Comfort

Go somewhere you know well to ease yourself into the process, whether that's a local café, a park or bookstore.

2 Start Small

Think small and grow from here. This could be using a small sketchbook or creating quick, timed sketches. This also refers to the location: choose a calm, contained spot so there isn't too much activity or extra details to distract you.

3 Use Limited Colors and Materials

Only bring a couple of your favorite materials to speed up the decision-making process. You can even pick a limited palette (see page 37) before you go on location so everything is ready and you can just focus on drawing.

4 Plan the Trip

Plan the transport or walking route to get to the location. Think about where there is a restroom nearby if you are staying a while. What will the weather be like? Do you need to bring anything extra because of this? I usually stand up when drawing on location, with my sketchbook leaning on my left arm, tucked against my stomach. This means I can move around the scene more easily. However, if you would like more comfort then bringing a stool or choosing a location with seats is preferrable. Feeling prepared is going to make the drawing process a lot more relaxing.

5 Stay Safe

When drawing, you are preoccupied, so your things are more vulnerable. Try to keep your bag as empty as possible with minimal valuables. You don't want your drawing session to end with a disappointing surprise.

Also think about the time of day you are going and how long it takes to get there. If you are in a new city by yourself, you may want to keep your drawing session to earlier in the day, so you aren't traveling back in the dark.

6 Wear Headphones or Sunglasses

If you don't like the feeling of people watching you while drawing, music and sunglasses may help. They create

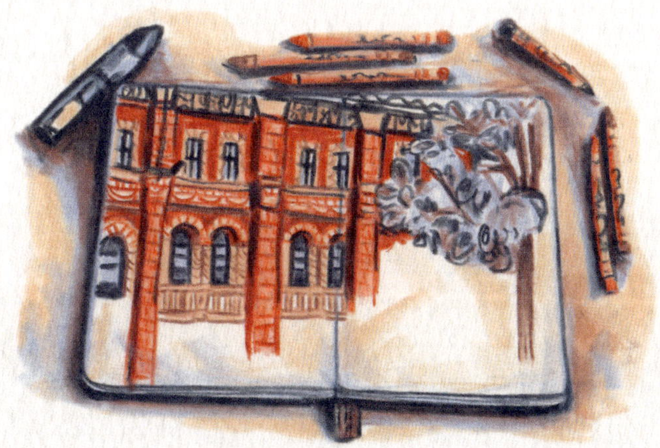

a slight boundary to support you. Just remember that while this extra boundary can help you feel more at ease, always stay vigilant and aware of your surroundings to keep safe while drawing.

7 Sketch With Others

Drawing with other people helps create a sense of community. It becomes a shared experience which can make you feel less observed. When traveling I always enjoy joining drawing groups; it enables you to create in a supported space while exploring a new city. The lovely 'SketchBreakfast' group I went to while living in Barcelona is a great example of this.

You can find similar groups by looking on social media for drawing meetups or artistic opportunities in your area. Use keywords and hashtags such as #urbansketchers, #sketchgroup and #artmeetup. You can also be more specific by adding your location at the start, such as #londondrawinggroup. Don't hesitate to send a message expressing your interest, ask for more information, and see whether it feels like the right fit for you.

8 Observe First

It is important to fully understand the scene before you pick up your pencil. Start with a walk around the location. Get comfortable with your environment, decide which areas interest you, find the focal points and the story and atmosphere you want to capture.

While walking, look out for a comfortable spot for drawing. Is there shelter? Can you sit down? Would you feel comfortable drawing there? Now you know your surroundings better, you can go with confidence to your location and start drawing.

9 Celebrate the Imperfections

Remember to celebrate and enjoy the creative process. The value is in the process, experimentating and spending time on your craft.

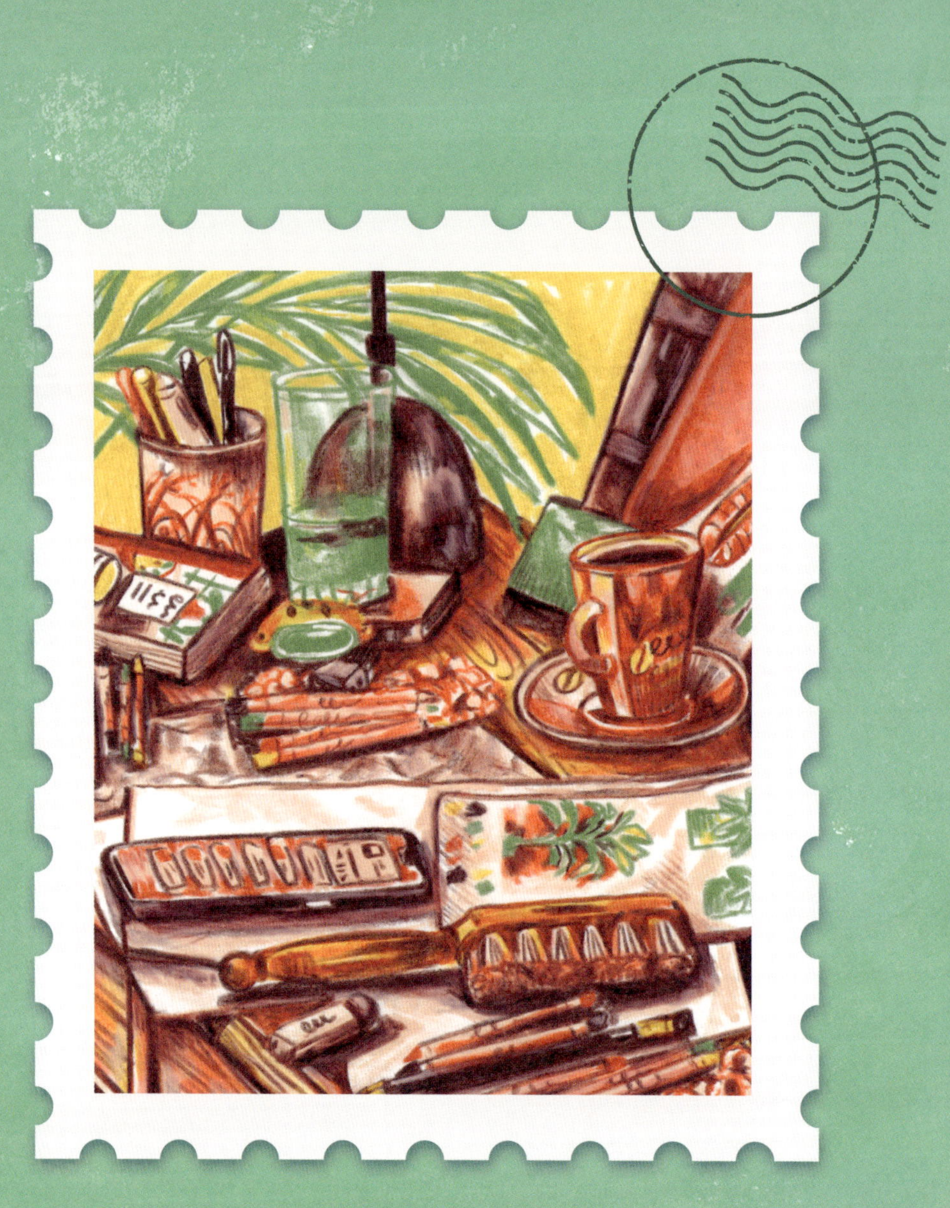

CHAPTER TWO

Illustration Fundamentals

DRAWING TECHNIQUES

HOW TO USE YOUR PENCIL

Your artistic style isn't only developed through your chosen medium, but also the way in which you approach that medium. How you use a pencil will have a big influence on the emotions and atmosphere evoked in your drawing. When using pencils, you are going to need to think of three special words: angle, pressure and speed.

Angle
A shallow pencil angle is going to increase the surface area of the pencil lead in contact with the paper - great for creating flowing, broad marks or shading in large areas. The steeper the angle, the less lead will be in contact - perfect for those precise architectural details.

You can also play with your finger position. The closer your fingers are to the lead, the more rigid and strict the mark-making. The further away from the lead, the less control you have, which will create more fluid and looser marks.

Pressure
The greater the pressure you apply to the pencil, the stronger the marks, creating confident and energetic drawings. The lighter the pressure, the softer the marks - an ideal choice for natural landscapes.

Speed
If you have done timed drawings (see page 14) before, then you will probably have seen the difference between these and your non-timed sketches. If you want drama and confidence, experiment with fast marks which will have a lot of energy. If you want feelings of stability, order and balance, then use slower marks.

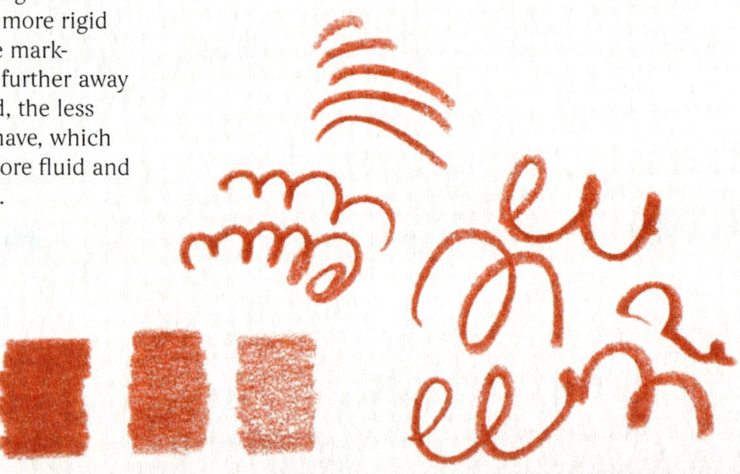

MARK-MAKING

Mark-making refers to the process of making patterns, lines, textures and shapes using your medium. Your marks help convey emotions, communicate your style and add detail to your drawing.

When creating your marks, always think about the direction of the lines. Examine the subject, the shape, texture and form and draw your lines following the direction of the surface. This will help create a three-dimensional appearance.

The easiest way to picture this is by describing water. Water flows one way with a distinct direction of movement. To show this movement, you would draw lines following the direction of the water.

Things to think about:

- **Shading lines:** Drawing all of these in the same direction will create a sense of structure and uniformity.
- **Cross-hatching:** This can be used as a shading method for adding depth. For this technique, draw lines horizontally and then add a layer of vertical lines on top.
- **Your lines do not have to be straight:** If you are drawing a natural subject, such as trees in a city, straight lines wouldn't complement the texture or shape. Instead, you can focus on curving marks to mirror the subject.
- **Be playful:** Explore as many different marks as you can think of, from dots and lines to swirls. You don't have to stick with the traditional straight lines for shading.

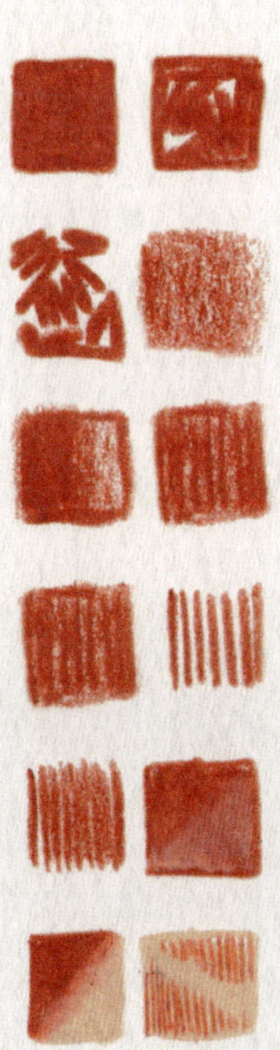

BLENDING

Blending is a drawing technique used to soften the transition between colors, shades or tones (see page 35). Successful blending creates smooth, gradual gradients that can help suggest depth, form and texture.

Smooth blending depends on both the quality of the paper and how you use the pencil. The paper can only withstand so many layers. Start soft and gradually change the pressure for each layer.

For a smooth finish, focus on circular motions. You can start with light to dark colors, or go dark to light, using your lightest tonal value (see page 37) to blend everything together. Move the pencil in a circular motion while gradually adding more pressure.

If you want to add more textures after blending, go on top with a darker color and add in shading lines. This will help layer up the drawing, adding depth and detail.

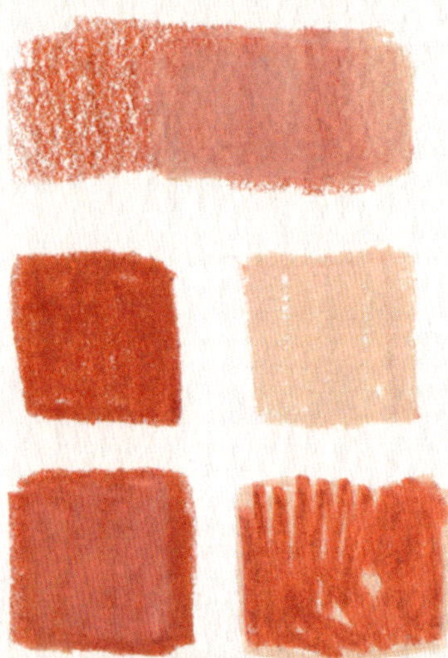

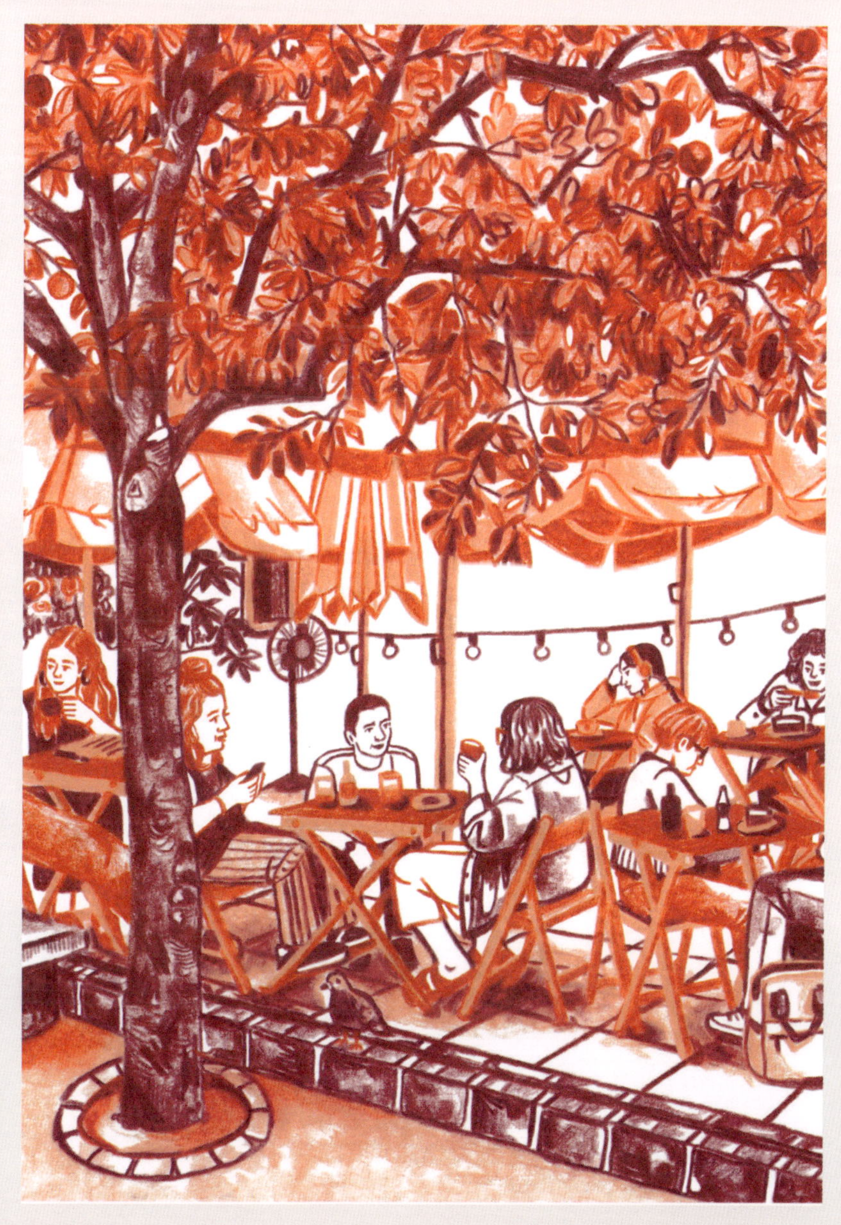

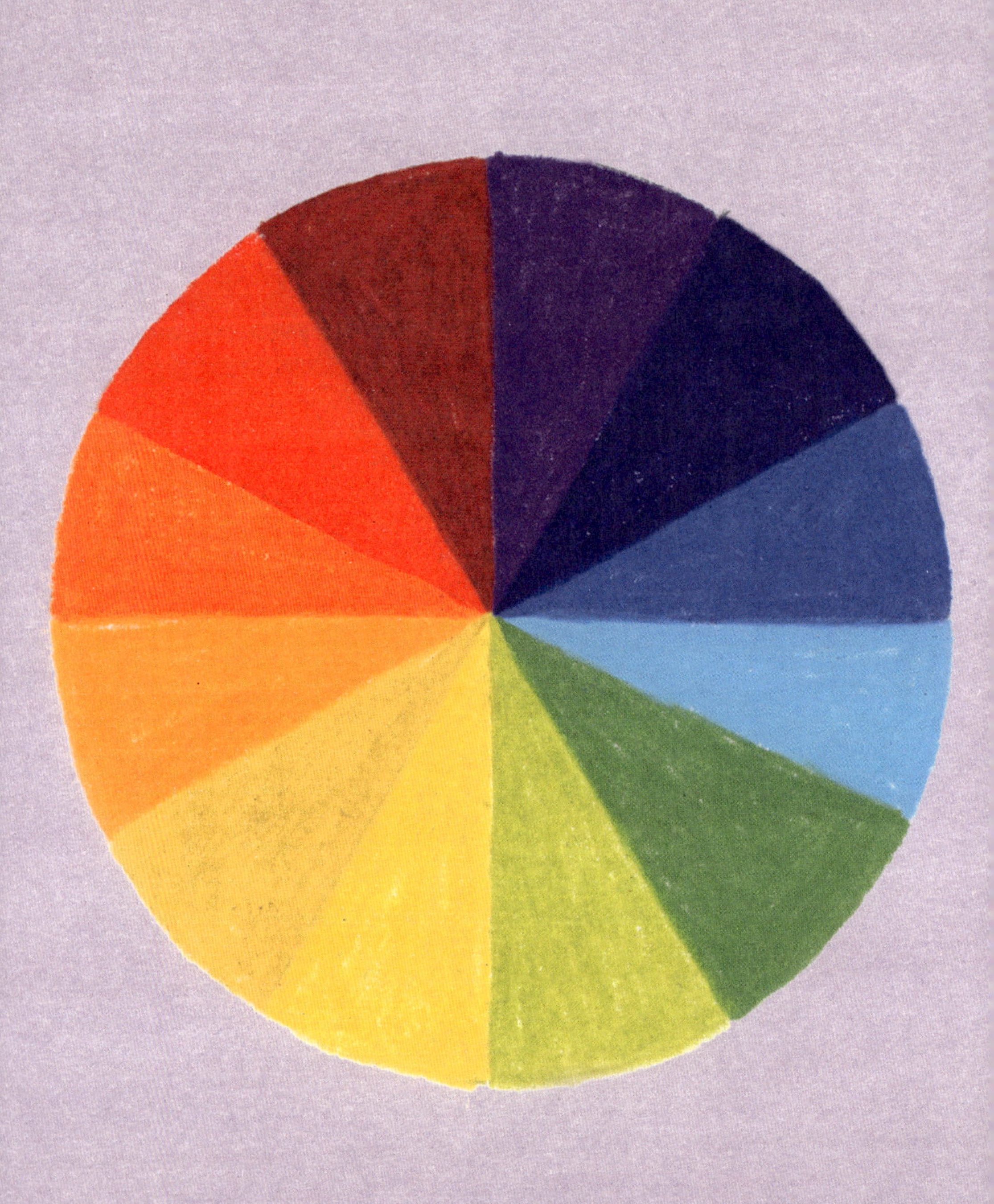

COLOR

Color is such an important part of illustration to evoke emotions, tell a story and create a balanced composition. Color theory is both an art and a science, all about how we perceive colors and the messages they convey. Below are color essentials to help you successfully choose a palette.

THE COLOR WHEEL

The basic color wheel is split into three sections:

Primary colors
Red, blue and yellow. These colors cannot be made by mixing other colors together. Primary colors are combined to make every other color.

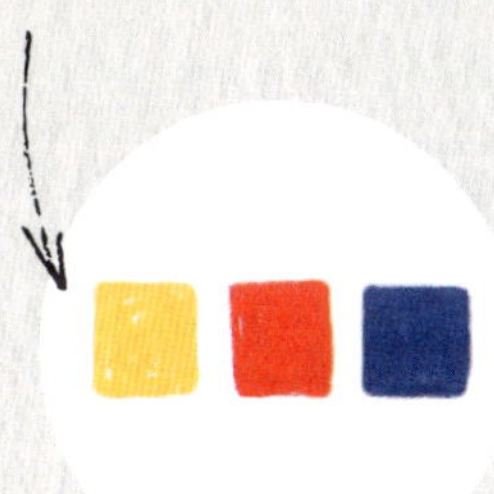

Secondary colors
Green, orange and purple. Create these by mixing two primary colors together.

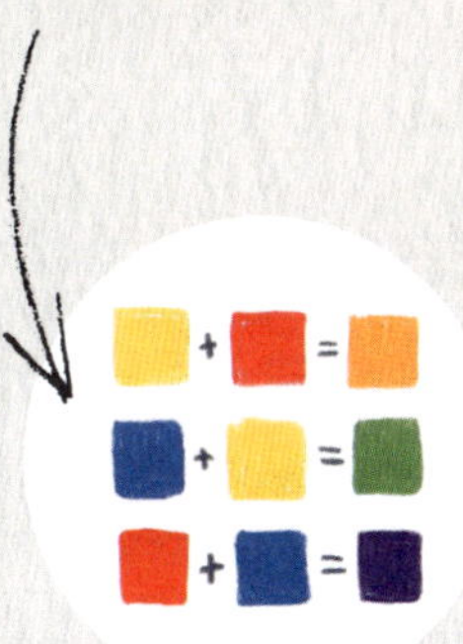

Tertiary colors
These are created by mixing a primary and secondary color in equal amounts. For example, combining the primary color blue and secondary color purple to make violet.

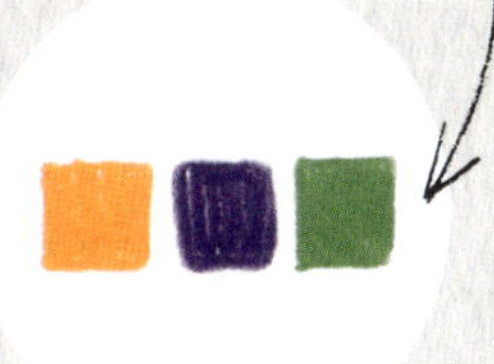

Understanding color variations
Once you have mixed your color, it is important to understand how colors change when combined with white, black or gray. These variations are known as hues, tints, shades and tones:

- → **Hue:** The pure color that appears on the color wheel
- → **Tint:** Add white to a hue to make it lighter
- → **Shade:** Add black to a hue to make it darker
- → **Tone:** Refers to how light or dark a color is (often created by adding gray to a hue)

COLOR TEMPERATURE AND PSYCHOLOGY

The color wheel is split into three temperature categories: warm, cool and neutral. The temperature of the color palette you use will have an influence on the emotional response of people who engage with your art.

Color psychology explains how each color has symbolism and connotations attached to it. For example, the color red stimulates energy and increases heart rate, perfect for grabbing your attention and creating a sense of urgency. Blue, on the other hand, is linked with serenity and sadness, lowering your heart rate and reducing stress.

→ **Warm colors:** Red, yellow and orange - energy, optimism, excitement
→ **Cool colors:** Blue, green and purple - calm, sad, peace
→ **Neutral colors:** Brown, gray, black and white - grounding, linked to the earth

When choosing a color palette that is not monochromatic (a single hue), it is a good idea to think about the balance between the color temperatures. This helps bring harmony to the drawing. Choose a primary color, such as red, and then a secondary color, perhaps orange, and now add a color with a cool temperature like purple to balance out the design.

Remember: you don't have to use all of the colors in front of you. By creating a selective palette, you can influence the way we read the drawing and what you want to say about the location.

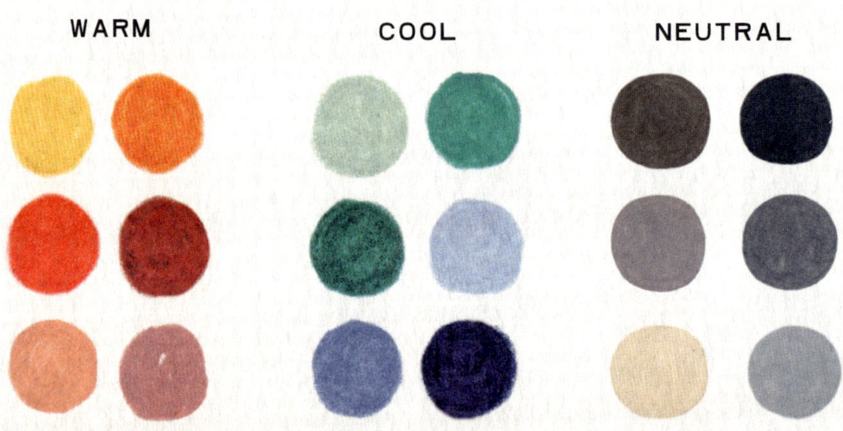

LIMITED PALETTES

Limited color palettes involve reducing the number of colors in the scene to a considered selection. This helps create a more cohesive and harmonious design, while encouraging you to experiment with color psychology. When on location, limited color palettes also speed up the drawing process, as you don't have to worry about using every color you see. How do you know which color to use for each subject? The answer to this is tonal values.

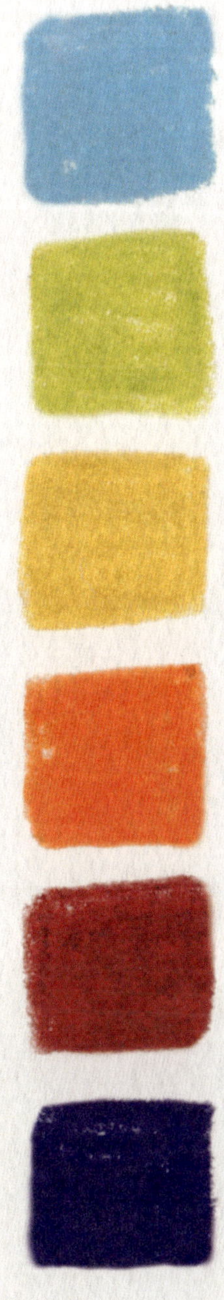

Tonal values

'Tonal value' refers to how light or dark a tone or color is. Every color has a tonal scale, from light to dark. Artists use these values to show form and to represent light and shadow. When drawing, you need to make sure you have a variety of tones to create depth, contrast and a stronger sense of three-dimensionality in your illustration.

It might seem strange, but you are going to want to view your scene in terms of black, white and the gray scale. This allows you freedom from the restrictions of needing to use a specific color for each object. Instead, focus on using the relevant tonal value from your palette to match the subject.

The best way to view the location in tonal values is to squint at the scene. Let your eyes go blurry and then examine which areas are most prominent and which fade away. This helps you split the image into three different tonal values - light, medium and dark.

If you want to check the values, take a photo of the location and switch the saturation to -100 or turn it into black and white. Now do the same for the photo of your color palette and compare. This becomes your reference tool.

Let's say blue is your darkest color and in the scene the windows are the darkest subject: you will use blue for the windows. It is like a matching game, slowly piecing the puzzle together through tonal values.

TYPES OF COLOR PALETTES

Knowing how colors interact with each other is important to create harmonious color palettes. Below are a few combinations you can try.

Complementary colors
These are colors opposite each other on the color wheel, so will add energy and high contrast. When combined, these pairs will cancel each other out, creating a dark brown or black.

When choosing complementary colors, pick one prominent color to use in most areas, and the other as a highlight. This imbalance in the proportions is essential to make sure they don't feel like they are in competition. These are contrasting colors, so they create a lot of tension. You don't want the drawing to look overwhelming.

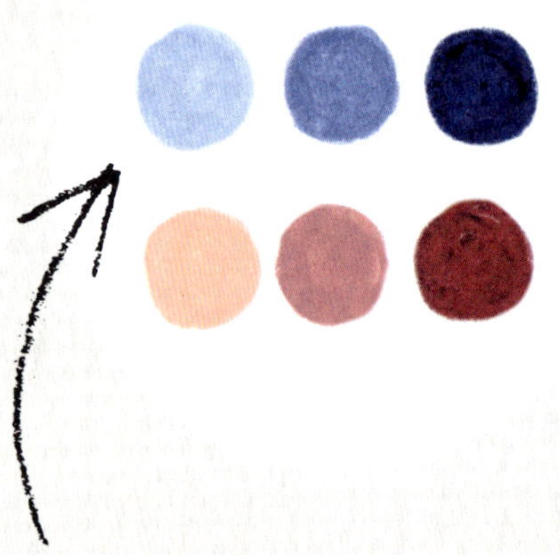

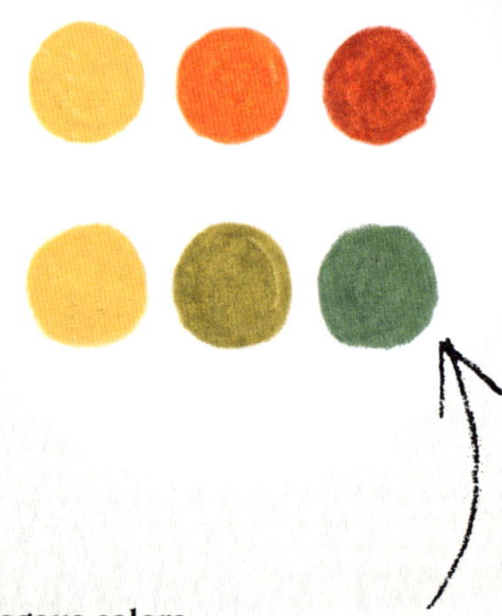

Monochromatic colors
A monochromatic color palette involves different tones and shades of a single hue. This palette will be harmonious as you are just playing with the tonal range. Make sure to have a light, mid and dark tonal value to create depth and contrast.

Analogous colors
These are colors that are next to each other on the color wheel, such as green and yellow. This will be a harmonious and balanced combination as there isn't much contrast.

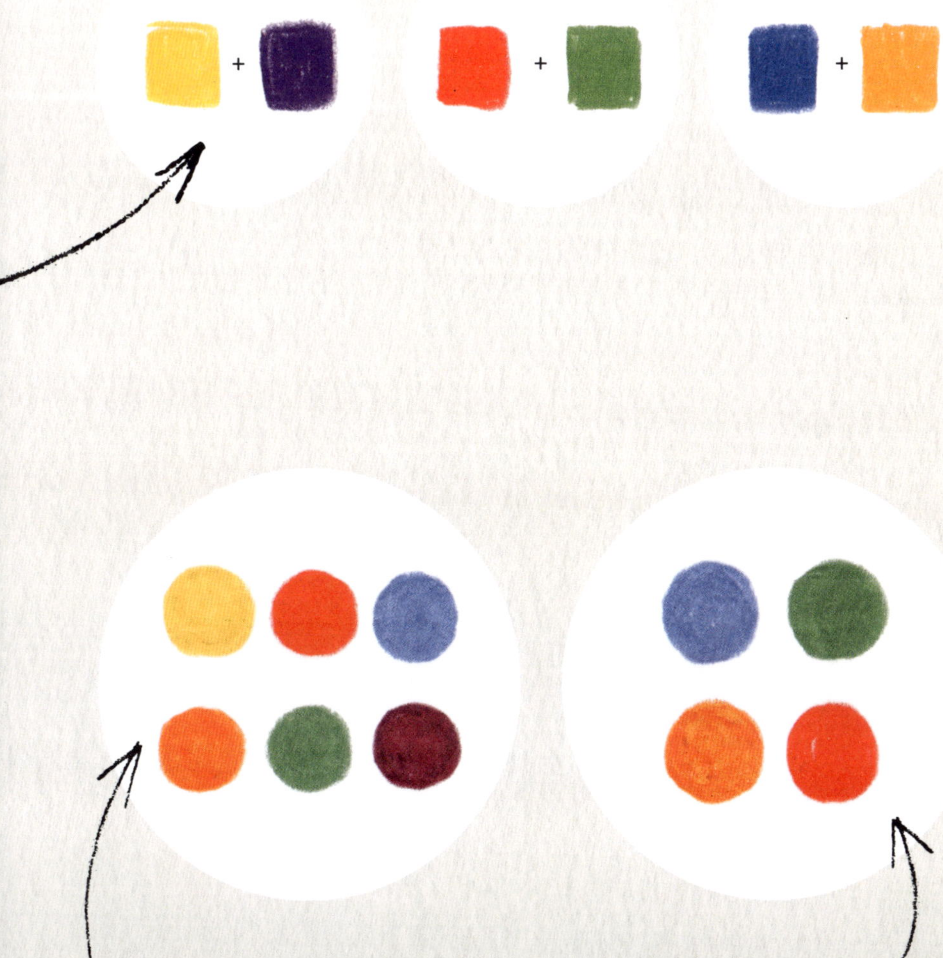

Triadic colors
Use three colors that are evenly spaced across the wheel, such as red, yellow and blue, to create a balanced look while using a larger selection of colors.

Tetradic colors
Four colors that are arranged into two complementary pairs, such as blue and orange paired with red and green. Again, for this type of palette, pick your dominant color, use two as accents and then one as a supporting color.

COLOR FOR DEPTH

To add depth to your illustration, you need to have contrast in the color temperature, saturation and tonal values.

Saturation
Saturation refers to how vibrant a color is. A pure hue is the most saturated version of a color - this is the color you get straight out of a paint tube. The more saturated a color is, the further forward it will appear in a drawing.

To increase the saturation of a color, simply apply more pressure when using your pencil.

Tonal values
If you want something to appear distant, use lighter tonal values, and darker tones for bringing the subject forward.

Color temperature
A warm color will come forward and a cooler color will appear more distant. This is a great technique to use for your focal points (see page 44). If you would like a character to be brought forward, then use warmer colors for the person and have cooler surrounding elements.

HOW TO PICK A PALETTE

Every time I travel to a new location, I love observing the colors. Each place has its own unique palette influenced by the culture, history, climate and people.

Here are a few color swatches I have picked up on my travels, showing how each limited color palette can transport you to a different location.

My favorite way to create palettes is to go for a 'color walk'. Walk around the location and swatch colors that frequently appear in the scene. You can do this by taking a photo and then using Procreate, or another graphics software, to digitally swatch the colors from the image. Or use pencils to match the colors and then keep these swatches in a 'color inspiration' section in your sketchbook.

This will be a great starting point to make a harmonious palette, while also trying to reflect the city. When creating your own drawings, try limiting your color choice to five or six. Remember to think about contrast, balance and incorporating a light, mid and dark tone and then you are good to go. If the palette seems too overwhelming, try reducing the saturation of some of the colors or adding in the opposite color temperature to balance it out.

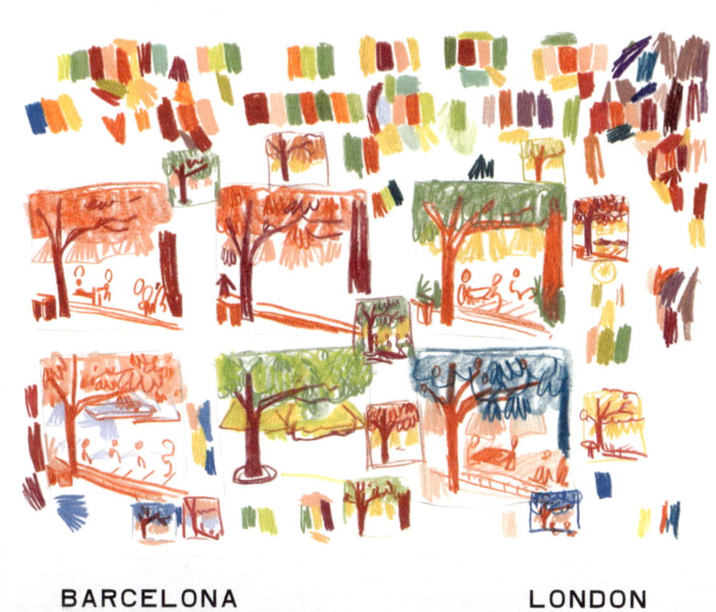

BARCELONA

LONDON

BERLIN

MARRAKECH

MILAN

GOZO

ELBASAN

PARIS

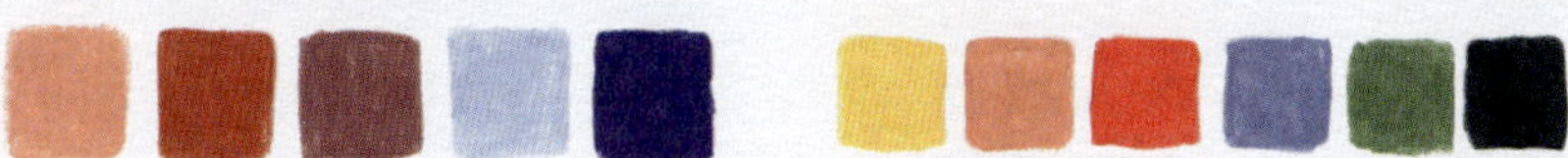

THE 60-30-10 RULE

If you would like a mathematical guide, then you can use the 60-30-10 rule. For this rule, use 60% of your main color, 30% secondary color and 10% accent color. If you have more than three hues, then you can use different tonal values of the same hue and fit those in each percentage: for example, 60% are your red hues, 30% orange and 10% purple. By establishing a hierarchy of colors, it will help achieve balance and harmony in the drawing.

Main color/ Primary color
The dominant color in your design, it sets the atmosphere and tone. In this rule, it is around 60% of the overall illustration.

Secondary color
The next prominent color, covering around 30% of your design. This color is used to support the primary color without overpowering it.

Accent color
A color used for only 10% of the design - small but impactful. The accent color draws attention to focal points, highlights details and guides the viewer through the illustration.

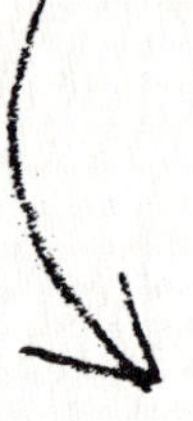

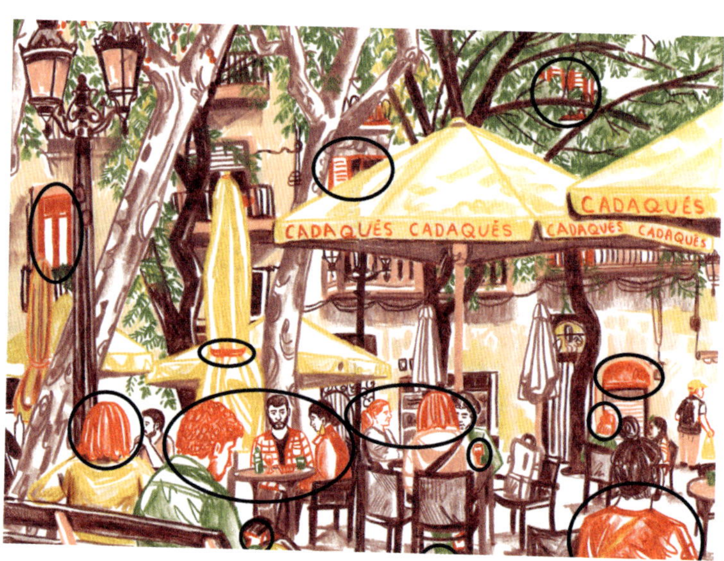

LIGHT AND SHADOW

Color is not the only illustration topic you can use for capturing atmosphere, adding depth and conveying narratives. Understanding how light and shadow work is another important tool to strengthen your drawing. To determine where to include areas of light and shadow, you need to be aware of the light sources.

When on location in a city, light sources could be from a mixture of artificial lights in buildings, electronic signs, screens, streetlights and sunlight. The number and intensity of light sources will influence the size and direction of the shadows created.

→ **How Do Shadows Work?**
Light travels in a straight line. When a light source is blocked by an object, it will form a shadow, called a cast shadow. This is the dark shape cast onto another surface. The size and shape of the shadow produced is a direct response to the object being hit and the intensity and position of the light source.

→ **Light Intensity and Shadow Quality**
Light intensity refers to the strength of the light source. An intense light source would be a bright lamp placed close to an object or peak sun during a clear sunny day. Whereas a soft light can be seen during sunset or on overcast days. The greater the light intensity, the sharper and more defined the cast shadow will be.

For example, just before sunset, when the sun is low in the sky and lighter in intensity, the shadows will be long with soft edges and a small tonal range. Whereas, if you were drawing during midday, when the sun is above the subject and very intense, it will produce a short, crisp shadow with strong tonal contrast.

Being aware of your light sources and the influence they have on the shadows formed will not only make your urban sketches more accurate, but also let you share greater context as to the time of day, the weather and the mood of the city.

COMPOSITION

Composition is a great way of capturing the viewer's attention, creating a narrative and a visually appealing illustration. The term composition refers to the placement and relationship of objects and elements within the scene.

HOW CAN YOU ACHIEVE A BETTER COMPOSITION?

1 Know the Story You Want to Share

Knowing this will give you the context you need to decide the composition. Here are questions you should think about to set the scene:

- **What is your focal point?** A focal point is an area of the artwork you draw the viewer's attention to, through color, composition and contrast. To pick a focal point, look at the scene and think: consider is the most important part, and what grabs your eyes? Is this a person, an interaction or an object? You can then use the composition to guide the viewer to this point.
- **What emotion do you want to convey?** Is it a peaceful or energetic location?
- **Where is the scene taking place?** Context for the culture, season and time of day.
- **Are there any objects you need to add to show the story?** Consider their placement as part of your overall composition, using the following techniques to help you.

2 The Rule of Thirds

The rule of thirds is my favorite technique to use. It is a great tool to create balance and inform where to place your focal points to guide the viewer through the scene.

For this technique you need to divide your page horizontally and vertically into three, to create a three-by-three grid. Now using your grid, place any focal points in the intersection of these lines or along the lines. You can also place your focal point, such as a figure, so it fills an entire row or column.

In this illustration of Mesón del Cafè 1909 (the oldest café in Barcelona) the rule of thirds grid has been placed over the scene to show how I used this compositional technique to create a harmonious drawing.

Let's take a closer look at this composition:

- The figures are the main focal points, so I placed them both within the central column of the composition. Their heads align with a horizontal third line while their bodies are placed on the vertical third lines. This gives the figures visual weight without placing them directly in the center.

→ The hanging lamp is placed just above the horizontal middle line, again in the central column of the illustration. This anchors the upper third of the drawing and guides the viewer's eye upward.

→ The shelves intersect at points on the horizontal third lines, adding structure to the background, without distracting from the figures below.

→ The top of the doorway sits on a horizontal third line, leaving the top third of the illustration as negative space for the roof, beams and light details. This creates breathing room in the composition.

This drawing uses the rule of thirds to highlight focal points while encouraging movement that naturally guides your eye through the scene. It helps maintain a visual balance as you intentionally place the objects to create a lyrical and dynamic image.

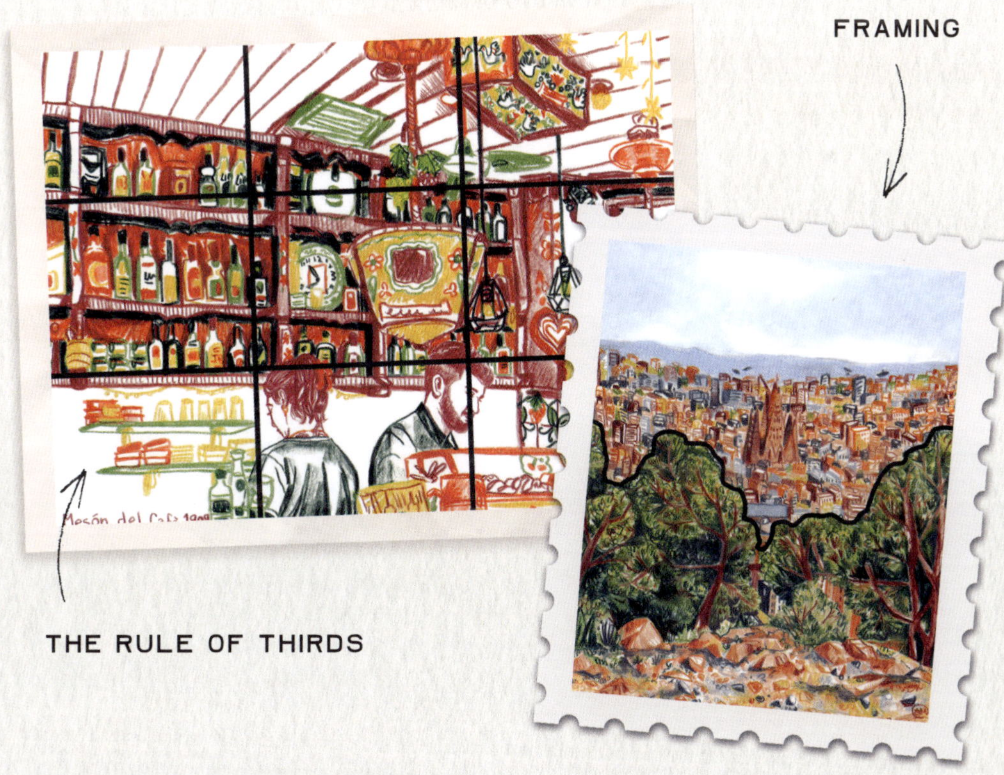

Think about where new sections start in the location. How can you utilize these transitions in the composition? A great example is placing the edge of a building along one of the third lines to start a new section in a harmonious position.

3 Diagonal Lines and Intersections

Diagonal lines are great for adding energy, conflict and a sense of direction. When viewing images, we generally read from left to right, so we want the movement to follow this direction. You can add points of interest across a diagonal line to subtly guide the viewer from the top left to bottom right corner of the drawing.

That said, the direction of image reading varies across countries. In most Western cultures, people tend to process the image from left to right. In contrast, in right-to-left reading cultures (such as Arabic or Hebrew) the visual flow may naturally move from right to left. Traditional Chinese, Japanese and Korean texts follow a top-down reading pattern, however, in modern print, horizontal left-to-right reading is now common. It is important to be aware of your intended audience, so you can adjust your composition accordingly to create the most engaging illustration - one that reflects how the viewer naturally reads an image.

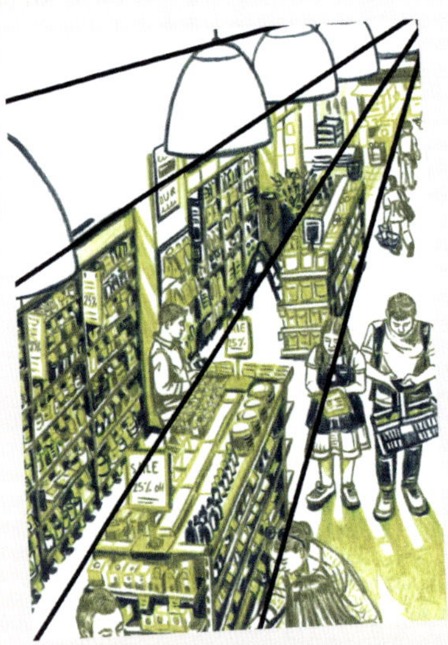

4 Negative Space

A good composition will create a balanced illustration. Space is a key aspect of composition, to create the illusion of movement, provide context, suggest distance and convey emotions. The positive and negative spaces in your drawing are as important as each other. Negative space refers to the white space in between each element. You need this balance between detail and space to let the illustration breathe.

5 Color Balance

You can play with lines of color to guide the viewer through the drawing. Pick a highlight color to add to objects across the leading lines of the scene. When choosing the color, make sure it isn't one of your prominent ones. You need it to stand out. Whether this is through using complementary colors, warm and cool temperatures or changes in saturation, there needs to be contrast (see pages 36–42).

6 Framing

Framing is a great technique for emphasizing a focal point or creating an edge to the scene. Cities are a perfect location for seeing framing in action through arches, windows and doors. These subjects create the idea of movement, offering a glimpse into a hidden scene and making the viewer question what is beyond.

Trees and bushes are another great framing subject (see page 45). By adding trees as a frame in the foreground, it gives something to look through and builds a sense of depth and perspective.

7 Open or Closed Composition

An open composition is used to emphasize movement, space and an immersive scene. Elements of the drawing go off the edges of the page, letting the scene continue beyond the borders. A closed composition creates the idea of boundaries and a more static scene, as all the elements are contained within the frame.

8 Perspective

Perspective is an art technique that uses lines and angles to create the illusion of three dimensions and depth on a flat surface. To understand perspective, you need to focus on three elements: depth, horizon lines and vanishing points.

Depth refers to the visual illusion of distance and space. When you look at paintings, you will notice how some objects appear closer than others – this is depth. Artists create this illusion by adjusting scale: objects closer to the viewer are drawn larger, while those further away are smaller. For example, distant trees in a landscape are much smaller than trees in the foreground.

NEGATIVE SPACE

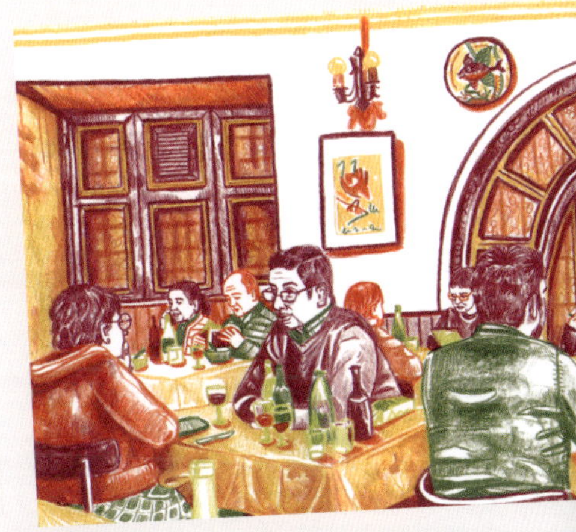

A horizon line is a horizontal line in a drawing that represents the viewer's eye level. An easy way to picture this is to think about where the sky meets the ground or water.

A vanishing point is a point on the horizon line where parallel lines appear to converge. There are different types of perspective depending on the number of vanishing points in the scene. One-point and two-point are the most common perspectives.

- **One-point perspective** involves one vanishing point, such as the end of a road or path. When you look at a straight road, the edges will appear to meet at a point in the distance. This is a perfect example of one-point perspective.
- **Two-point perspective** has two vanishing points. Picture a building on a street corner. If you place the

building in the center of your page, you will have two vanishing points where the roads lead. To find these points, draw your horizon line, then mark a point at the top center of the building. Draw two straight lines from this point to the horizon line on the left and right. Repeat this step from a point on the bottom center of the building. Where these lines intersect on the horizon line are your two vanishing points.

The steeper the angle of your lines, the closer the vanishing point is to the viewer. Once you have the guidelines, you can start adding buildings, using these lines as your dimension guides.

Perspective also refers to how you view things. It is important to consider how your position on location will affect the way in which the scene is interpreted. If you want a person or building to appear imposing, then try a perspective looking up at the subject. This position will create a sense of power as the subject looms over you. If you use a bird's-eye view, such as looking down at the subject from a balcony, it will create the idea of space, emphasize the scale of the location and introduce a feeling of movement.

You could also position yourself in the midst of the activity to draw if you want the viewer to be immersed in the scene, rather than observing from a distance.

9 Proportion

Proportion refers to the relative size of elements - such as the size of a window in relation to the building. Thinking about proportion in your drawings will create accurate angles and scale to help form a realistic illustration.

However, as the artist, you don't just have to stick to accurate proportions. Proportions can be manipulated and exaggerated to affect how the viewer interprets the subjects, to create a more stylized appearance or draw attention to focal points.

ONE-POINT PERSPECTIVE

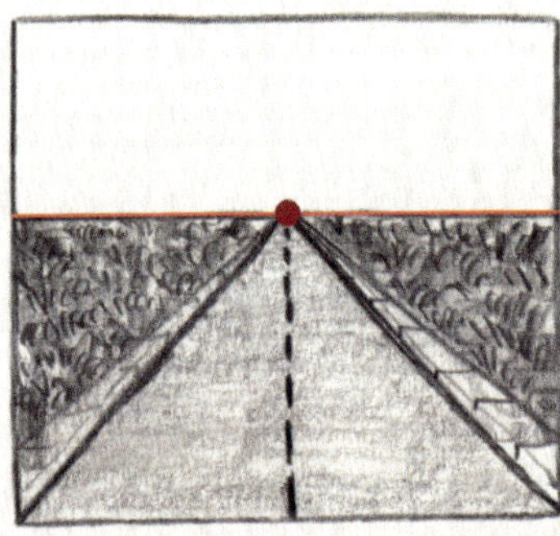

TWO-POINT PERSPECTIVE

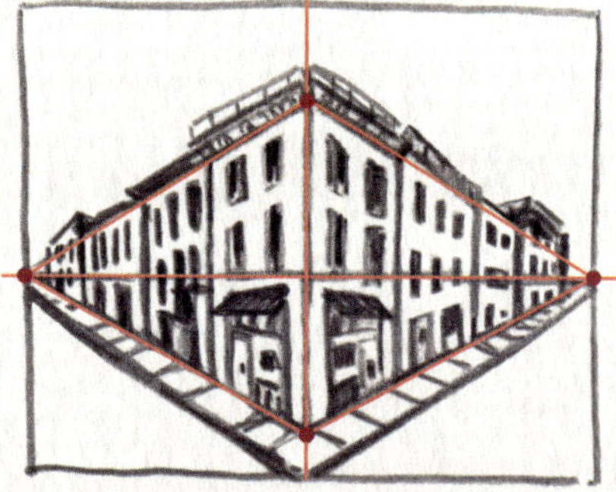

BRINGING IT ALL TOGETHER: HOW TO START YOUR SCENE

When deciding how to start a scene, think in layers: foreground, middle ground and background. This will help create depth and structure, guiding the viewer through your scene.

→ **Foreground**: This is the area closest to the viewer. You can include objects in the foreground, such as trees, to frame the location, add context and lead the viewer into the scene.

→ **Middle ground**: This is the transition space between the foreground and background. You will usually place your focal points in this section - this is where the main action is.

→ **Background**: The background is the furthest part of the scene. This could be distant buildings, landscape features or shelving details in a café interior. These details will help show the scale and context of the location.

Before beginning your drawing, you need to plan the composition. Walk around the location to observe points of interest and decide what story you want to share. Now use your composition knowledge to work out which tools can help guide the viewer through the scene - such as diagonal lines and negative space. Finally, look if there are any natural frames, intersections or strong compositional features (such as the edge of a building) that you could use to build a successful composition.

Next, you can do three quick 'thumbnail' sketches - named for how small and fast they are - to decide on potential designs. These sketches will be used to explore different focal points and framing, and help you decide what to include and leave out to best depict your narrative. Try varying viewpoints, zooming in and out and changing up your main subject.

To make a thumbnail sketch, use a graphite pencil to draw a rectangle. Now, split this into a 3x3 grid, so you follow the rule of thirds while deciding your layout. Then do a quick one-minute sketch inside each rectangle to experiment with different compositions. Concentrate on the basic shapes and scene structure, without adding too many details. Once you have experimented and chosen your favorite, you can tackle the final drawing.

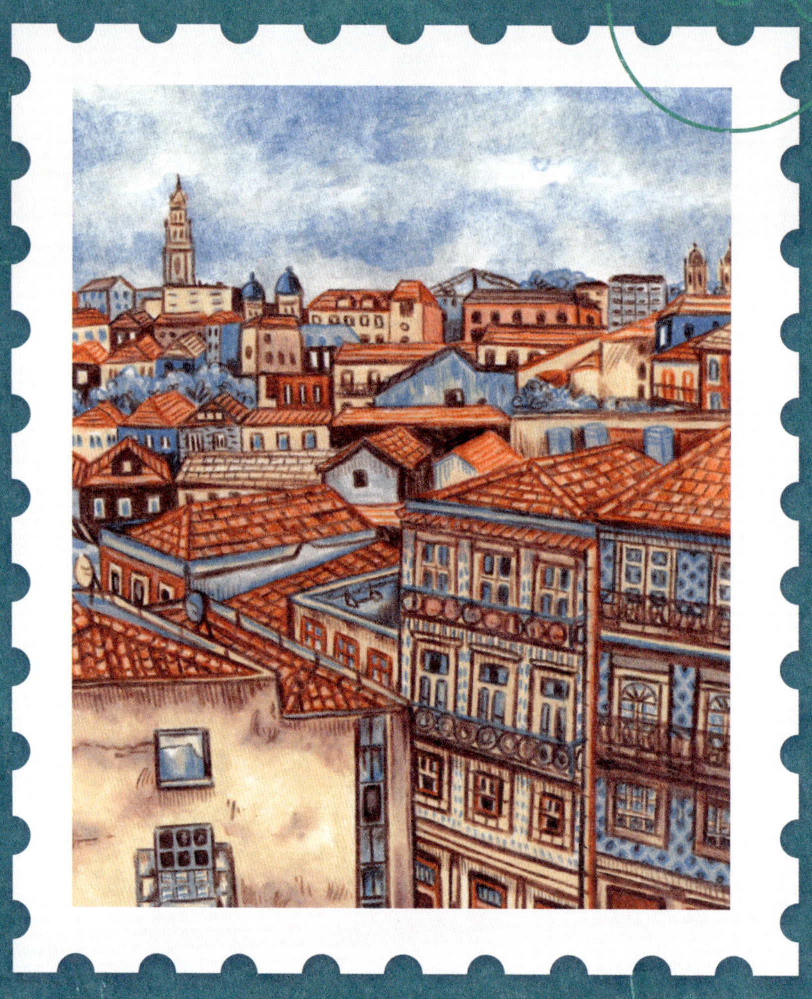

CHAPTER THREE

Architecture

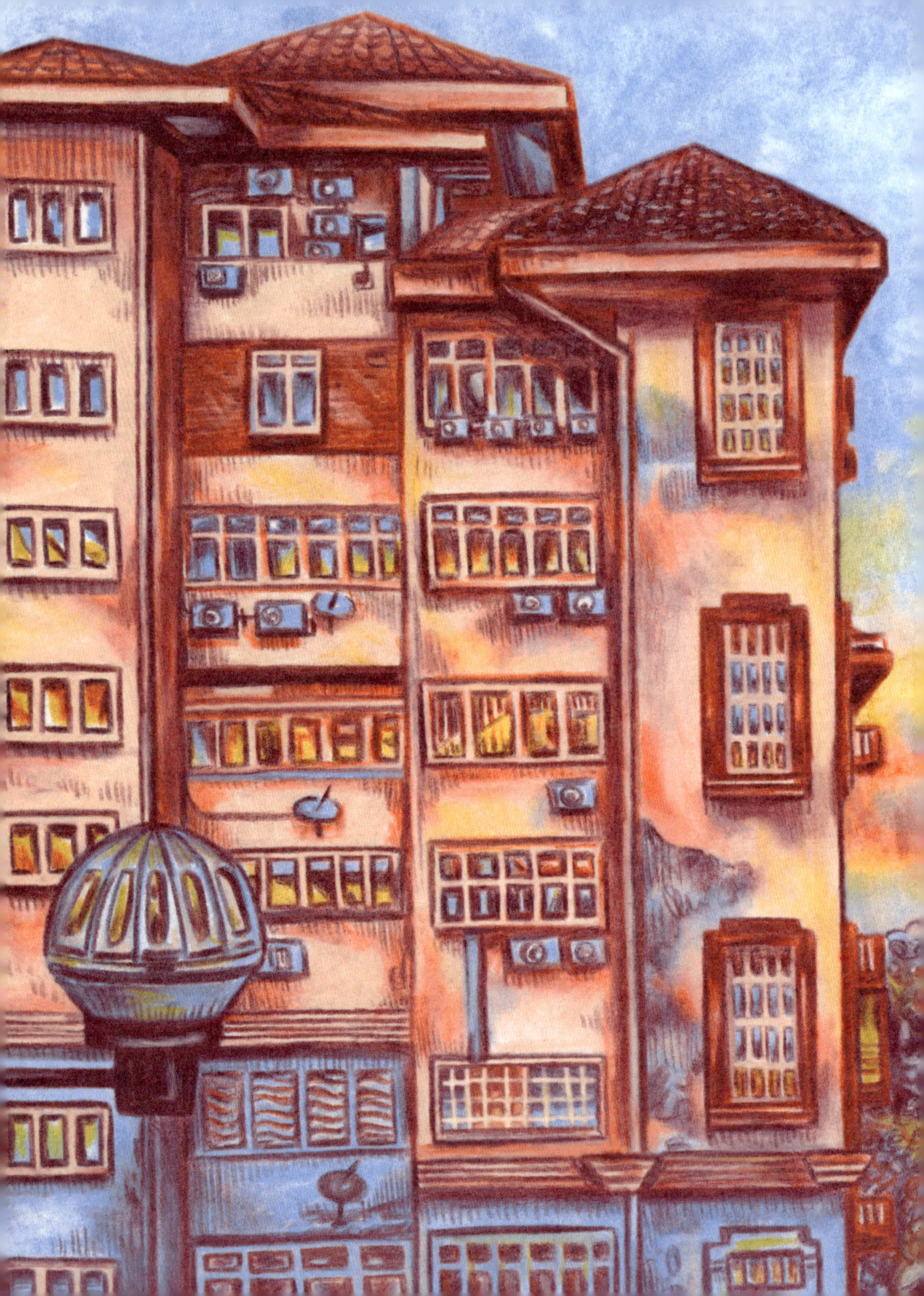

Now you have learned all about the fundamentals of illustration, let's dive into different city subjects.

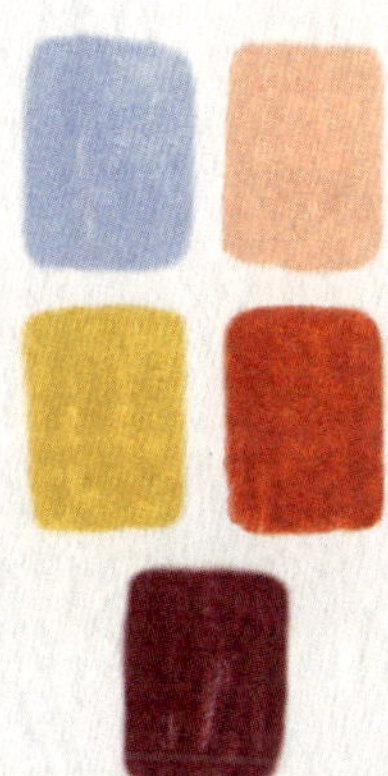

Architecture gives you an insight into the culture, history and daily life of a city. Every building is part of the jigsaw, each with a unique character and story. Buildings and other structures are also visually interesting, an opportunity to play with texture and composition, and to practice perspective. Even better, buildings don't move, so you can sit and focus on all the details you would like to capture.

Before talking generally about drawing architecture, I want to share some tips for tackling detailed subjects.

1 Use Your Pencil as a Guide

Your pencil is your best friend when it comes to perspective and proportion. If you are on location and struggling with deciding how big each section of the building should be, use your pencil.

Hold your pencil a straight arm's distance away, close one eye and align your pencil with one of the building lines, such as the angle of the roof. Now, keeping your pencil at the same angle, bring it down to your paper as a reference line and draw the roof line at the same angle as your pencil.

2 Pick an Object as a Reference for Proportion

To judge proportions accurately, you can use your pencil again as a measuring tool. For example, if you are drawing an architectural scene and want to understand how big a window is in relation to the rest of the building, hold your pencil at an arm's length and close one eye. Align the pencil up against the side of the window and see how much of the pencil is equivalent to the window length. Use your thumb to mark where the bottom of the window falls on the pencil.

Without changing your grip, move your pencil to other parts of the building – how many windows fit into the height and width of the structure? This technique will ensure your drawing is proportionally accurate, as it helps you work out the relative size of one element compared to the whole scene.

This isn't about counting the number of windows – it is about using one familiar object as a reference measurement to compare the sizes of other elements.

3 View the Building in Simplistic Shapes

To make buildings less overwhelming, view each section as simple shapes. Think triangles, squares, rectangles and circles. Now put the building together by drawing the simplistic shapes and then add details from this foundation.

Walls

Walls are great fun to draw. They are full of texture, comprising different materials from wood and bricks to intricate stone details. Here is a sketchbook drawing I did on location at Piazza Santo Stefano in Bologna, Italy. This location was perfect for exploring surface textures: cobbled floors, brick walls, arch details, tiled roofs and greenery creeping through in the background.

As seen in this drawing, I start by creating a warm base. Soft earthy pinks are my go-to colors for the background. Use the side of the pencil to draw broad marks to block out a large area quickly. This will also help to create a nice textural background.

Then go on top with a mid-tone - here I am using a terracotta shade and a muted grayish violet - and start marking out a few lines as brick suggestions. You can interchange between a couple of colors to mix up the tonal values and create more natural color variation. When drawing brick walls, you don't want to draw every single brick. Instead, take an approach that suggests the brick wall, but is more subtle and manageable on location.

On the left-hand side of the drawing, the wall is solid plaster. To show the differentiation between the two surfaces, you need to change up your marks. I like to stick to using the side of the pencil for the background and then layering up with strong, energetic marks. Raise the angle of the pencil and follow a motion of constant zigzag strokes, varying the direction of these. This adds more texture, referencing the cracks and imperfections across the wall.

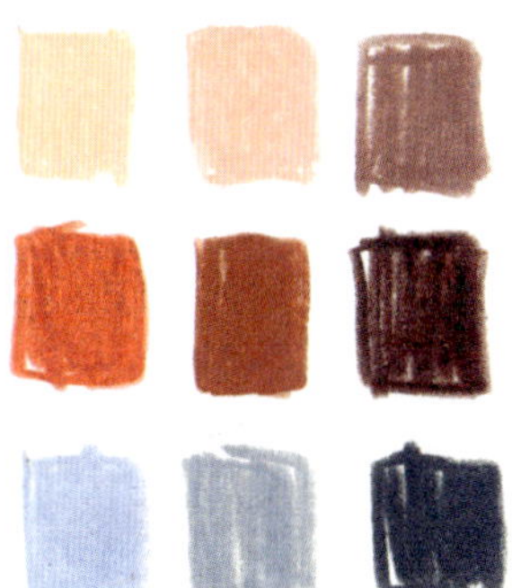

For the highlights on plastered walls, finish with the lightest color. Use strong zigzag marks to add suggestions of the light hitting the wall, while slightly blending the colors to soften the gradient.

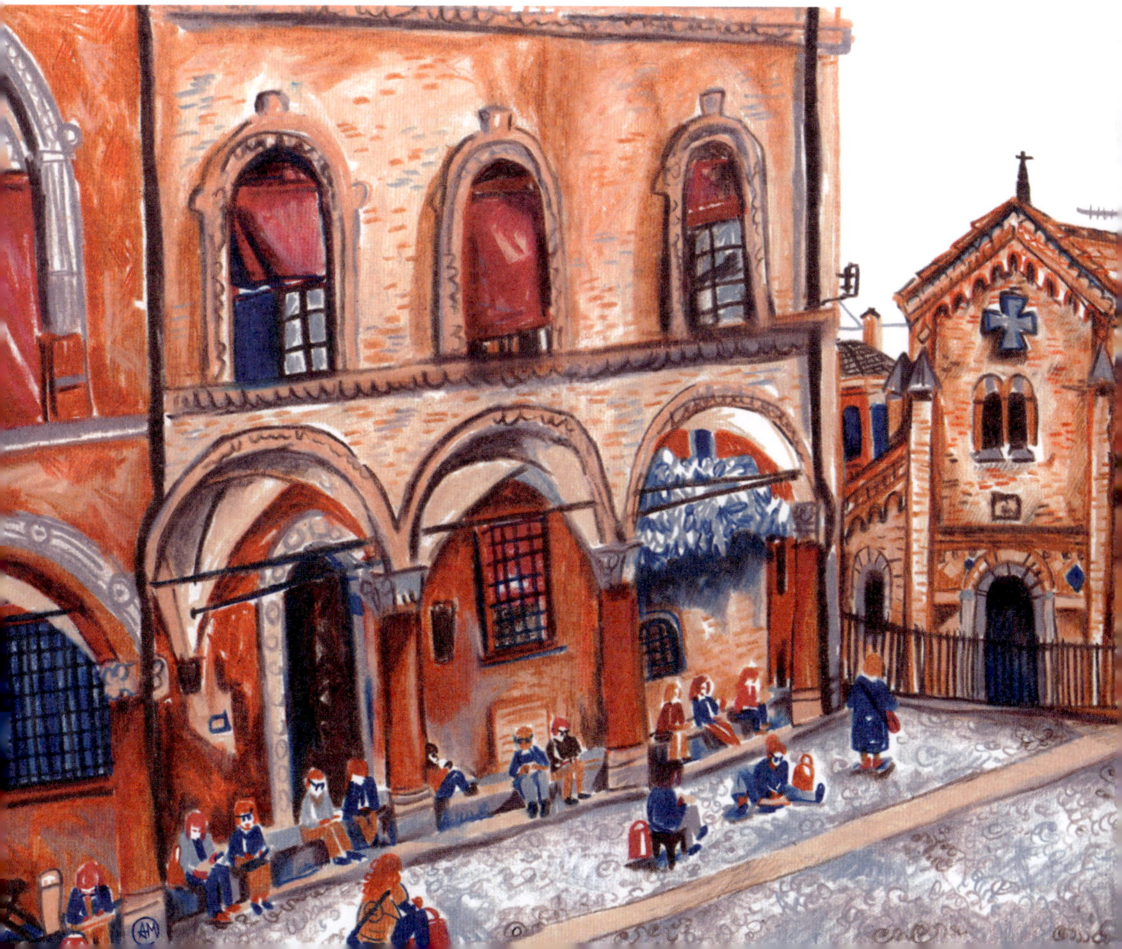

Doors

Barcelona, Spain, is a great city for seeing exquisite architecture. This illustration is a collection of various beautiful doors I came across when living there. You can see the thought and craft that has gone into each design, with the wooden panels, curving stone arches and intricate metalwork.

A composition like this is always a wonderful idea for a city illustration. Pick a topic that captured your interest during your visit, such as people you saw or food you ate, and draw variations on this subject in a collage composition. You could even make a version for each new location you go to, forming your own illustration series.

For wood I will immediately grab my warmer hues, going for soft pinks, oranges and browns. Blue hues are great for capturing the reflective material of glass, and soft sandy colors are perfect for the surrounding stone blocks.

Drawing wood involves exploring layers and innovative mark-making. Use the pencil like a paintbrush, layering up each stroke to replicate the marks and fluidity of the wood textures.

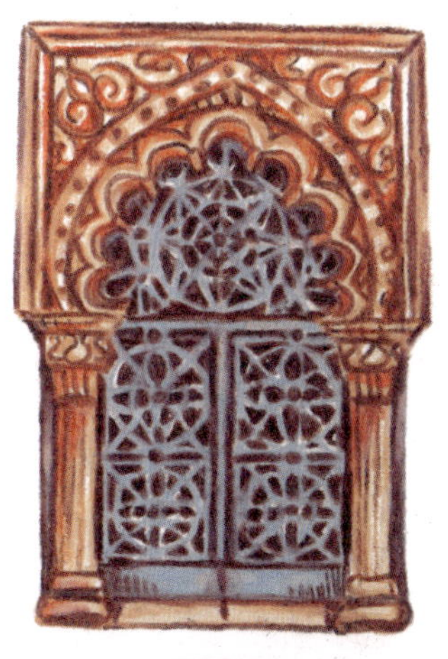
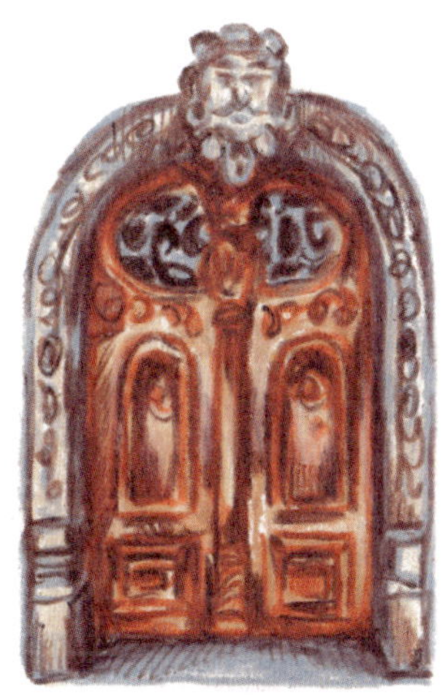
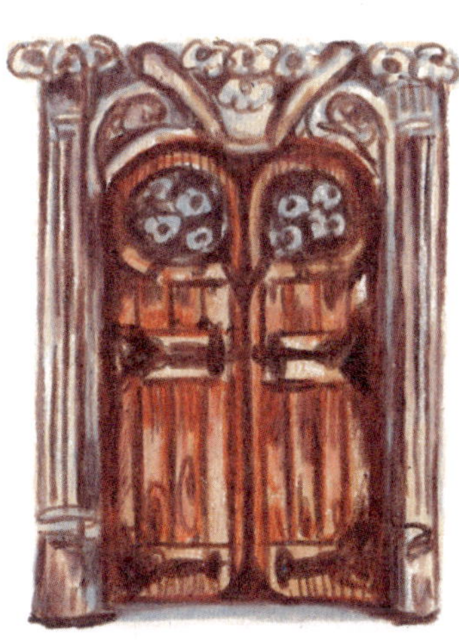
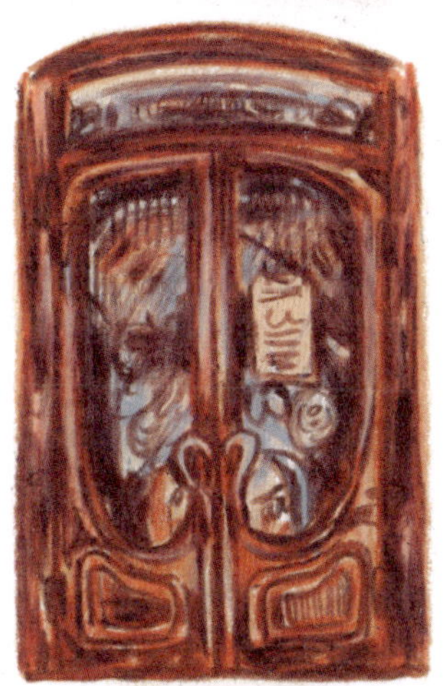
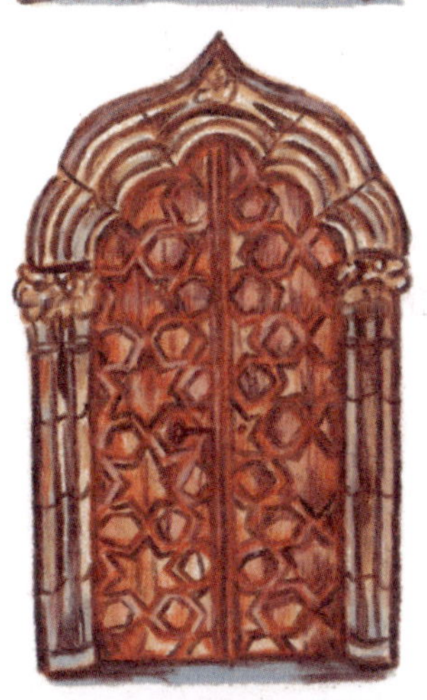
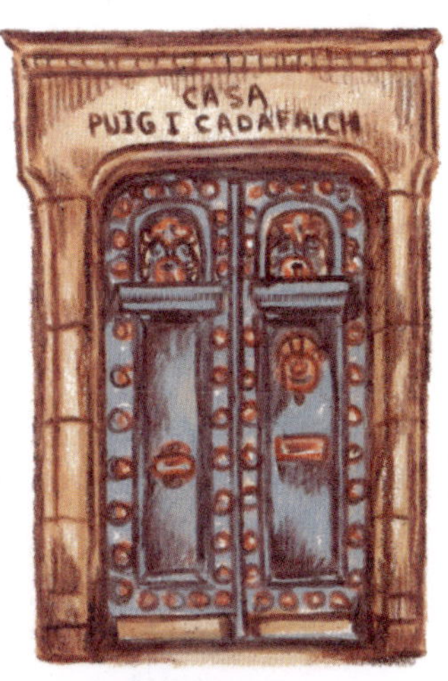
CASA
PUIG I CADAFALCH
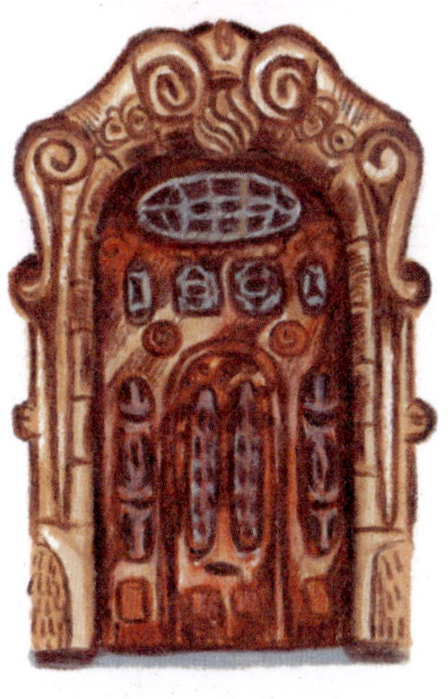
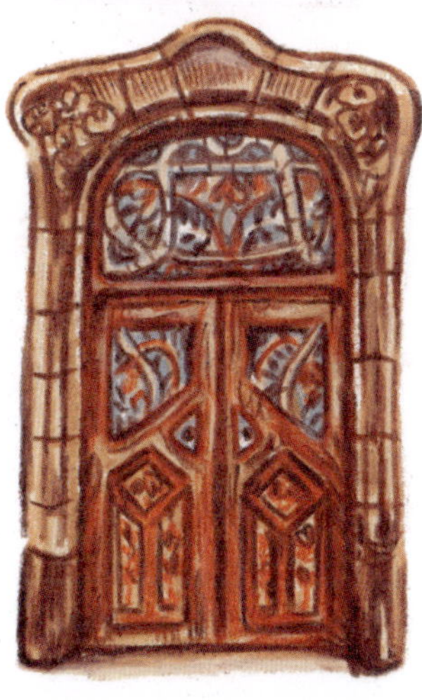
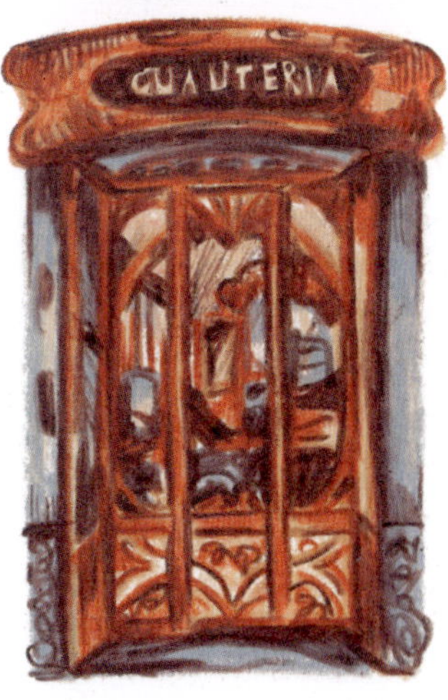
GUAUTERIA

Let's go through the drawing steps for this lovely door I saw in Porto, Portugal.

STEP 1

When drawing subjects with textural details, you need to focus on layers. Each layer is an opportunity to play with the pressure and angle of your pencil while changing the mark-making to add details.

Start with the light layers. Select the main colors you see in each area of the door and apply a wash of color to the background. Use the side of the pencil to slowly and softly build up the color.

STEP 2

Continue drawing broad marks with the side of the pencil, now with more pressure. For the stone areas, every time you see shadows apply more pressure – try and move the pencil as if you are the material. Think about whether the material is fluid, soft, reflective or hard, and then try and move the pencil in the same way.

For the wooden door, to add areas of shadow, continue using the side of the pencil while applying more pressure.

Change the direction and speed of your pencil strokes often to create textural marks that reflect the pattern across the wooden surface.

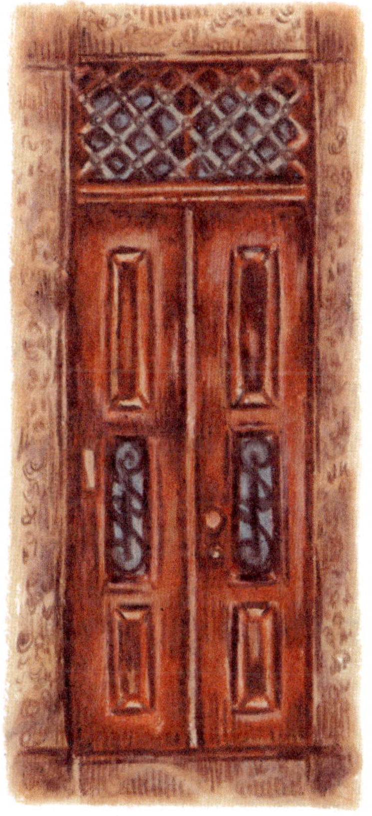

STEP 3

Now move on to blending and adding details. Using the soft cream color for blending, change to a steeper angle and apply more pressure. To add the wood texture, go in with the darkest tone and experiment with shading lines in the shadow areas – play around with the mark-making. For the stone texture, add smaller curved marks in dark brown, mirroring the lines in the material.

STEP 4

In the window panel, contrast is very important. On the light-blue background, add the lines of the metal pattern in soft cream. Now add dark brown to fill in the squares and create tonal contrast.

STEP 5

The final touch is to go back in with the cream color to add highlights. Apply strong marks in areas where the light catches the surface.

Windows

Windows involve a variety of different materials, so let's talk through each surface.

Drawing windows involves understanding not only their shapes and proportions but also the materials that define their character. They can be framed with wood or metal, have shutters or curtains, feature stained glass panels, or be surrounded by carved stone architraves or lintels.

Accurately representing these materials helps convey depth and realism, so let's talk through each surface.

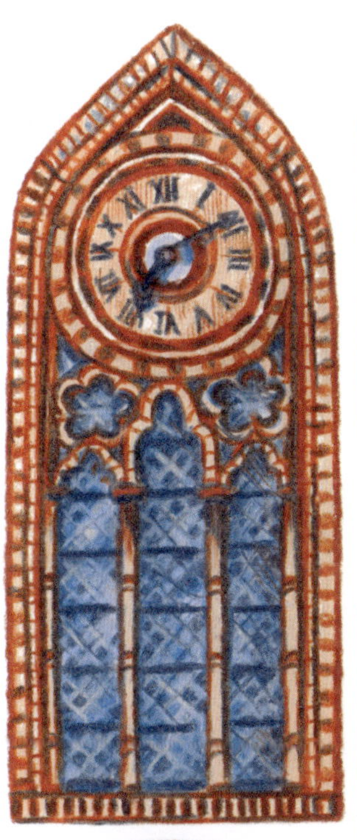
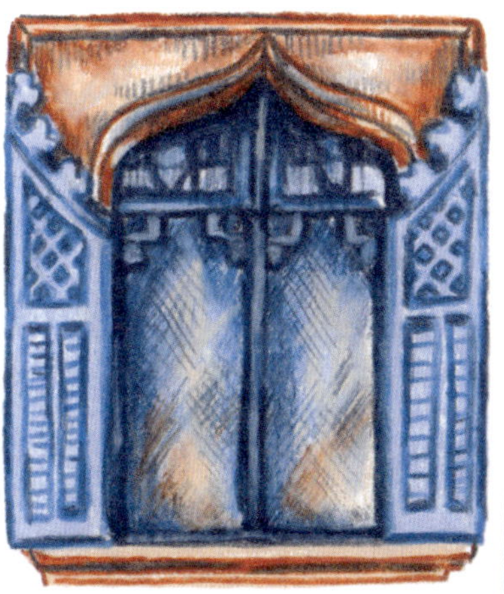
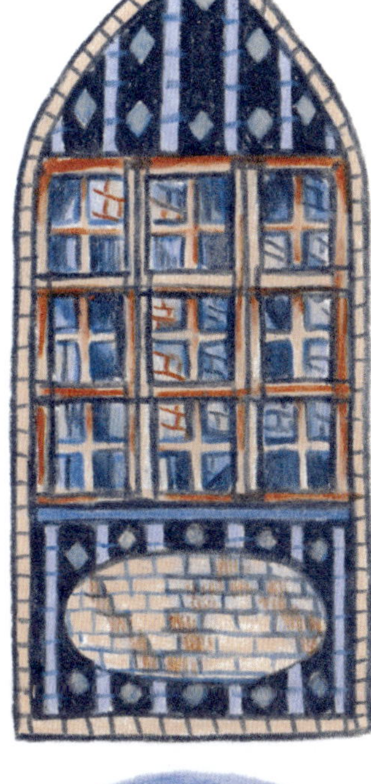

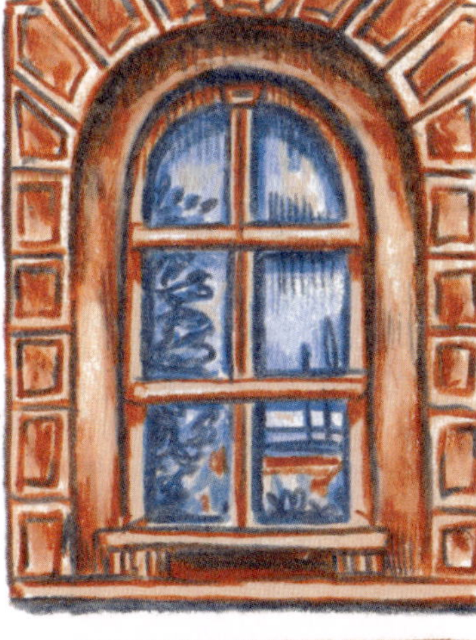

Frames
Window frames can be made from wood, metal, plastic or stone. I often like to use a contrasting warm color, such as russet or an earthy tone, so the frame stands out against the cool blue glass.

Start with a light sandy color to block out the frame shape. To add depth, introduce the darker earthy tone in the shadow areas, such as a russet color. Go back in with your lightest color to blend the transitions. Use a dark brown or dark blue to outline the details and add straight lines for shading marks - across these window drawings I am using charcoal gray.

Surrounding stonework
If the window has surrounding brick or stone details, follow the same layering technique. Start with the soft sandy color to block out the stone design, then use warm russet to outline the brick shapes and add a few shading lines. If you want to add more detail, then go back in with charcoal gray to outline the shapes and add a few subtle lines to introduce suggestions of the stone texture.

Glass
For glass, the focus is on creating the illusion of transparency. I like to use blues for this, starting with light blue for the background and then layering darker blues on top. Remember that glass is reflective, so you need to add colors from the surroundings that would be reflected off the window. If there are trees nearby, add a few subtle green marks; if there are buildings in front, add warm brick colors. Analyzing and incorporating these reflected hues will help the glass feel real rather than flat.

For the final details use your darkest blue to add a few shading marks. This could be a mix of cross-hatching, straight lines or some curved lines for flowing reflections.

Curtains
To draw curtains, you need to focus on capturing the appearance of fabric. For this, begin with sandy pink to block out the curtain shape; remember you are drawing fabric, so use flowing lines. Then add a few lines in russet to imply the folds in the material. Continue with this russet to add areas of shading, especially near the window frames and either side of the curtain folds, remembering to think about the direction of the light source and where the shadows will be. Finally, use sandy pink for blending to soften the gradient transitions.

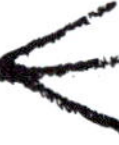

FRAME

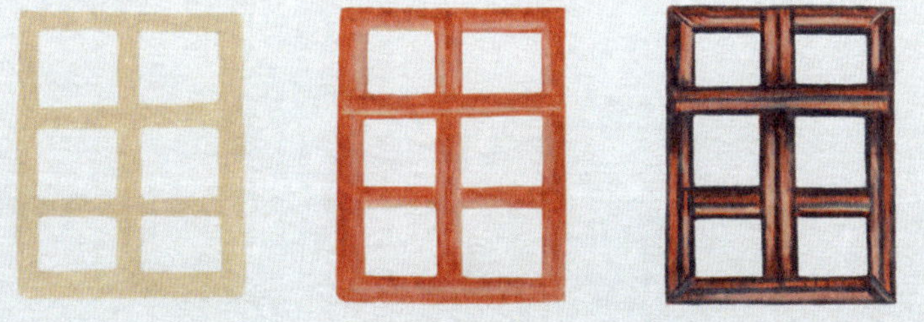

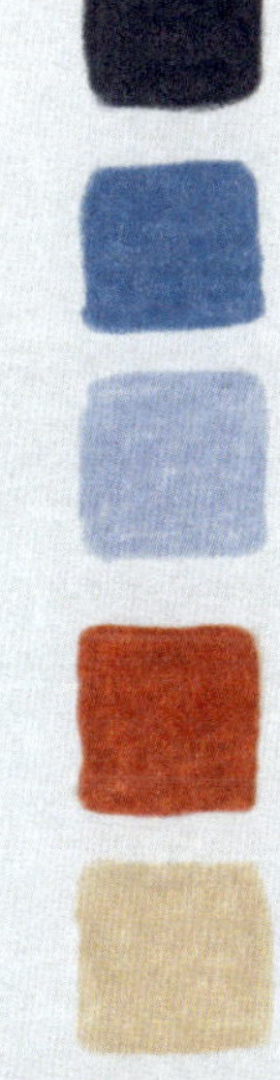

STONEWORK GLASS

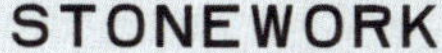

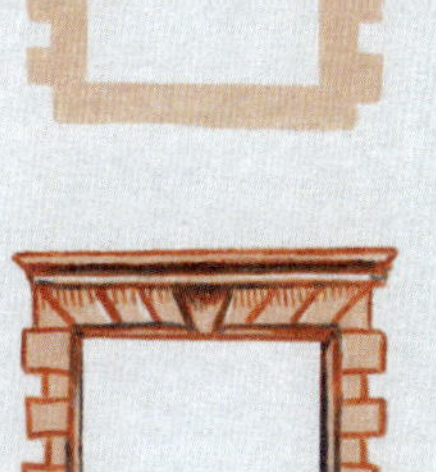

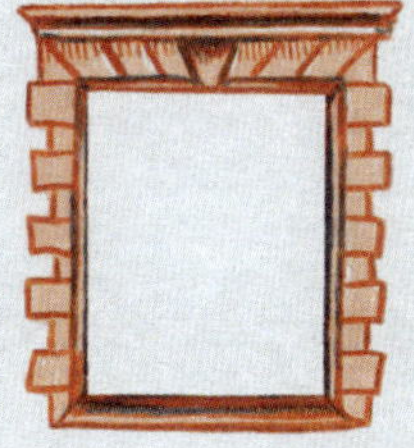

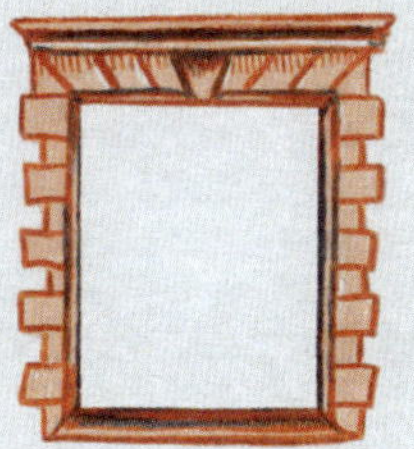

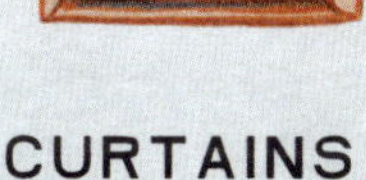

CURTAINS

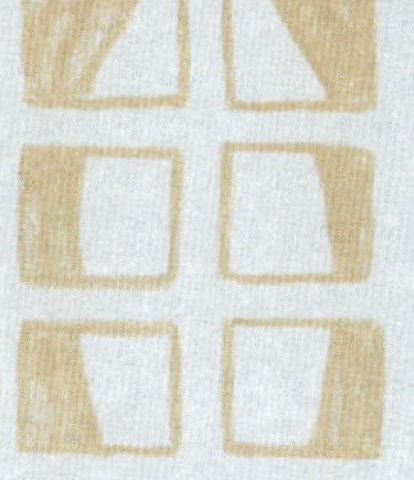

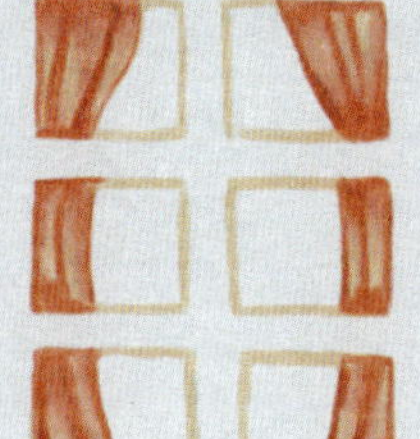

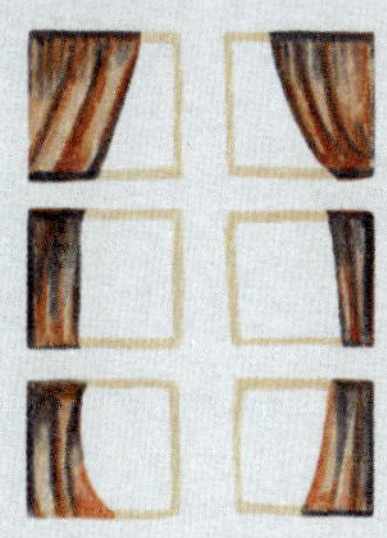

Roofs

One of my favorite memories of drawing in Marrakech, Morocco, is of an evening I spent overlooking Jemaa el-Fnaa square, listening to the sounds and watching the vibrant city beneath me. There was something so beautiful in the seemingly mundane rooftops that I couldn't help but bring out my sketchbook.

Roofs are a great subject for playing with lines and shadows. When picking the shadow color, think about the temperature. Are the shadows warm or cool? Here I noticed a cool shadow, so I opted for purple.

For a compositional technique, I used diagonal lines to add energy into the drawing and guide the viewer through the illustration. The diagonal central roof helps lead us from one corner to the next, creating a sense of movement.

I will now demonstrate a couple of different ways to approach roofs, depending on the tile style and your distance from the subject.

TILES

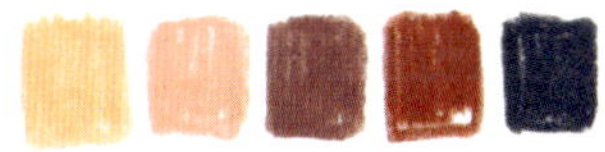

STEP 1

Start by using the lightest color to block out the roof shape - here I am using pale yellow. Go on top with a slightly darker soft pink to add the tile suggestions, using the side of your pencil with more pressure in curved marks.

STEP 2

Now build up the tile details with the mid-tones. I have added a warm reddish-brown (dark russet) for the tile shadows, still using curved marks. Then add a soft purple shadow in between the tiles.

STEP 3

Bring your pale yellow back again and use circular motions to blend the colors together. This is going to produce a softer gradient to create the smooth tile texture.

STEP 4

Finally, add your darkest color for the details. Here I am using a dark blue-gray, which is one of my favorite colors for adding contrast without using black. Add this dark tone in the cracks between the tiles, where they overlap and for any areas of noticeable shadows. Remember to continue following the shape of the tile with your marks. If you want to add highlights and a pop of tonal contrast, use yellow again with a lot of pressure.

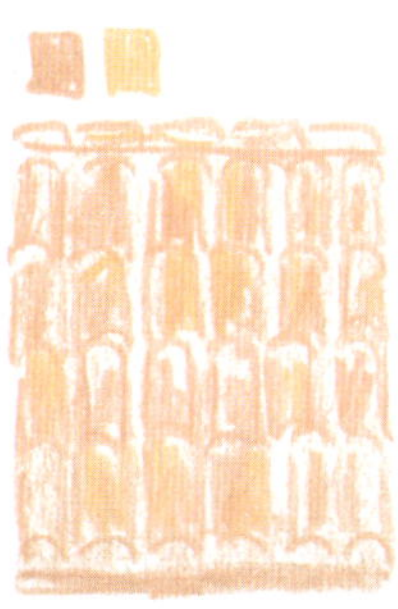

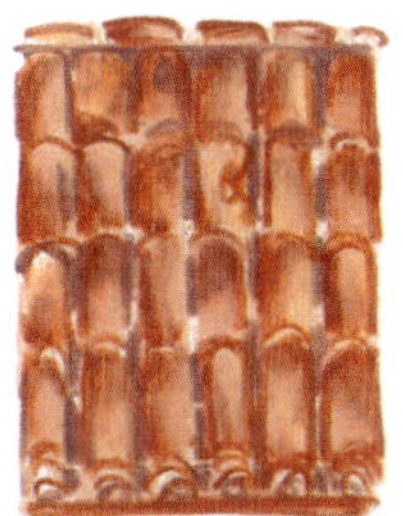
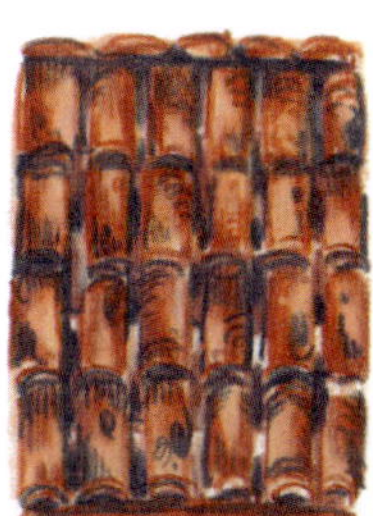

Here are the marks and layering techniques used throughout this process to achieve the various textures.

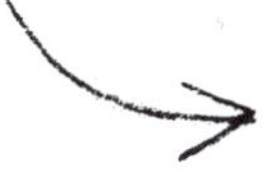

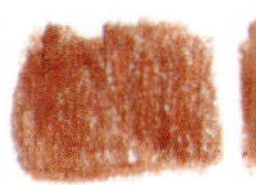

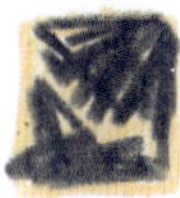

ROOFS FROM A DISTANCE

When drawing the roofs of buildings that are farther away, I like to take a simplistic approach, using a single-color line drawing. I do this to make sure it doesn't distract from the more important parts of the scene. It is all about creating the impression and essence of what you see in front of you.

Here is an example of a location drawing done in Elbasan in Albania. For the main building, I used a dusty mauve to add the horizontal lines implying the roof shape.

For the foreground roofs, I went in with a russet color and drew the individual tile shapes. This adds a bit more detail, visual interest and structure against the fluidity of the surrounding trees. In both areas, I am not worrying about using a variety of colors to add depth or detail, instead focusing on the main shapes and lines.

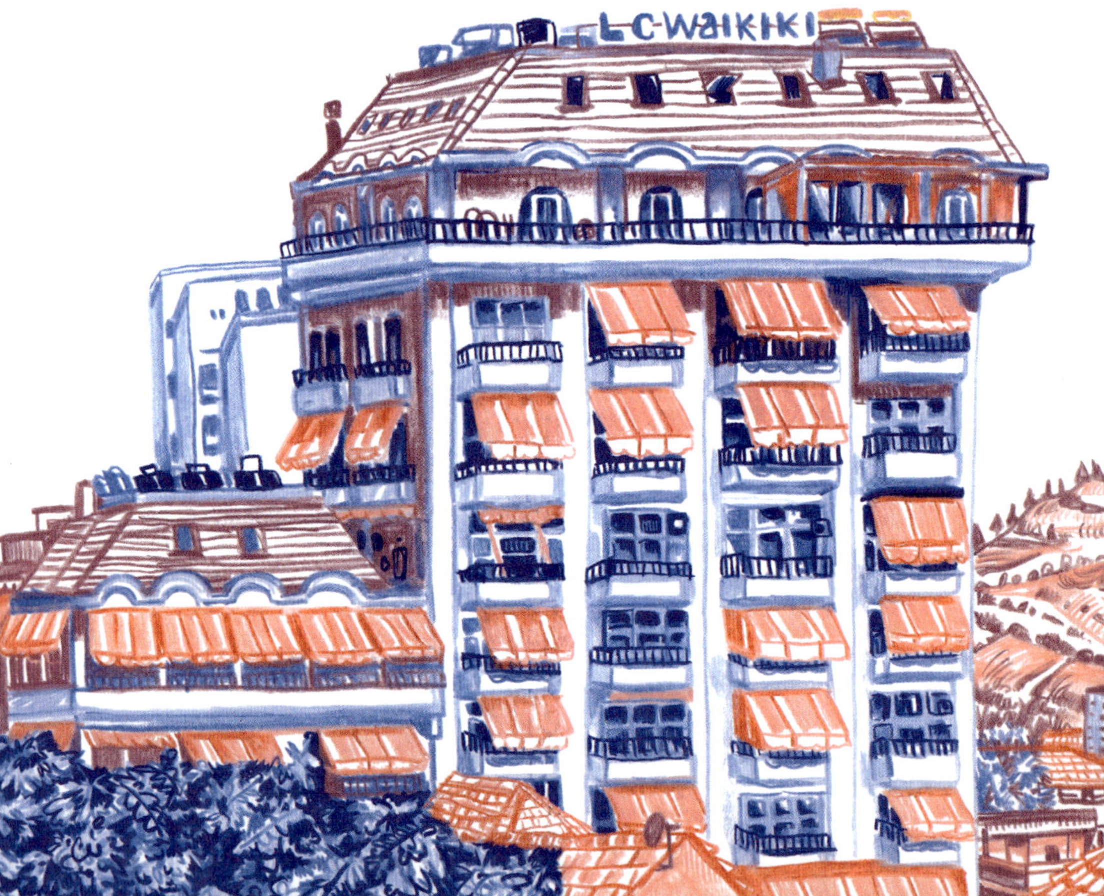

ROOF DETAILS

Across your travels you are sure to find beautiful roof details, such as the intricate wood carvings on traditional buildings in Malaysia. This vibrant dragon carving in Kuching is an example of the craftmanship, care and appreciation of art within everyday life in Malaysia.

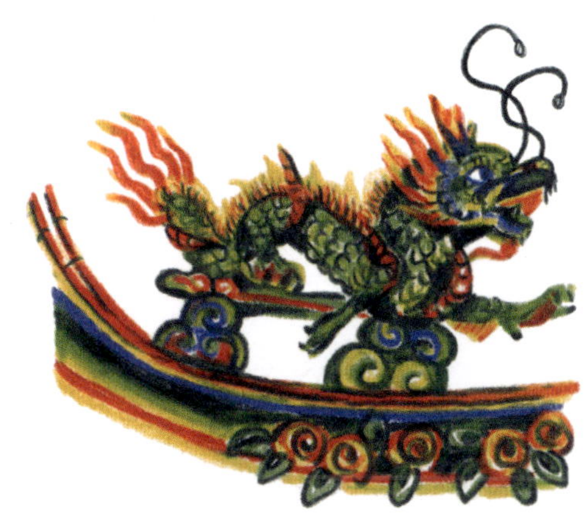

Most of this drawing is built up using block colors. The main textural detail comes from the scales of the dragon's body, using a drawing technique very similar to that of the first tile steps.

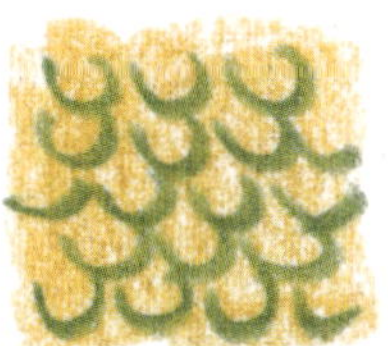

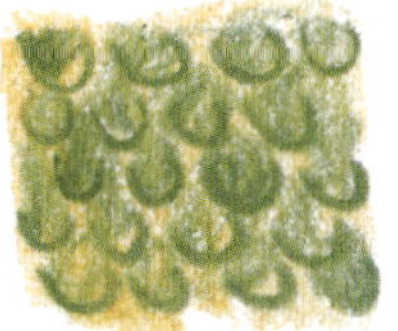

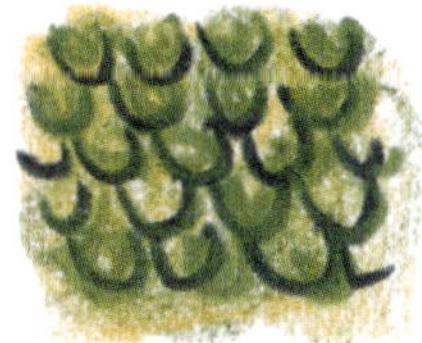

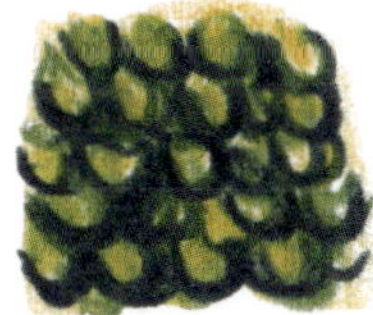

STEP 1

Start by creating a background wash of color using a warm yellow ocher. Then introduce the 'u' shapes across the design in soft green, making sure that they aren't completely uniform to add more fluidity.

STEP 2

Go on top with the same green, using the side of the pencil in circular motions to add tonal contrast and texture. Don't apply too much pressure, so you still get some yellow coming through.

STEP 3

Now add dark green on top, to redefine those 'u' shapes and add contrast.

STEP 4

Finally, look at the shadows within the design and introduce more of your dark green into these areas. Then go on top with yellow ocher, for blending and creating highlights across the scales.

Balconies

Balconies are a very popular recurring motif within illustration. Much like a window or door, a balcony is an opening into a new space, providing a glimpse into someone's daily life.

Drawing a balcony is often a very simple process. For metal balconies I like to use a single color to draw the outline as the final layer on top of the wall and window. This means it can be seen over the rest of the busy drawing.

These two illustrations are part of a T-shirt series I created in Barcelona called 'Sunday Love'. As these are screen printed, I kept to a limited monochromatic color palette of three tones.

These designs show how simply you can draw balconies, focusing on the linework instead of adding any shading details. For each composition, you can play around with the narrative through the character design, decorations and the activities people are doing.

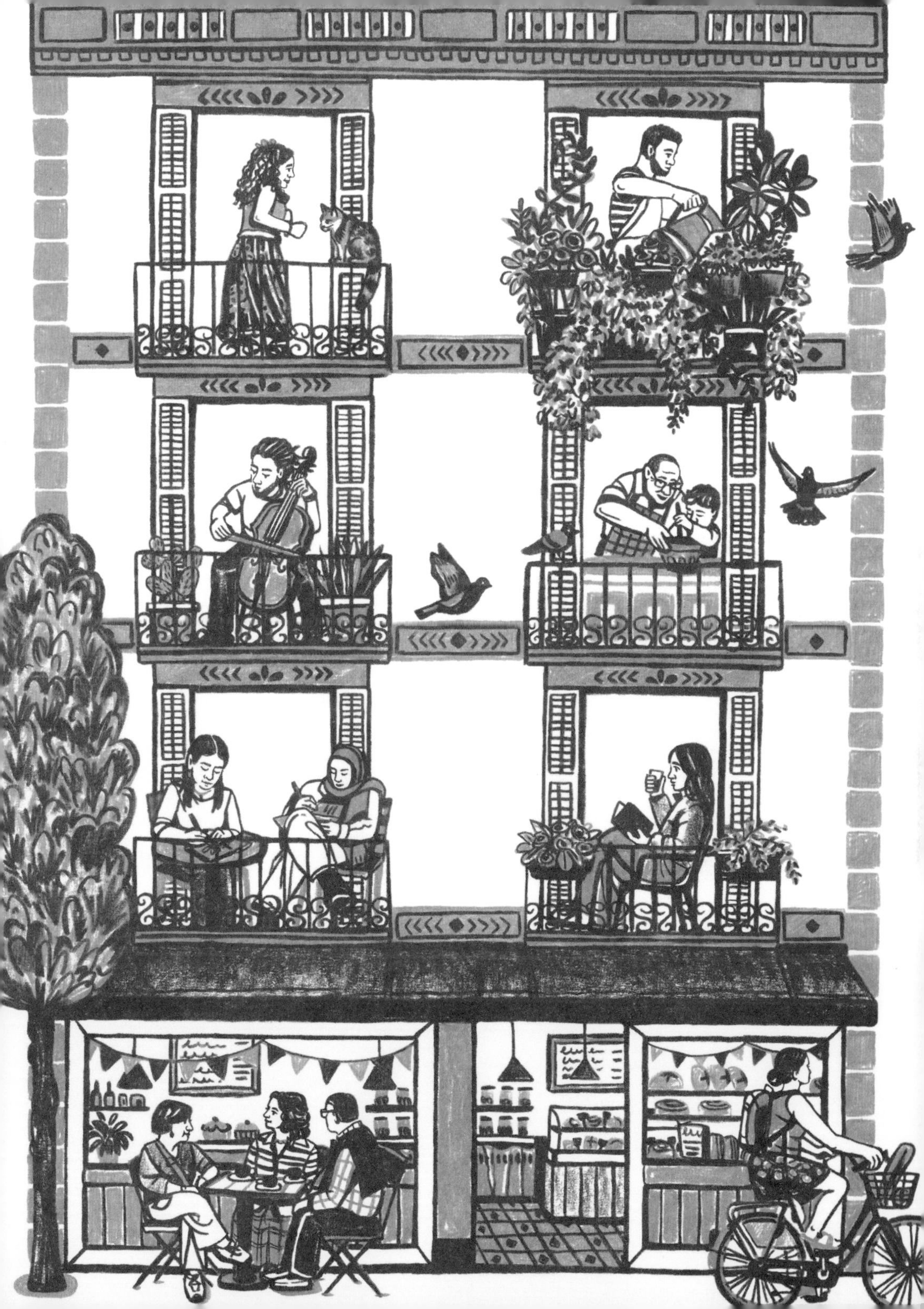

Fences *and* Railings

As with balconies, fences and railings are extra details within a scene, so I like to keep the color usage to a minimum. I will usually stick with the same technique of a single-color line drawing.

If you want to make the railing more of a feature, you can play with adding an extra darker tone for the shadows. Here is an example of a lovely railing design in Berlin, Germany, drawn in a monochromatic palette.

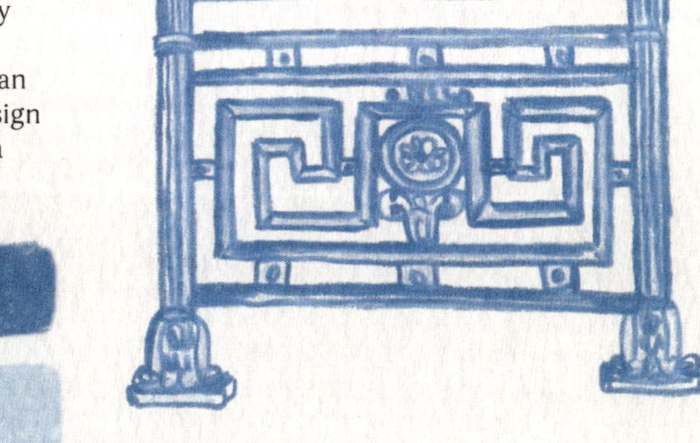

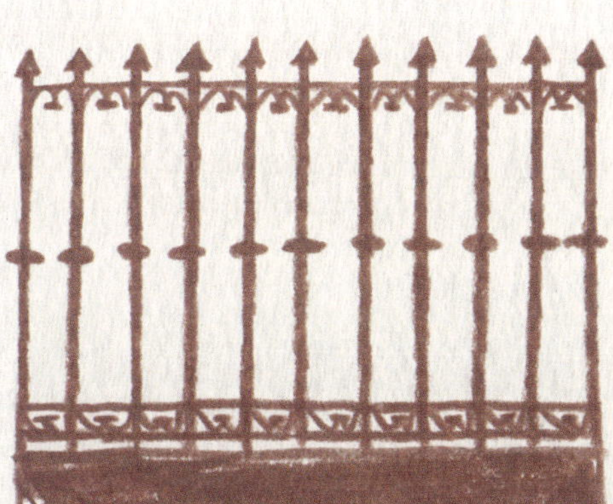

Draw the main shape in your lightest shade, such as a soft sky blue. Then add a deeper cobalt blue (the darker tone) to outline areas, add shadows and mark out any details. Otherwise, you can keep to a single hue - like this drawing of a delicate railing design I saw in Copenhagen, Denmark.

Purple is a great color for black railings, while light blue and pink are good options to use for white or pale railings.

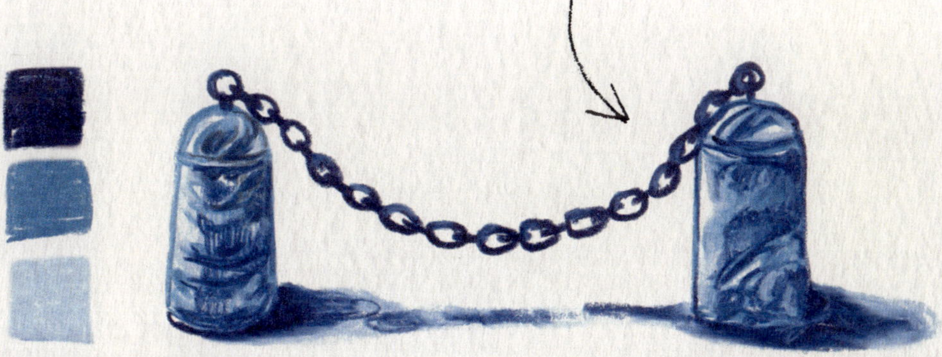

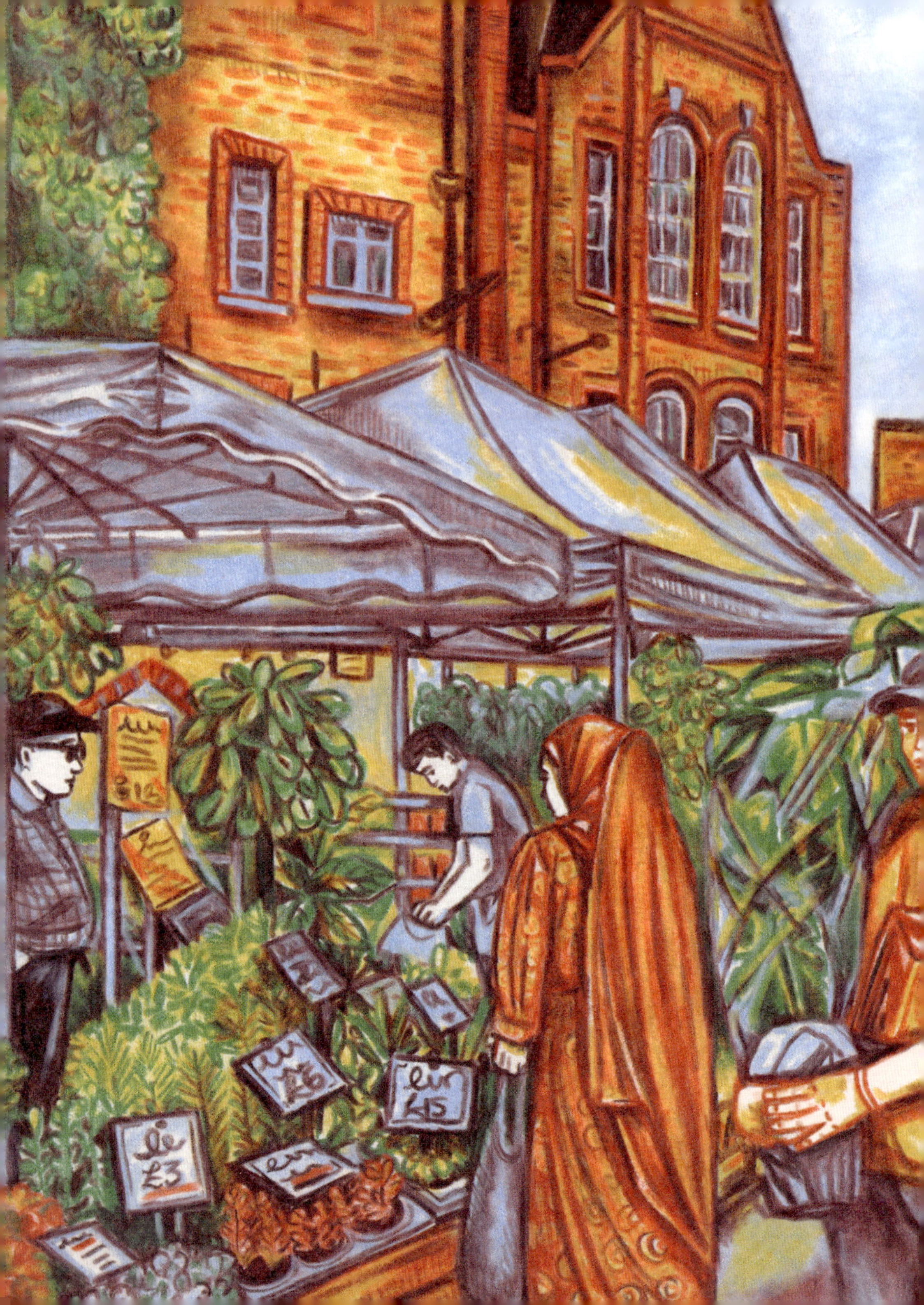
£15
£3

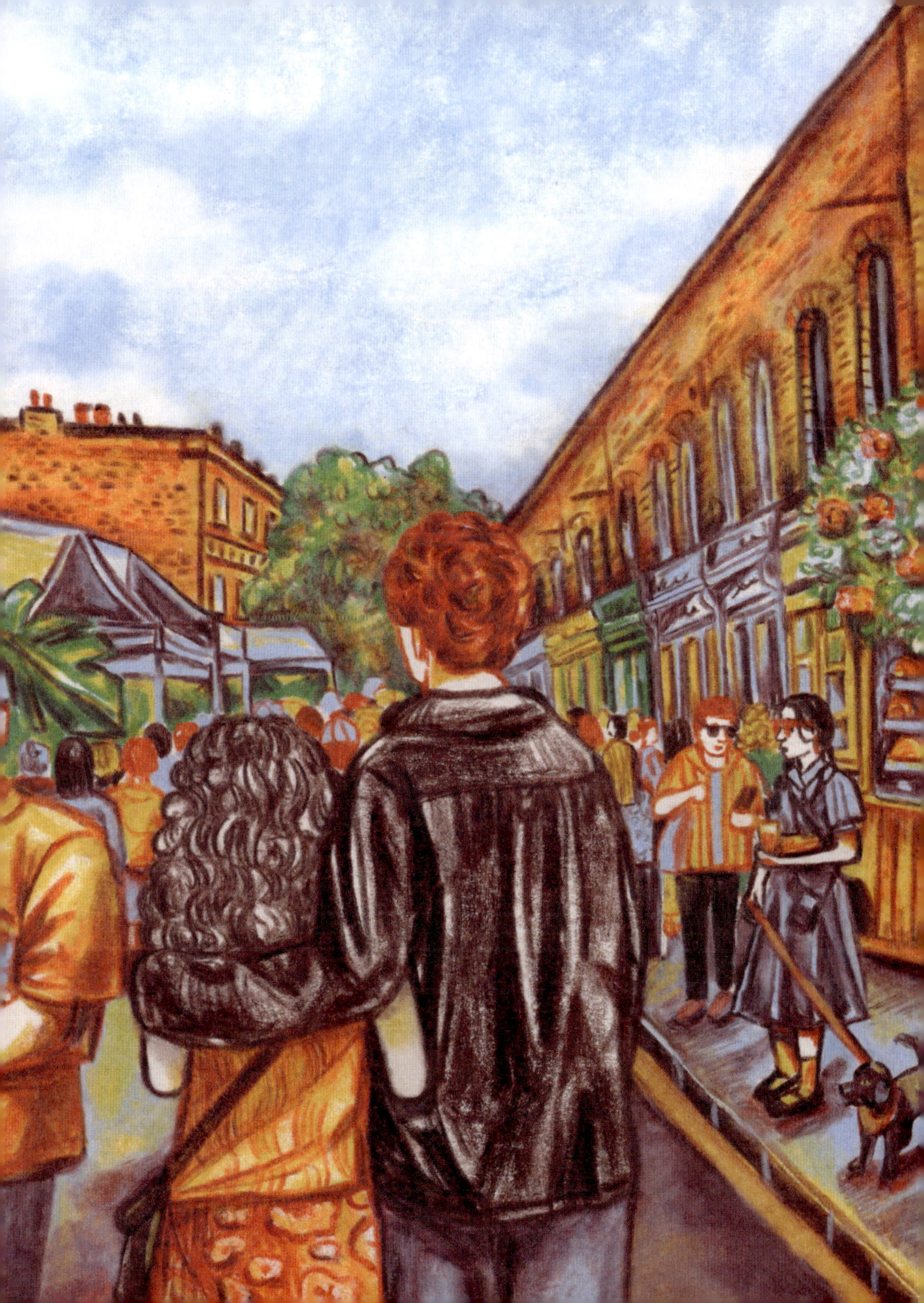

Floors

Every city has its own visual aesthetic and design, which includes the choice of materials for the roads, streets and sidewalks. Whether these are old, cobbled lanes, modern asphalt or large stone slabs, each surface has a different texture that you need to tackle.

Streets made from small bumpy stones, like a pebbly beach, are a joy to draw. You might come across this surface in old buildings, around statues or in traditional squares.

COBBLES

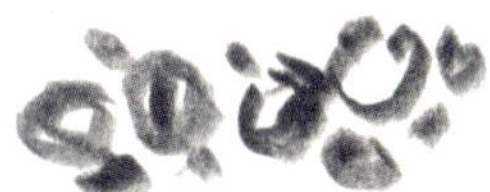

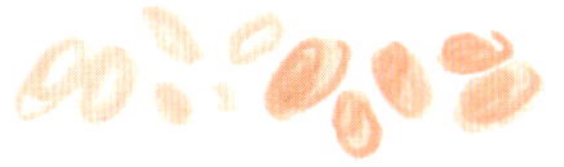

This is a drawing of a pebbled floor I noticed in the Pinacoteca di Brera in Milan, Italy. If you love traditional architecture and galleries, this should be on your Milan list. It houses one of the most important collections of Italian Renaissance art.

Here I have shown the final drawing with the layers needed to build it up. I stuck with soft colors to match the natural color of the surface – light blue, soft pink, dusty mauve and charcoal gray. You are going to want to randomly combine all these colors throughout the design to create the mix of colored stones.

Start with the side of your pencil in light blue, using circular motions to build up the suggestion of stone shapes. Vary the pressure to get a range of tones throughout.

Then introduce your other colors, using a mix of oval marks and rough outlines. You can bring in your darkest color (charcoal gray) to add shadows in between stones. Layering all these marks will create the impression of an uneven surface.

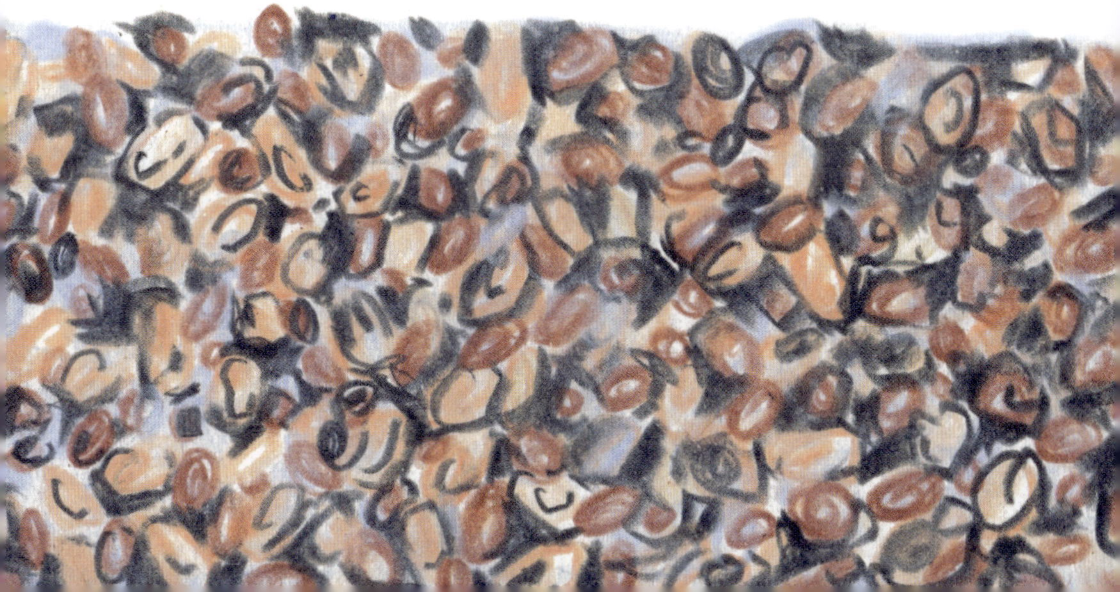

STONE SLAB FLOOR

To capture the appearance of soft stone, I like to use an analogous palette (see page 39) with pink and purple as the main hues, varying the tonal values to create contrast.

STEP 1

Use the side of your lightest-color pencil (the warm sandy color) and draw out the stone shapes. Maintain light pressure and move your pencil in a variety of directions to help form the different textures.

STEP 2

Now introduce your next tonal value - a soft pink. Continue with the side of the pencil in faster motions, almost like you are scribbling across the surface. You want to try and create those swirls and tonal variations you see in the stone. You can also softly outline the edges of the slabs in the pink.

Sometimes it is nice to stop here, with just two colors - simply as a reference to the stone slabs without all the details.

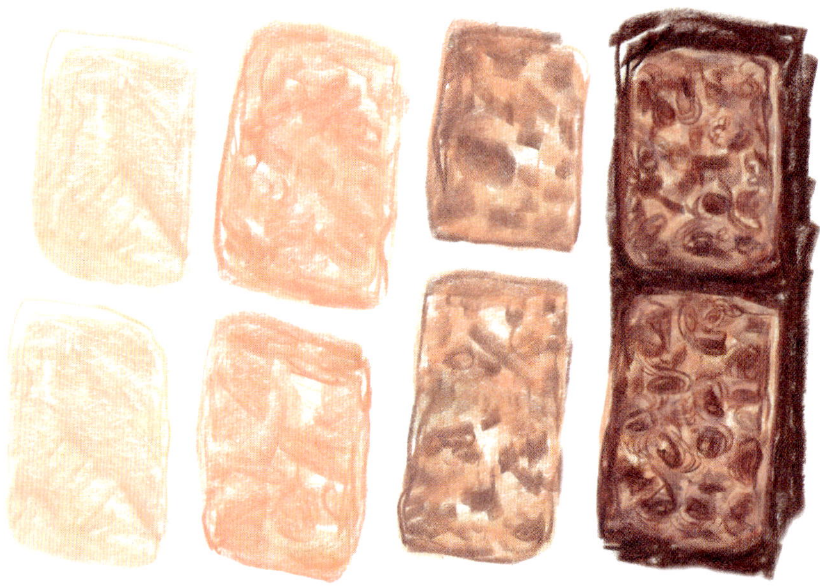

STEP 3

If you want to add more detail, move on to the next tonal value, bringing in dusty mauve. Here you can be a bit more decisive with your marks. Draw shorter, stronger marks to mimic the dips and cracks in the floor. To blend some areas together, use the warm cream pencil in strong circular motions.

STEP 4

For the final details, use your darkest color (a dark purple-brown) and play with the mark-making. Use your pencil at a steeper angle to add the curved marks around the different dips in the stone. Then you can blend sections again with your lightest tone.

For the dark gaps in between the slabs, continue with this dark color. Draw with the side of your pencil in strong and fast strokes. This will add energy to the design and leave the little stone imperfections.

Feel free to vary the level of detail. The stone slabs I observed had a lot of cracks and dark spots, which inspired the marked textures. Whereas this stone sidewalk has a more even surface, so I used less tonal contrast - mainly terracotta and pink for the slabs, with dark brown reserved for cracks and a few swirl details.

Apartment Building

I want to show how easily you can draw a building with only three steps. This is a reference from colorful apartments I saw in Kuala Lumpur, Malaysia. The exterior involves flat colorful walls, shutters and electrical details.

STEP 1

Start by drawing the outline shapes of the building, including the windows and floor dividers. I am using terracotta and pale yellow as my two color choices.

STEP 2

Use the side of the pencil with light pressure to shade in the thin rectangle areas above each new floor. For the main body of the building, use energetic and strong marks with a steep angle to cover the surface area. I like to keep the marks very intuitive, leaving occasional small white spaces.

Introduce a base color for the windows. If there are shutters, draw the outline and horizontal lines across to mimic the shutter lines and use the light blue for any glass windows.

STEP 3

Now add the shadows and details to bring the building to life. Use charcoal gray as the shadow color to go beneath floor dividers, windows and any dark areas, blocking out the shadow shapes. For softer shadows on lighter surfaces, such as the shutters and paler walls, use brown ocher (your mid-tone). Draw rough, fast marks in zigzag motions across the darker areas of the wall to suggest variations in tonal values and brick discoloration.

STEP 4

To finish, continue with your darkest color (charcoal gray) for the final architectural details: curving lines for the wires between windows; horizontal lines for shutters and rectangles or boxes to suggest fans. Focus on the outlines only. You can build up the apartments as much as you like, adding as many details as you feel bring them to life.

Use these same techniques for any similar building designs.

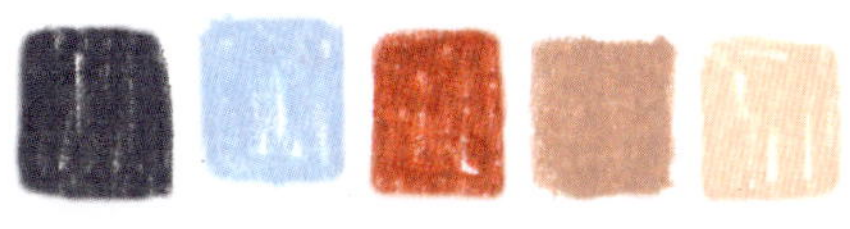

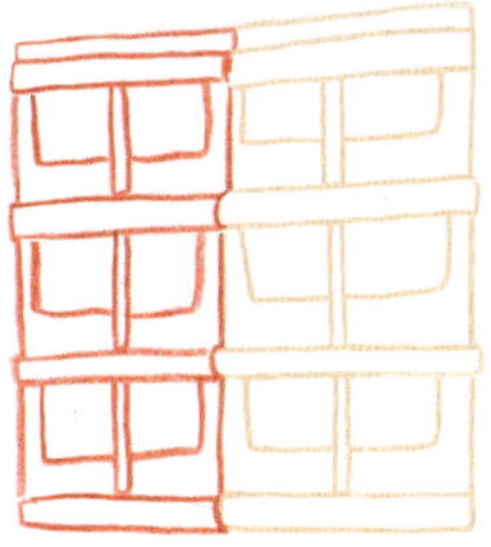

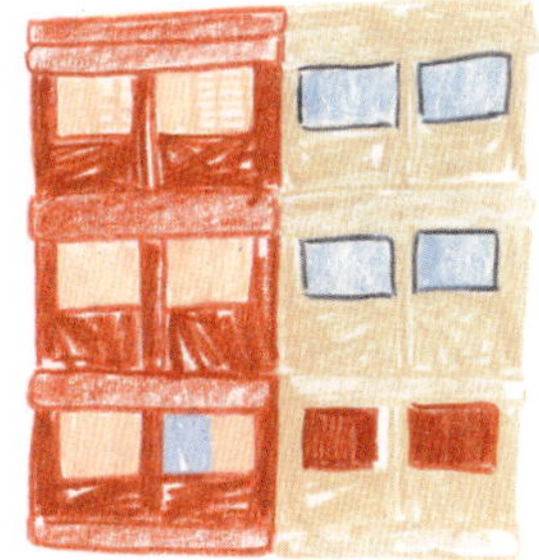

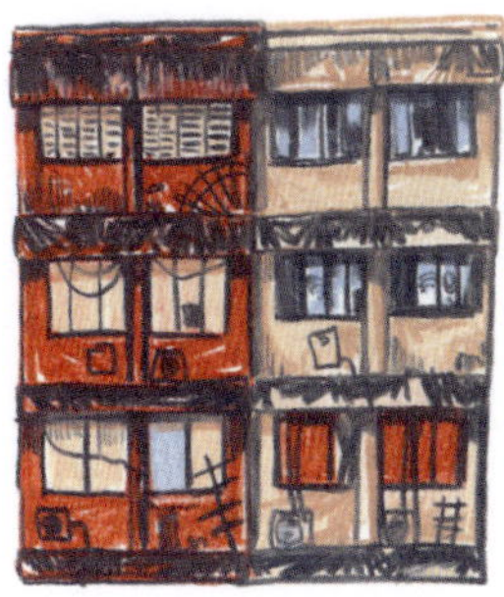

Architectural Details

When thinking about traditional architectural details like columns, arches and statues, I am immediately taken back to my travels in Italy. With so much culture, history and art embedded within their architecture, it is the perfect place to explore this topic. Cities like London, England, are also great case studies for these elements.

When drawing architectural details, the main thing to think about is the surface. What material is it made from? This will help you decide how to approach the drawing. Is it sandy stone, swirling marble or aged brick? Is the form curved or flat?

Now you have analyzed the subject and materials, it is on to the drawing phase. To simplify these intricate structures, you need to focus on the main patterns. Break down the details into a few simple shapes and lines.

This is a drawing on location in London at the V&A Museum. Not only does this building hold a beautiful collection of inspiring pieces from all different crafts and cultures, but the architecture of the building itself is a work of art and a great subject to study. Let's break down each of the individual architectural elements.

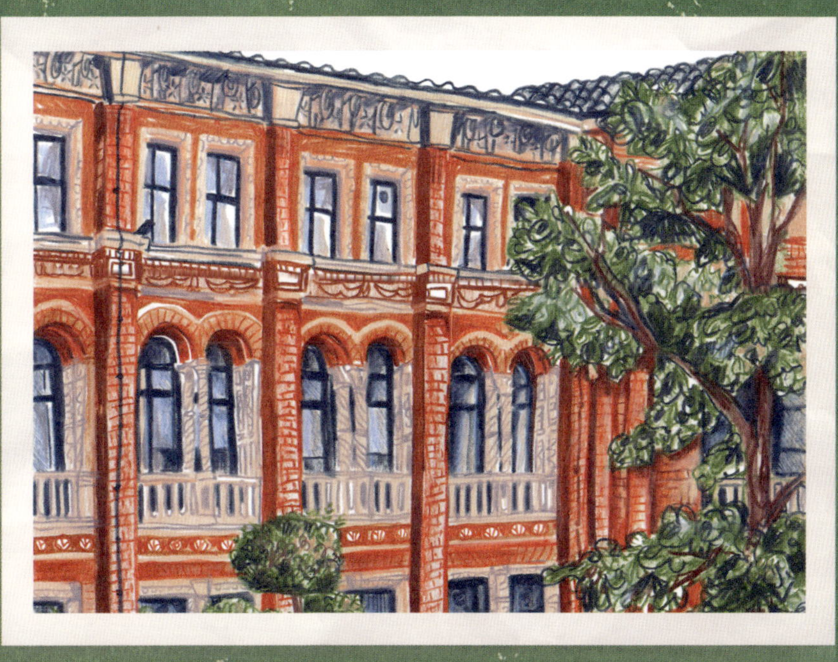

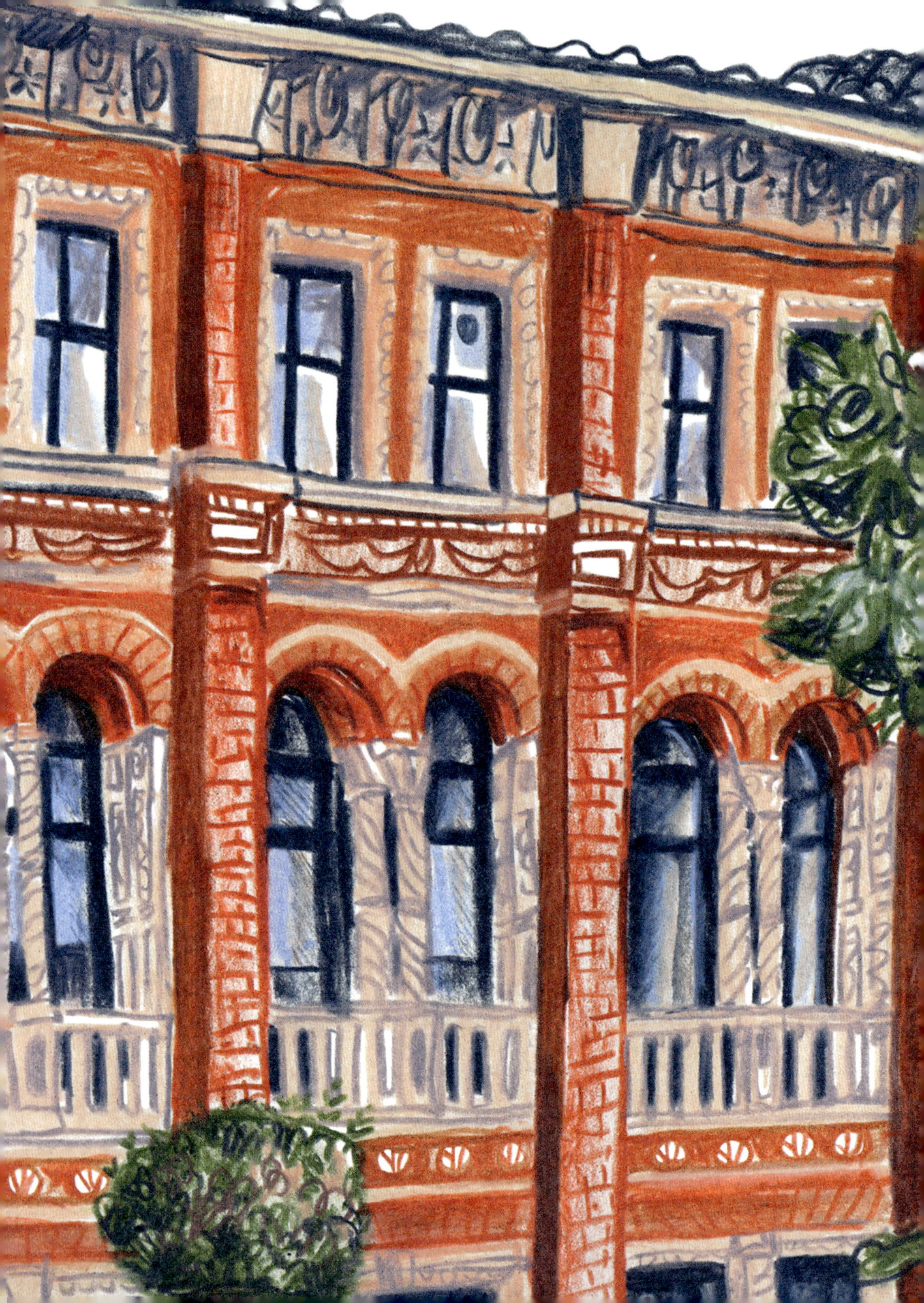

STEP 1

The curving archways around the windows are a key feature of the façade. For this I used a nice warm terracotta as the background and then added lines in a darker tone to suggest the brick details. Make sure to change the angle of your lines to fit the curving arch.

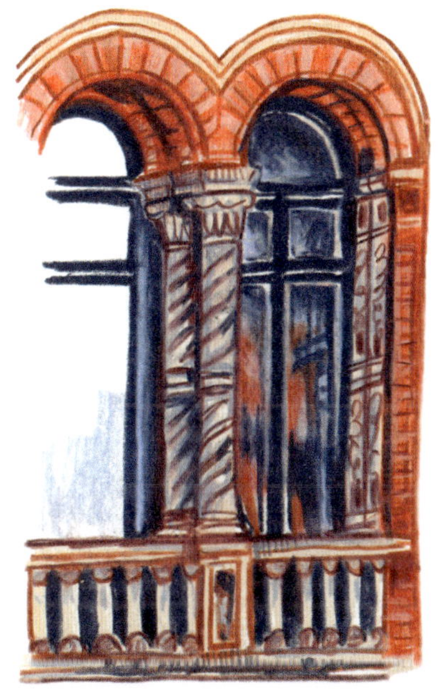

STEP 2

For the swirling columns in the center of the windows, it's again on to a two-tone approach. I used soft pink as the base color and then a gray-purple on top to outline the rough shapes. You need to look at the direction of the column pattern and simply add curved lines following this direction around the columns. This will help create the illusion of a three-dimensional form.

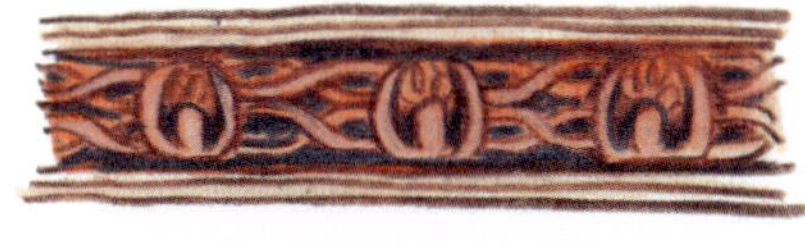

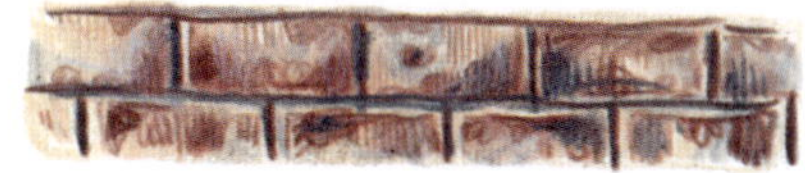

STEP 3

Under the roof and along the line dividing the floors are lovely tile details. As above, you can use a two-color approach. Apply a base layer of pink for the background, then add a darker tone for the details, using a variety of marks to create the stone patterns.

Bringing all these elements together helps build the impression of the façade while keeping it manageable to tackle on location. Suggesting details in this way also lets your artistic style and vision come through.

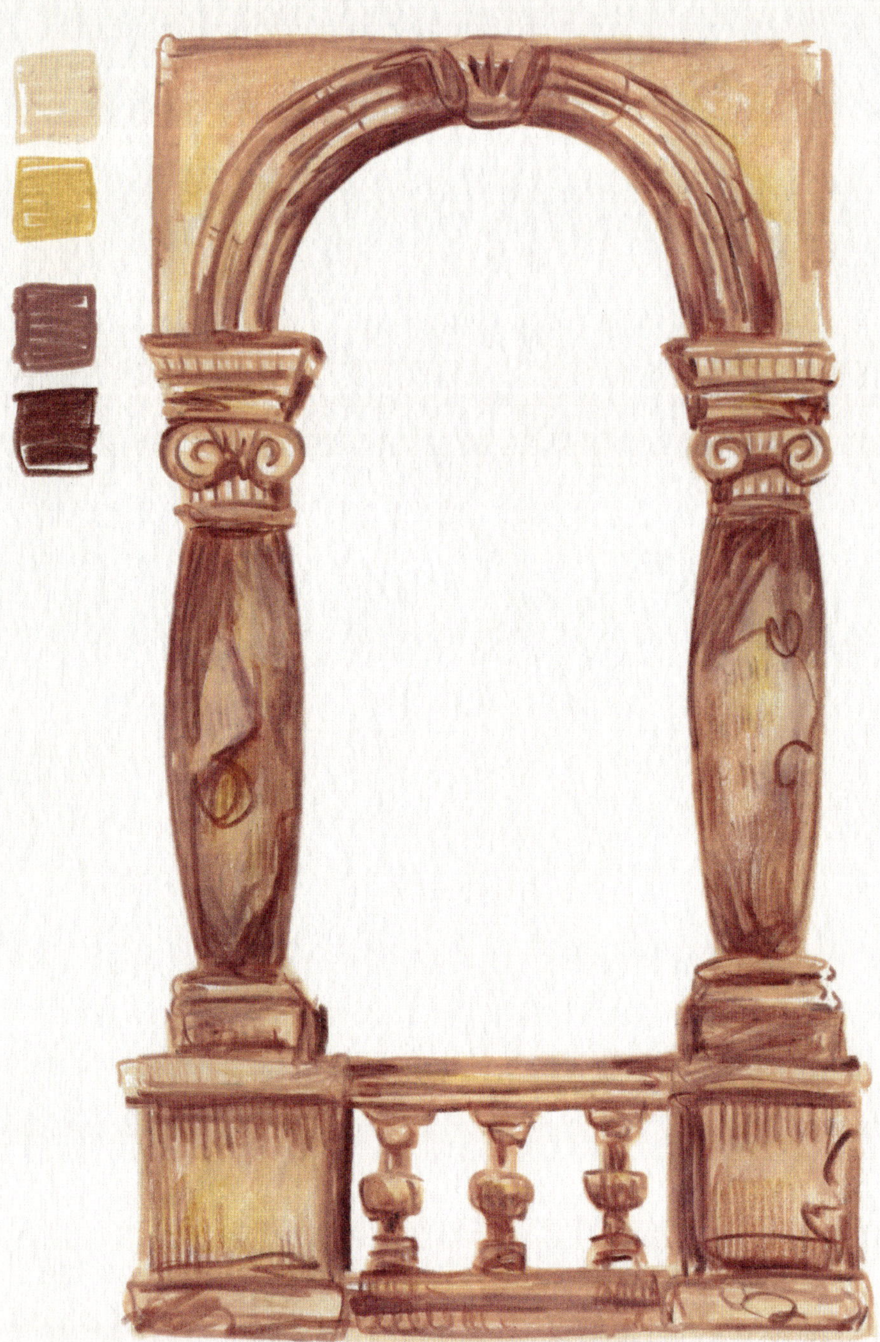

COLUMNS

Here are a couple of illustrations drawn on location at the Pinacoteca di Brera in Milan, Italy. Art, history and culture fill this place, creating the perfect atmosphere for an inspiring and beautiful drawing spot.

To simplify the column details, follow a two-color approach: one color for the background and one for outlining details. In the drawing below, I am using a soft cream color for the background and a dusty mauve for my darker outlines.

This subject requires a lot of thought on perspective. If you need help working out angles and proportions, go back to the tips at the beginning of the book, using your pencil as a reference tool (see page 53).

Start by blocking in the surface area of the subject with the lighter cream color, using the side of the pencil in varied directions to build up texture. Once the base is down, use the dusty mauve to define the shape with outlines. For any areas of dark shadow - under the arches or on the floor - fully shade these areas. And there you have it: a simplified way to capture a detailed structure.

If you want to dive in deeper with more depth and detail, introduce extra tonal values. The drawing opposite is also at the same lovely location in Milan. However, this time, I have introduced yellow ocher and soft pink for warm highlights and a warm dark brown to define shadows and add tonal contrast.

Begin with your lightest tone to shade the base of the structure. Now bring in your mid-tones with soft pink and dusty mauve. Add these in any areas you see shadow, to help build up the form - remember to have marks following the curves of the columns. Use warm yellow to add highlights where the sun hits the building.

To define the structure, outline the main shapes in dusty mauve and then use warm dark brown for the darkest areas. The final touch is to draw shading marks and fast, expressive lines to create energy in the drawing and reference the cracks and imperfections in the columns. Think about the direction of the light source so you know where to put the shadows in the design.

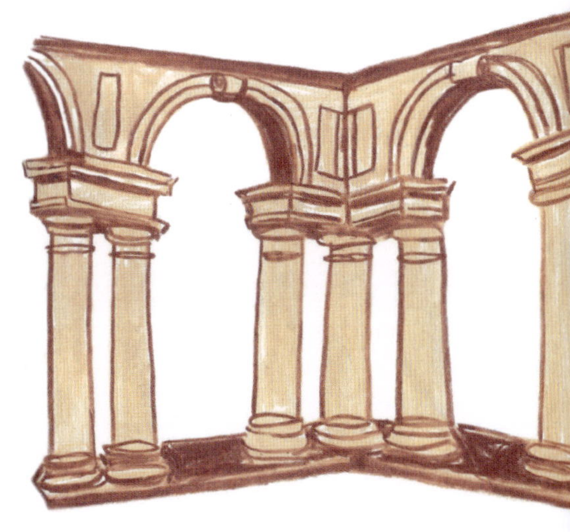

Street Furniture

A street scene comes together like a tapestry – all elements weaving together to add the details and bring the design to life. Even the less glamorous aspects, like streetlights, signs and traffic lights are helpful to build up the overall scene, giving context and a greater insight into daily life.

STREETLIGHTS

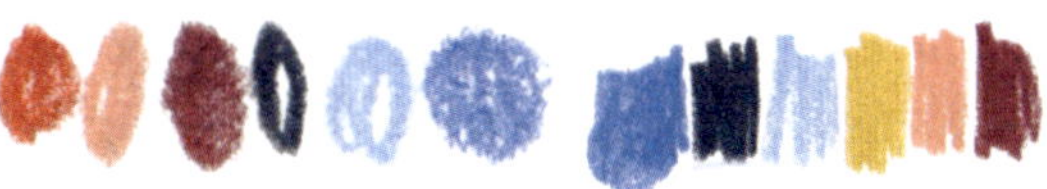

Streetlights are one of my favorite pieces of street furniture to draw. When traveling, I enjoy observing the variety in their designs - some sleek and modern, others aged and ornate.

For metal subjects, I tend to use my blues as I find these best replicate the material. Blue is also a lovely hue for monochromatic designs and blends nicely for the gradient effect you will be looking to achieve in your drawing.

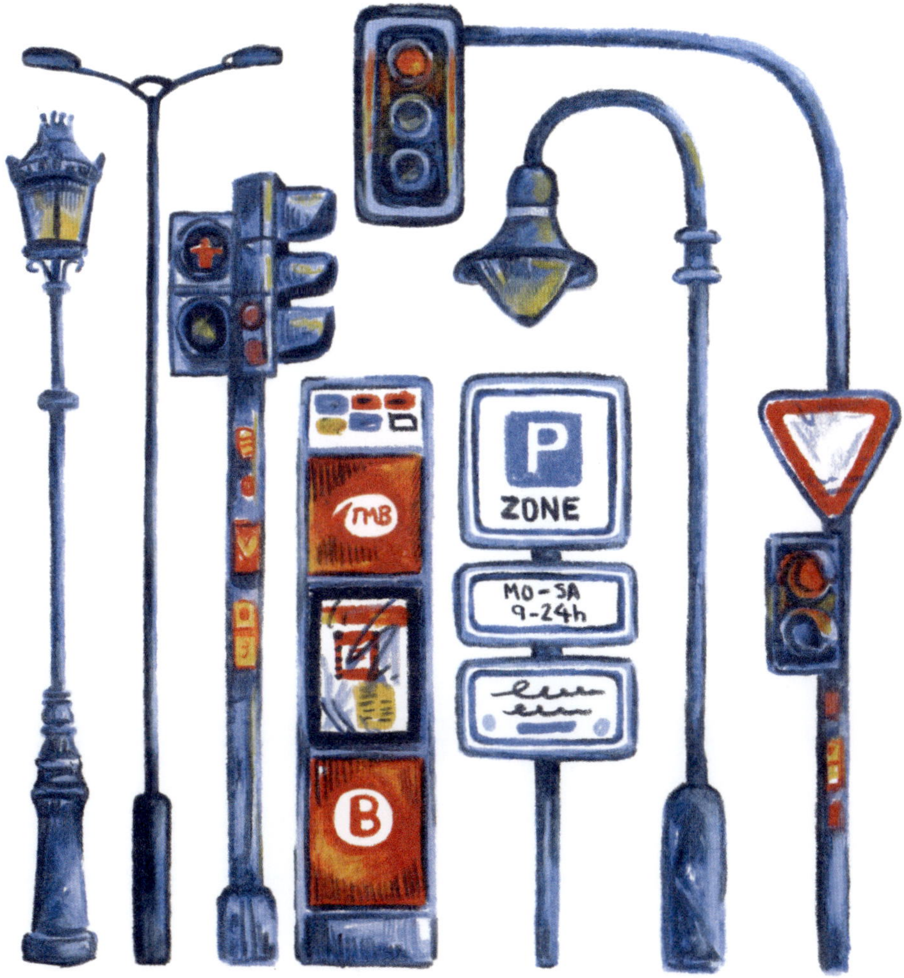

STEP 1

In this drawing I used a monochromatic blue palette. Starting with a light blue, map out the streetlight shape. Change the pressure of your pencil depending on whether the area is in light or shadow, keeping the top glass section very light.

STEP 2

Add your mid-tone (cobalt blue) to the areas of shadow across the body of the streetlight. Start with the side of the pencil and switch to a steeper angle when defining details in the shape.

STEP 3

Now introduce dark blue for definition, shading and contrast. Remember to think about the direction of the light source. Here the light is coming from the right, so the left-hand side of the streetlight is going to be in shadow. Lastly, bring back your lightest blue as a blending tool, drawing in circular motions to smooth out the colors.

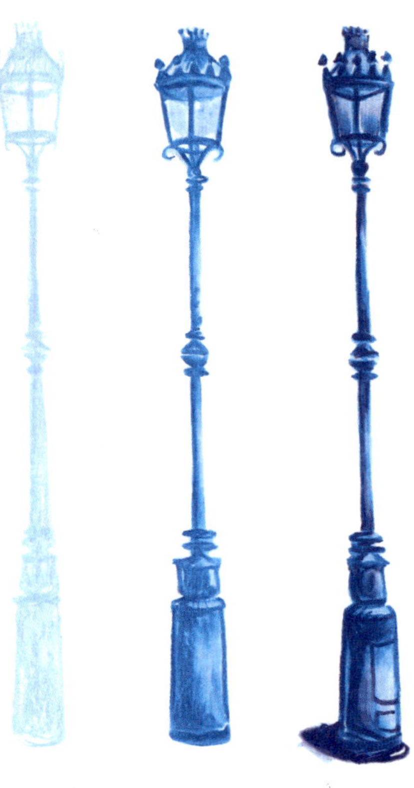

LANTERNS

During a summer in Malaysia, I was constantly drawing the world around me in my sketchbook. This encouraged me to observe the small details that made Kuala Lumpur unique.

The vibrant lanterns adorning streets in Chinatown were a delight to draw. The combination of bright yellow and red makes for a dramatic and energetic addition to your city scene.

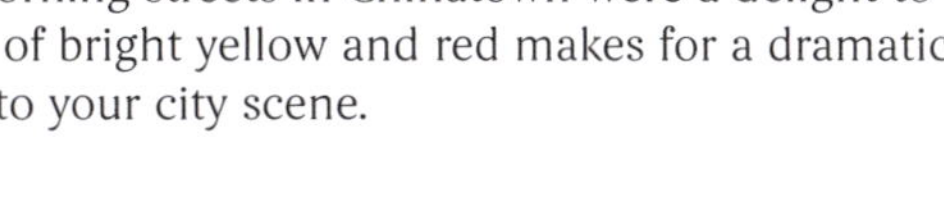

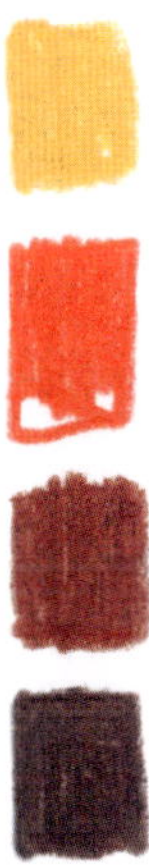

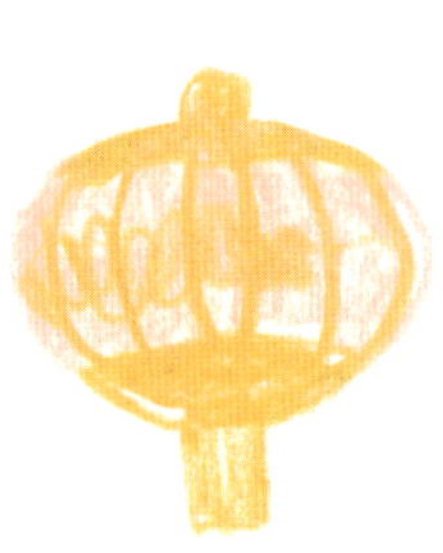

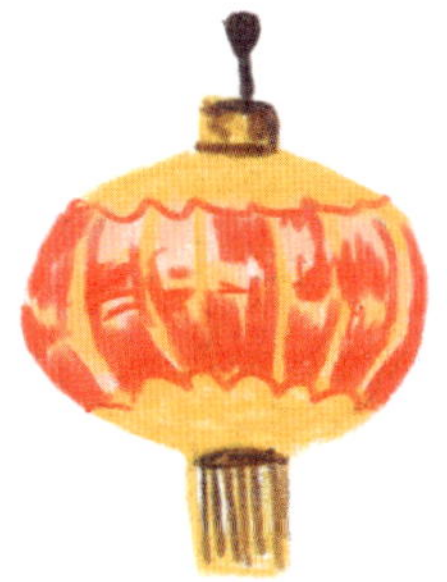

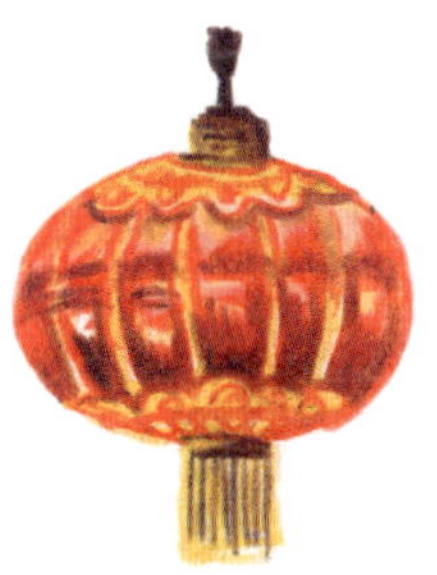

STEP 1

Using soft pink and warm yellow, create the foundation of the drawing. Make sure to leave gaps in the background as highlights, for the areas of white to come through.

STEP 2

Now introduce a vibrant scarlet for the main body of the lantern. Use a steep angle for the pencil to create those stronger marks, while making sure to still leave small white highlights.

STEP 3

For the yellow sections, you can use a warm dark brown to define the details. Add thin lines to create the suggestion of the tassels on the bottom of the lantern and the string coming from the top.

STEP 4

Bring in a dark red to start defining the curve. Shade the underneath of the lantern to create shadows and outline the yellow curved stripes going across the body. This tonal contrast will make these sections stand out. For the final touch, bring back your soft pink for blending to create a smoother transition.

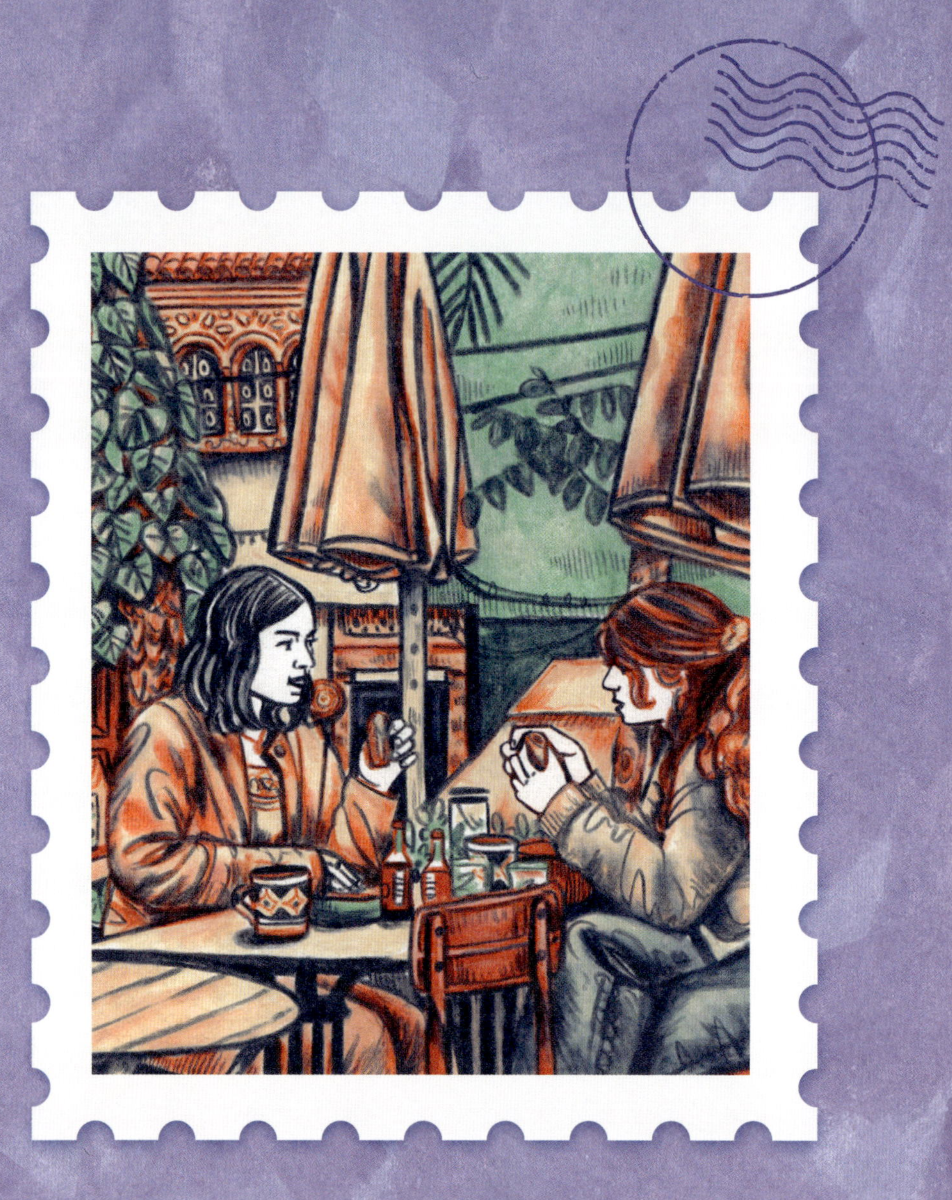

CHAPTER FOUR

People *and* Dogs

DRAWING PEOPLE

People bring the city to life. Characters reading, cycling, having conversations; every interaction, movement and connection tells a story.

The human figure is often considered a very daunting subject, especially when drawn on location. You need to find a way to quickly capture people, trying to mirror the realistic proportions, poses and character, all while they are in motion.

Here are a few tips for how to approach drawing people.

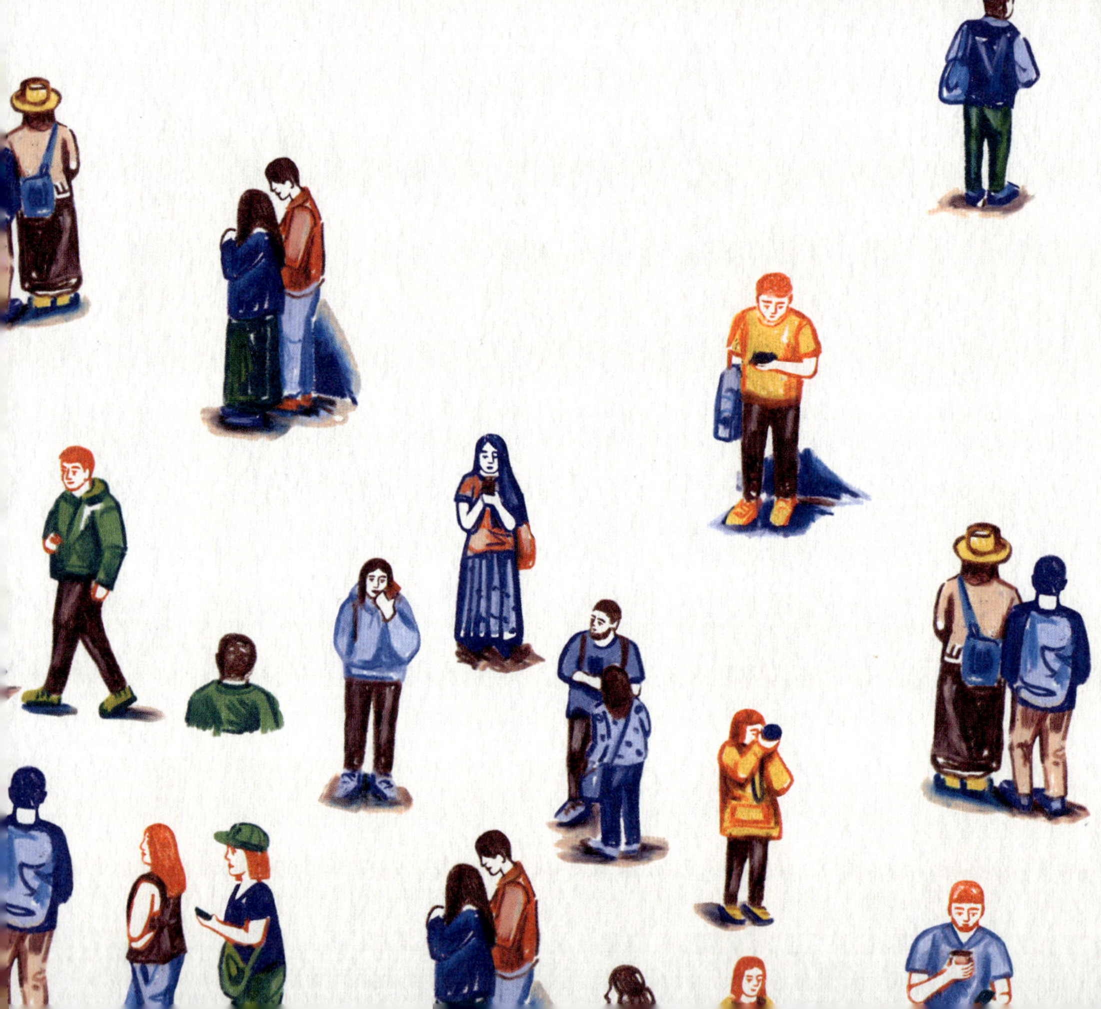

LINES OF MOTION

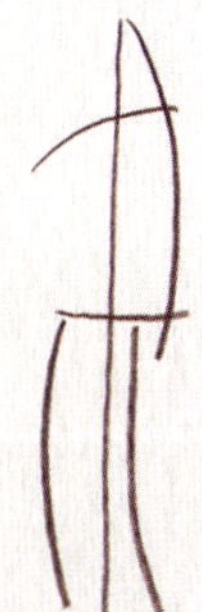

When viewing a figure, you need to be aware of the 'lines of motion'. These are lines across the body that capture the overall movement and energy of the pose. This helps establish the balance and structure of the figure.

Lines of motion include the line from the head to feet and across the shoulders, waist and arms. By working out the direction of these curves, it will help build a rough outline for the figure. You can practice by observing figures or using reference photos and doing quick 30-second sketches just capturing these important lines.

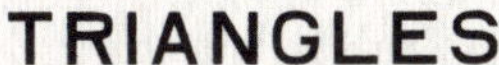

TRIANGLES

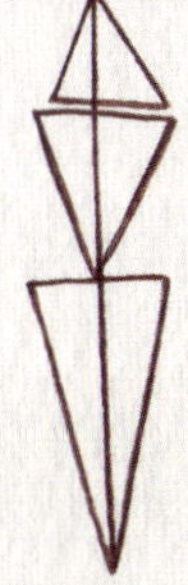

The triangle method is all about the relationship between different parts of the body. For this technique, you need to view the body in terms of triangles. The main triangles will be the head to shoulders, shoulders to waist and then waist to feet. To make sure the lines and angles are accurate, you can use your pencil as your measuring tool (see page 53).

USING THE HEAD AS A MEASURING REFERENCE

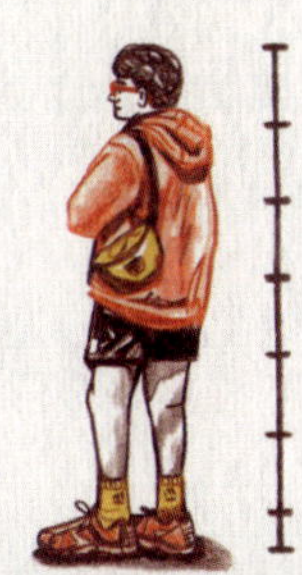

The head is a useful unit of measurement when working out body proportions. For this, look at how many times the head fits into the body. Generally, the average adult figure is approximately seven-and-a-half heads tall. However, this really depends on the height and build of the individual.

SIMPLE SHAPES

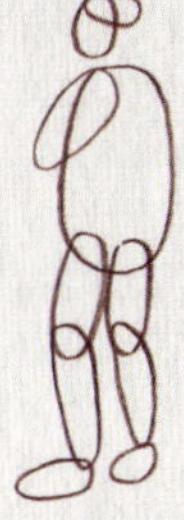

Map out the figure using simple shapes rather than focusing on body parts. These basic forms will serve as a guide to refine later. I use fluid oblongs and ovals, concentrating on key joints like the upper arm to the elbow, then the forearm to the wrist. Thinking in terms of joints and connections helps you better visualize how the figure moves.

CHARACTER

Facial expressions and body language are very important when trying to capture someone's character. Are they happy and talkative, tired and waiting in a long queue, or quietly enjoying a book?

Consider how the person interacts with their surroundings. Are they looking at someone, reading or eating? Are they closed off or open and confident? Drawing a figure isn't just about accurate proportions - it's about conveying personality. These observations bring your illustration to life and help the viewer feel part of the scene.

Eyes play a big role in expressing character. How you draw eyes not only determines the figure's focus but also their emotional state - tired with closed eyes or excited with wide, open ones. Try and observe where the subject is looking, so you don't default to a direct stare. The line of sight can also be a compositional tool, guiding the viewer through the drawing. These smaller details will strengthen the storytelling in your illustration.

FACIAL PROPORTIONS

In order to capture a person's face and expression, you need to understand facial proportions. Understanding these basic facial guidelines will help you be to quickly draw accurate faces when on location.

A common guideline is to think of the face as an oval shape. Start by drawing a circle to represent the forehead to the nose. In the middle of this circle, draw a horizontal line to place the eyebrows on and indicate the tops of the ears. You can then draw the eyes just below this horizontal line. Generally, the width of the face is equivalent to five eyes, and the eyes are placed one eye-width apart, halfway down the face.

The nose is positioned on the base of the circle line, with the edges of the nostrils lining up with the inner corner of the eyes. From this circle, extend the jawline downward to form the shape of the chin. The mouth will sit halfway between the nose and chin lines. When these guides become a habit,

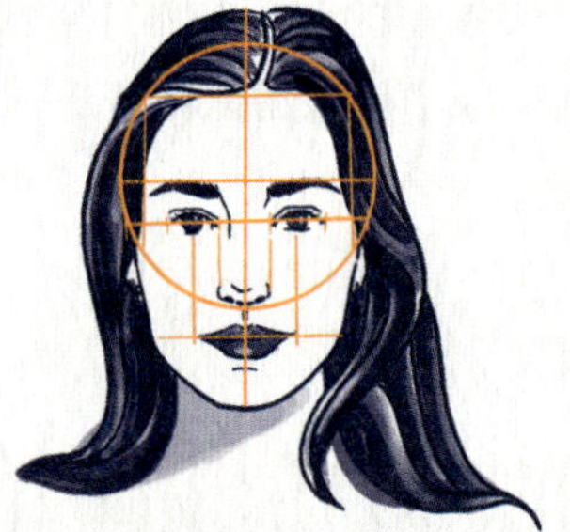

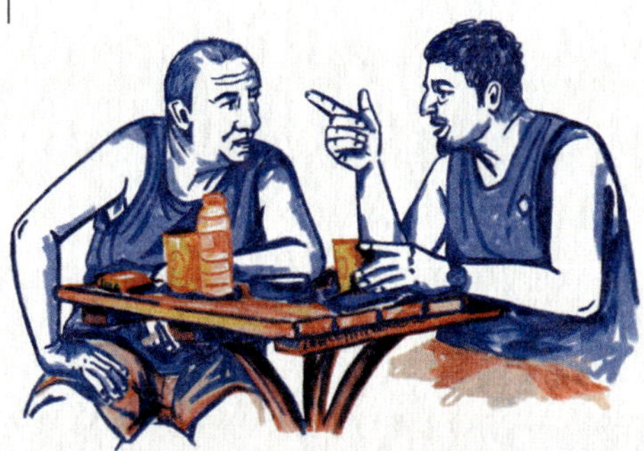

it will make it easier to play around and exaggerate facial features to capture different characters.

Here are a few examples of how I capture different facial expressions and perspectives when on location. You will notice that I focus on simplifying the form, using single lines and no shading. This approach allows me to quickly and intuitively portray a person's character on location, without getting caught up in the small details.

For talkative and expressive characters, I focus on open eyes, raised eyebrows and curved mouths - suggesting a smile or someone speaking. To show a more serious or tired mood, I lower the eyelids, draw the mouth in a neutral shape and minimize movements of the eyebrows.

If someone is looking down while reading a book, their eyeline will appear lower on the face as the viewer sees a greater proportion of the top of the head and forehead. For a side profile of people looking at each other while talking, you only need to draw one eye, and concentrate on how the shape of the nose and lips change from different perspectives.

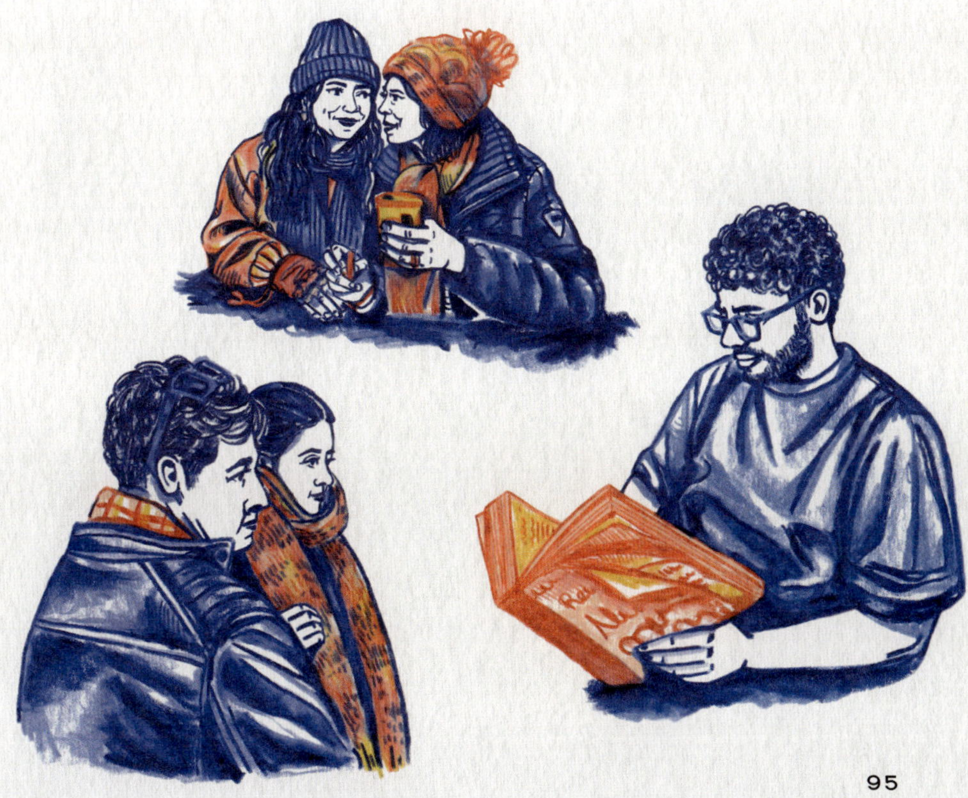

DRAWING PEOPLE, STEP BY STEP

Using this trio I saw at a flea market in Berlin, Germany, as a reference, I am now going to take you through the steps for drawing people.

STEP 1

Using the techniques just mentioned, start with the basic outlines of the figures. Think about the color palette and change colors where appropriate, depending on the clothing. Add a few line details for the folds in the clothes to suggest the fabric shape and material, and define where to shade in the next stage.

STEP 2

Now introduce the background colors. Use light pressure with the side of the pencil to block out the clothing, hair and boxes in the foreground. Make sure to vary the pressure to create the shadows.

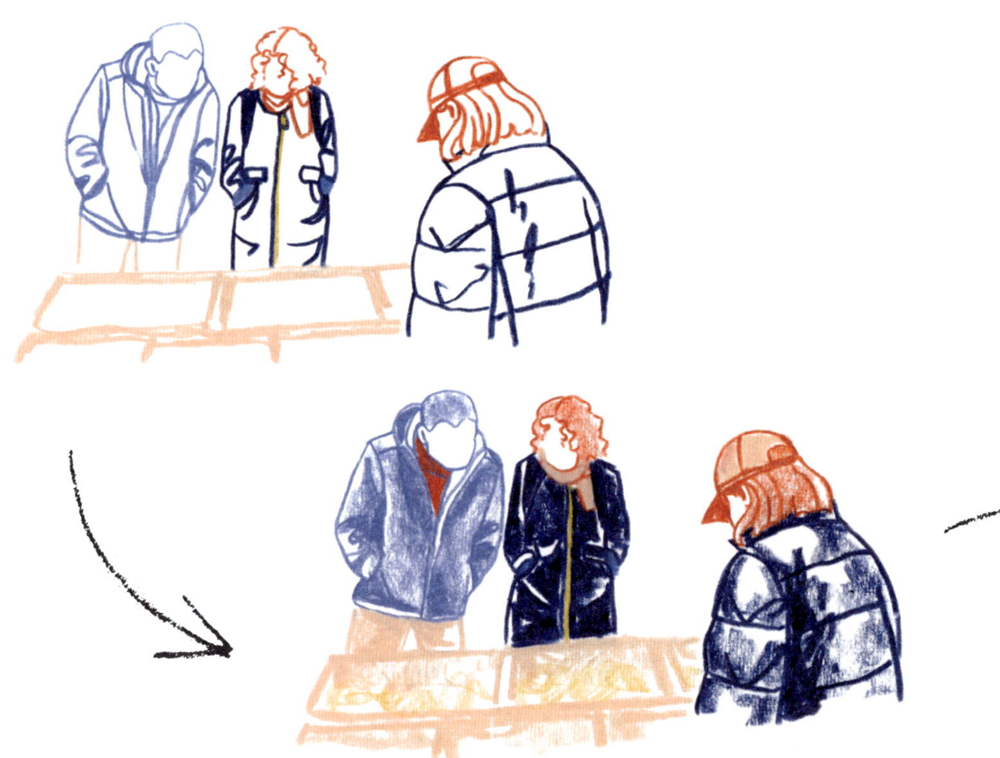

STEP 3

Go in with your other tonal values to build detail. I started with a mid-tone for the man's jacket, so here use a darker tone. For both women, I used my darkest blue for the background, so added a lighter blue to blend and highlight. Apply more pressure for blending and draw the outline details like folds, pockets, the zipper and hood.

Then add a few line details to suggest the hair texture and facial features – remember to think about where the people are looking.

STEP 4

The objects in the box are a variety of entangled jewelry. To create the impression of this subject, play with random swirls and patterns in a mix of colors. This creates a fun design and suggestion of necklaces while keeping it visually engaging.

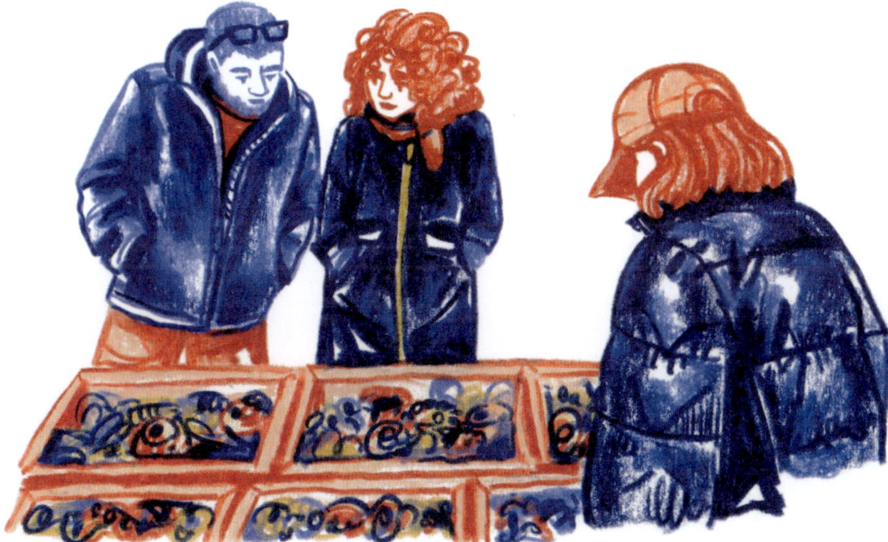

DRAWING DOGS

Drawing dogs is another way to bring life, character and movement into your city illustration. Whether they are sitting and watching the world go by, walking alongside their owner or relaxing in the sun, dogs add warmth and share a glimpse into urban life and daily routines in the city.

You can approach drawing dogs in a very similar way to drawing people. Look at the dog in terms of simplified shapes and build up the outline from this.

Below is a diagram showing how to view a dog in basic shapes: focus on perspective and the proportions of each part. When deciding what shapes to use, you need to first analyze how a dog moves: its natural rhythm and how each body part works in harmony.

Concentrate on the joints and hinge points, such as where the legs bend or connect with the body. These are points where your shapes should overlap. In this diagram, you can see how I use a mix of stretched, thin and wide ovals to represent the different muscles, all connecting at these points.

Once you have the main form in place, you can start layering color and exploring fur textures. By starting with observation and analysis, you will be able to accurately capture not only the likeness of the dog, but also its unique character.

When you are more confident with spotting key shapes, then you can start drawing these subjects without outlines. When I am on location, I always love to use the side of my pencil to map out the subject, rather than drawing outlines, which results in a more fluid and expressive drawing.

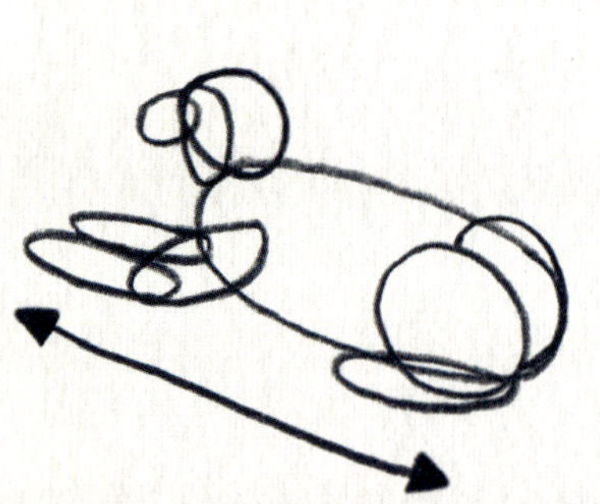

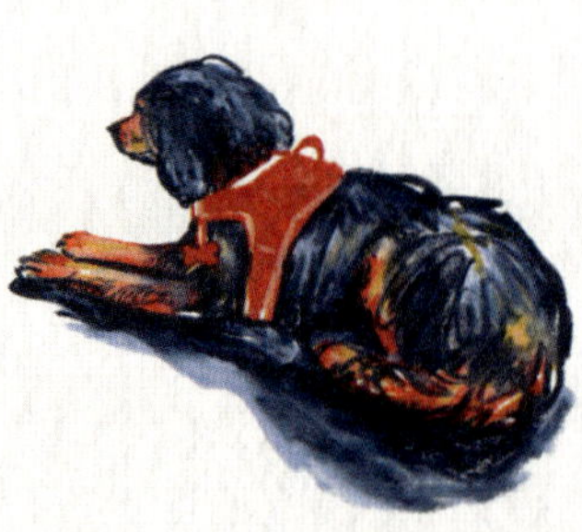

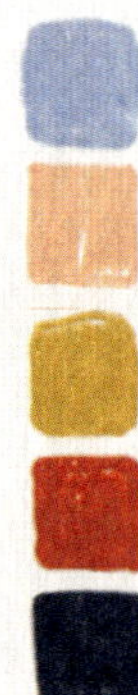

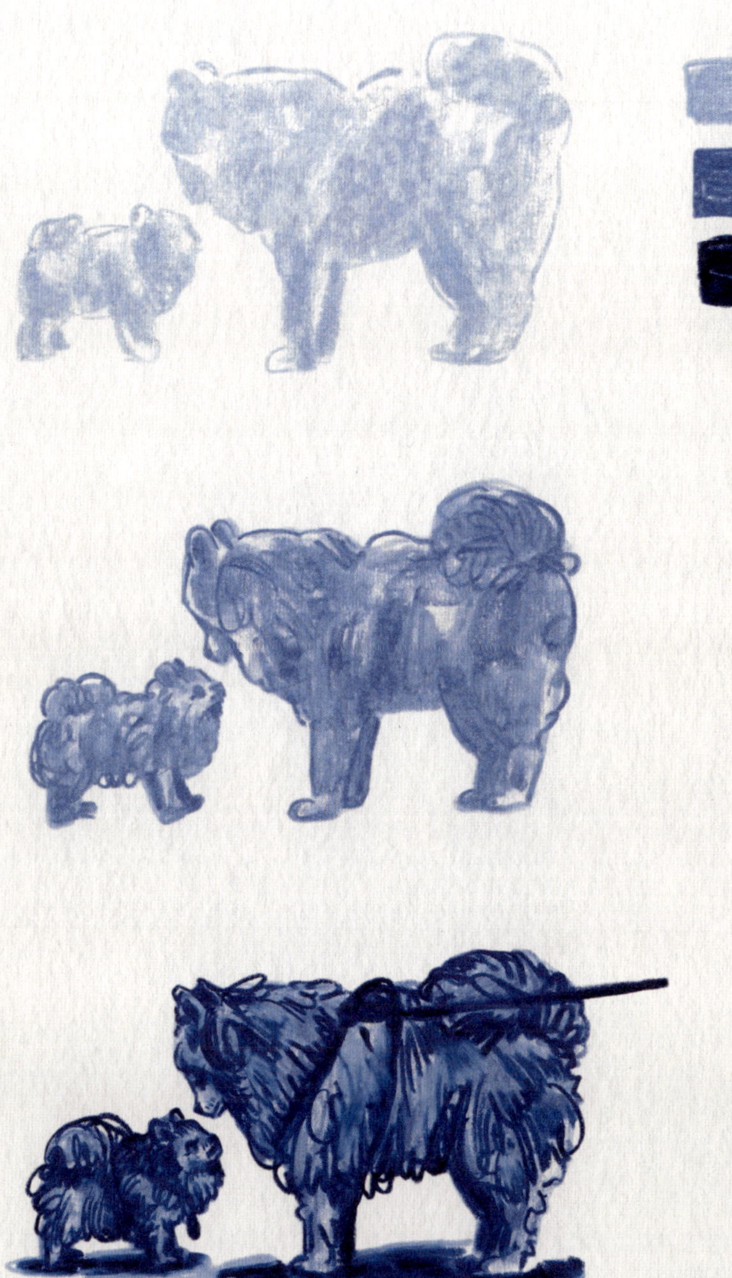

CAPTURING FUR TEXTURE

The focus here is on exploring different drawing techniques to capture the texture of fur. You will be using soft strokes with the side of your pencil, layering and playful mark-making to build up texture. Think about whether the dog's fur is long and fluffy or short and wiry, and how the marks you draw can best represent this surface.

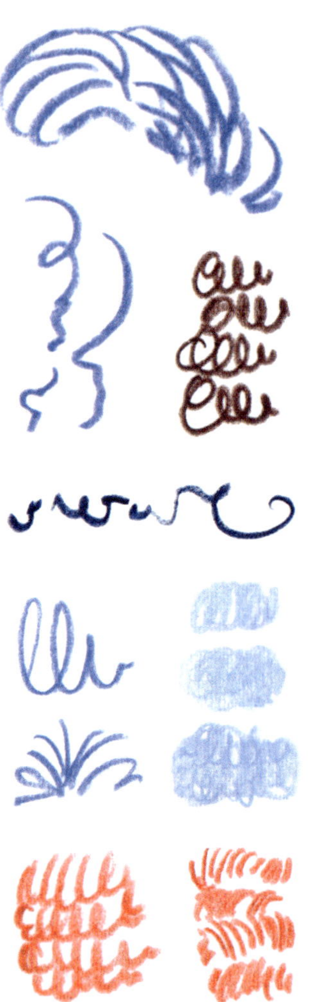

STEP 1

Start with the side of the pencil to roughly create the shape of the dog, as shown on the previous page. Move your pencil in circular motions to mimic the fur texture.

STEP 2

I am using a monochromatic palette featuring blues to suggest the cool temperature of the white fur. In this step you are going to bring in a mid-blue to draw the fur layers. Look at the areas of shadow across the coat and start applying more pressure with the side of your pencil to introduce tonal contrast. You can play with adding a few fur marks - think fluid lines following the fur direction.

STEP 3

Finally, draw the fur details, exploring different mark-making with curved lines and swirls. As these dogs are long-haired, I wanted to make the edges fluid to indicate the fluffy fur texture. For this, I like to draw these fun, swirly outlines.

When drawing the leash, make sure to add some of the lighter fur colors on top. This will show the overlapping fur, helping the leash blend in and look realistic.

DOG WALKERS

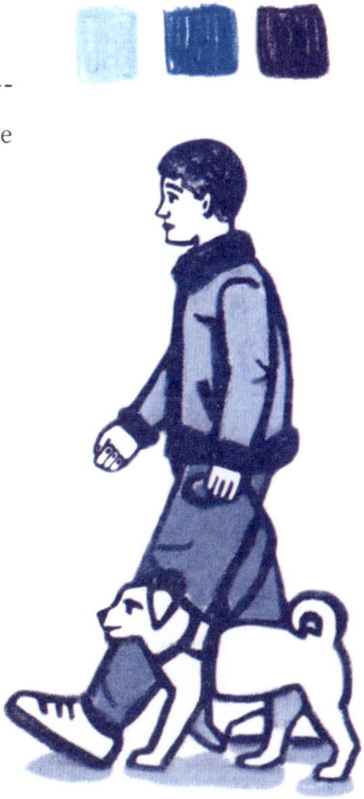

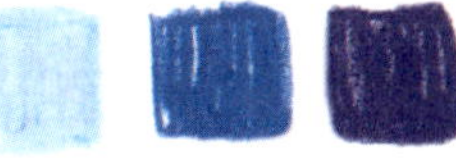

When drawing someone walking a dog, using the same colors for both the person and dog creates cohesion and shows they are a pair. You can either use the full-color technique just mentioned, adding all the fur textures, or you can keep it simple and draw just the dog's outline and block out any shadows. Be sure to pick a point on the figure as a measuring tool to keep the proportion of the dog accurate in relation to its owner (see page 53).

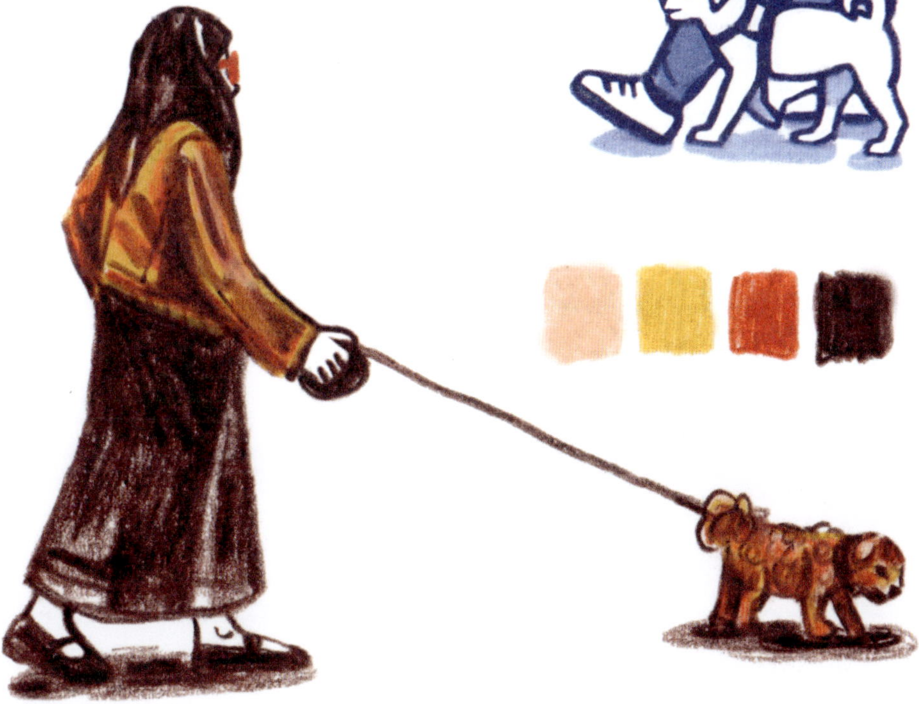

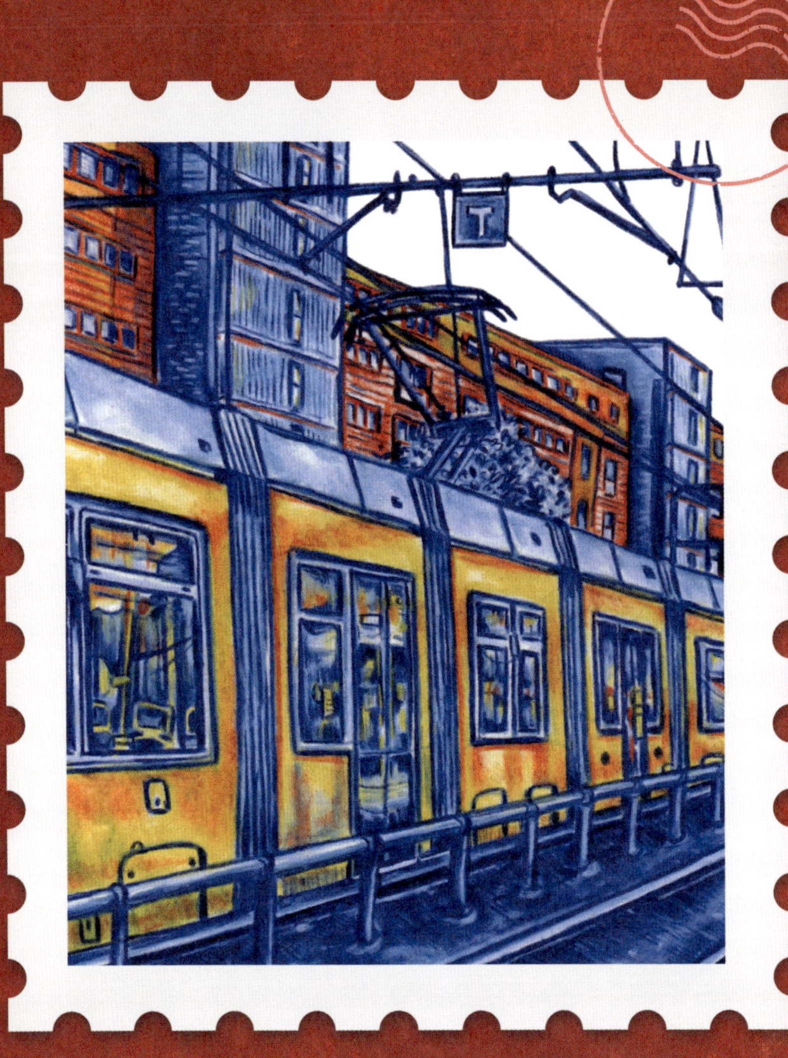
T

CHAPTER FIVE

Transport

Including modes of transport like bicycles, cars and taxis in your city drawings will add life and movement to the scene. It grounds your illustration in reality, as you capture the energy and everyday rhythm of urban life in a specific location.

Drawing methods of transport can be a mathematical process, focused on analyzing angles and proportions. In this section, I will show you how to break down vehicles into basic shapes. The suggested sequence of work is often to lay down the main background color, add a mid-tone for shadows, and finish with a clear outline on top to define the form and details.

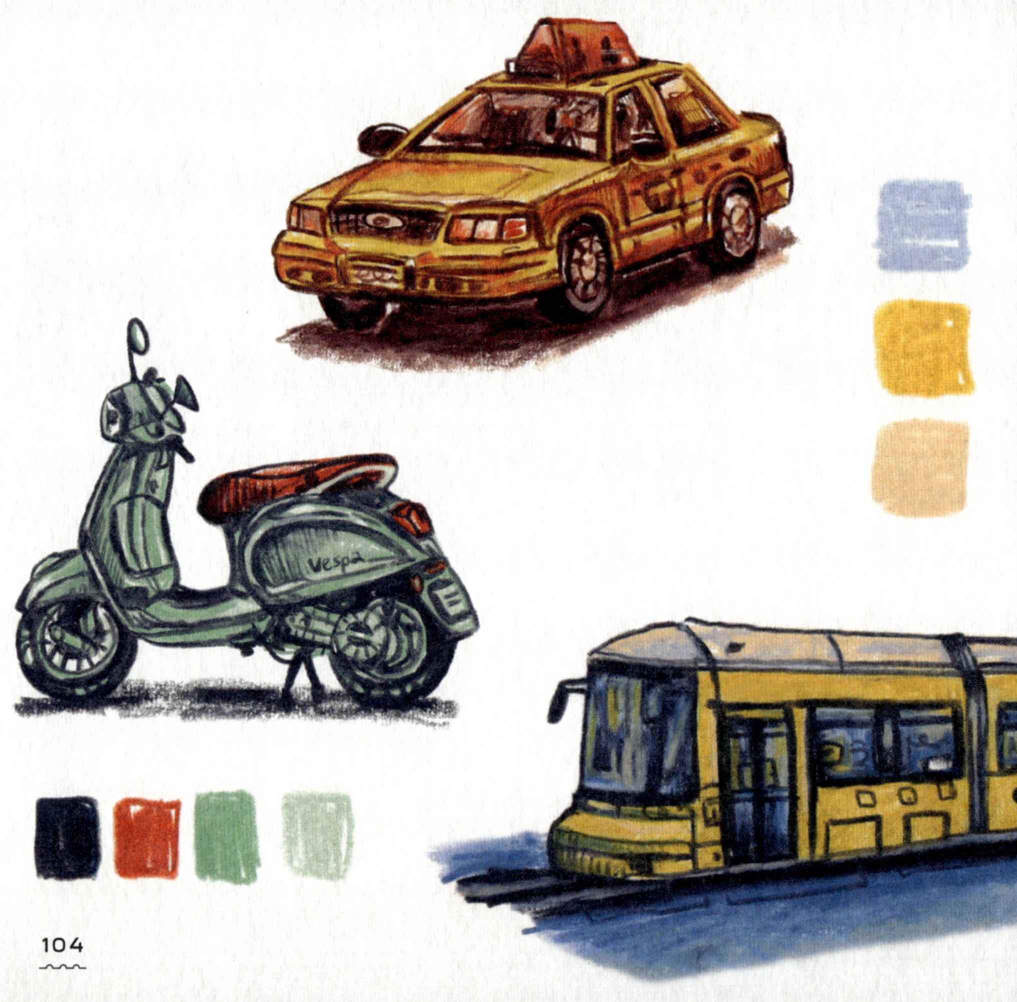

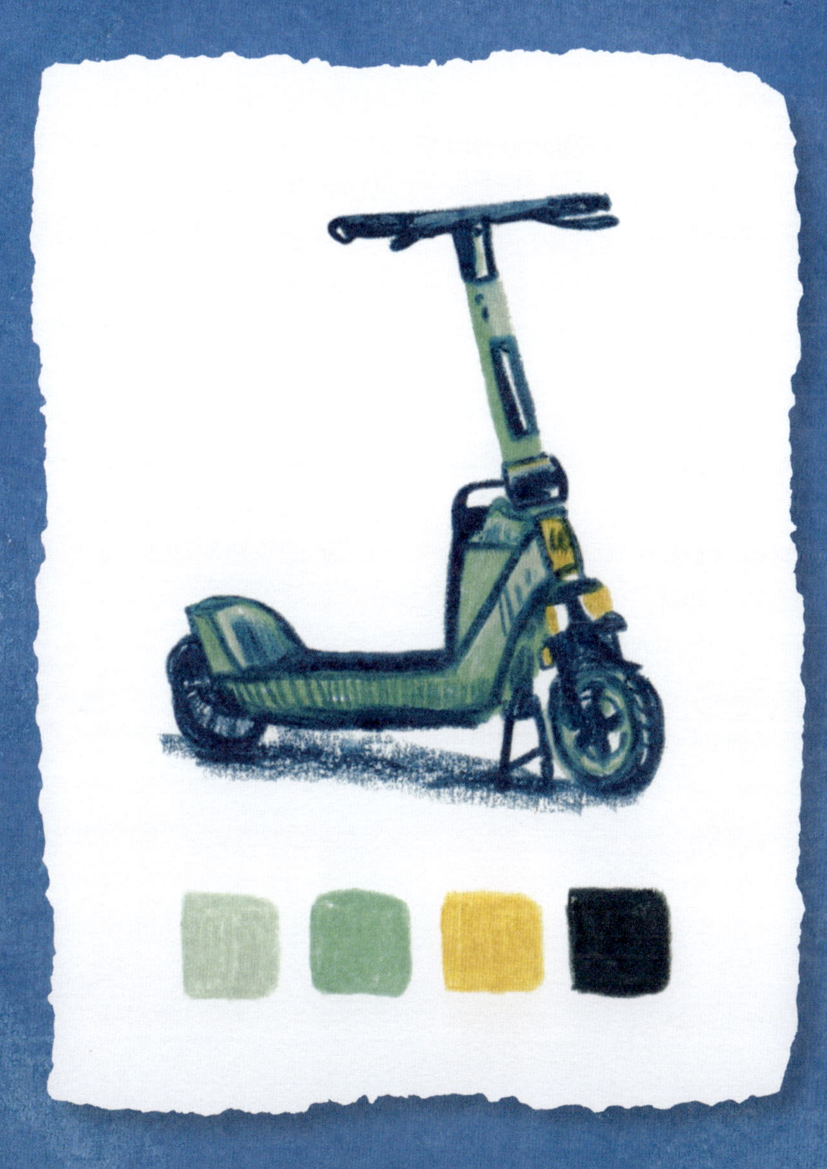

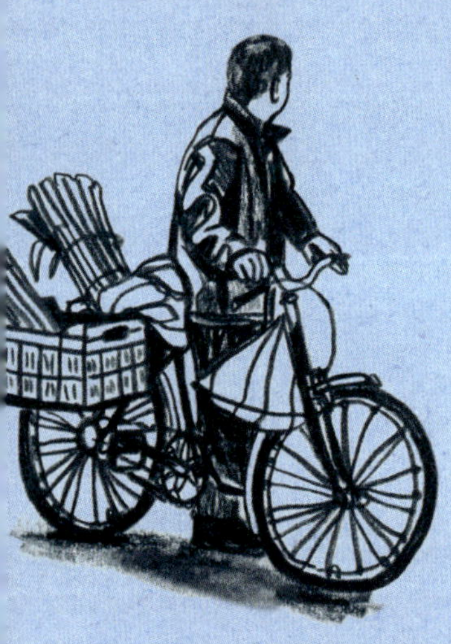

Bikes

Bikes are tricky subjects, especially when combined with a moving figure. To simplify, pick one part as your reference point for proportions, such as the wheel. Use its size to estimate how it relates to the rest of the subject, helping you work out the scale for both the bike and rider. How many times does the wheel fit across the width and height of the subject?

As the person is in motion when cycling, consider how the body moves. Your leg has two main sections – the thigh and calf – connected at the knee, a hinge point. Break the body into the main shapes, while identifying these hinge points to encourage you to observe and better understand the motion of someone cycling.

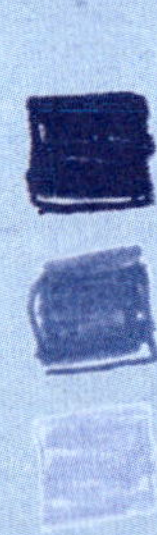

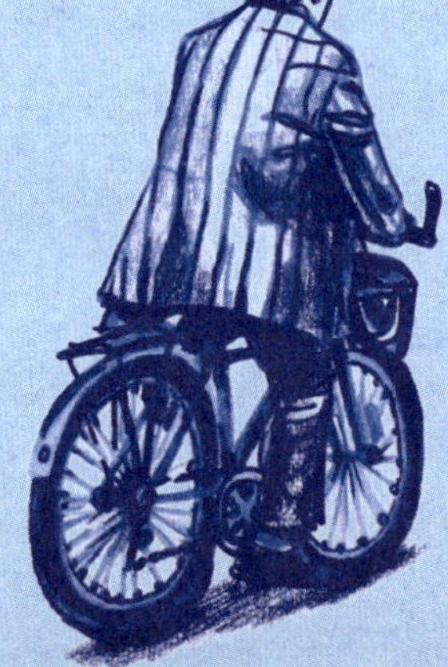

STEP 1

Start by drawing a circle for the front wheel and then following with the basic shapes of the bike and rider. As previously mentioned, use the front wheel as your reference point. For example: the shoulder height of the rider is two wheels, and the width of the bike is two and a half wheels.

For the figure, use your people drawing skills from page 93 to draw the lines of motion and the simple shapes of the person. Focus on building up the figure with various oval shapes and flowing lines. The person is leaning forwards on the bike, so their back will be curved. This fluidity in the lines will help create the idea that the figure is in motion.

Remember to draw the leg hiding on the other side of the bike. Imagine yourself riding a bike. Think about which areas of the leg would be visible and how it connects with the rest of the body.

STEP 2

Now you can add the shading and color details. I have drawn the figure all in a single color - adding form through the curves of the shirt and texture in the trousers using the side of the pencil. Add shadows where the clothing joins, on any hinge points - such as the arm and knee - and for the leg furthest away.

For the bike, use the warm orange to color in the main framework. Then add the light pink for highlight details and the dark purple for any shading. This tonal contrast will help create depth in the drawing.

For the final touch, use the side of your dark purple pencil to create a brushy shadow underneath. Think about the shape of the figure and where the light is coming from.

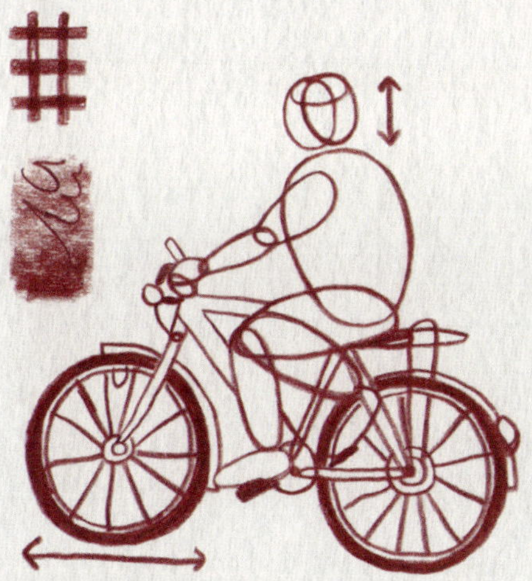

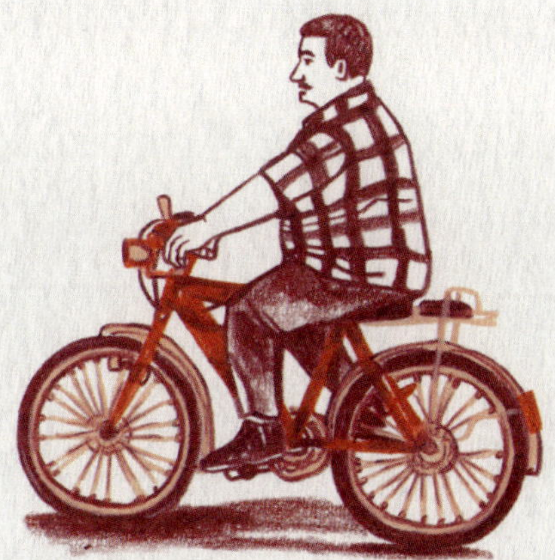

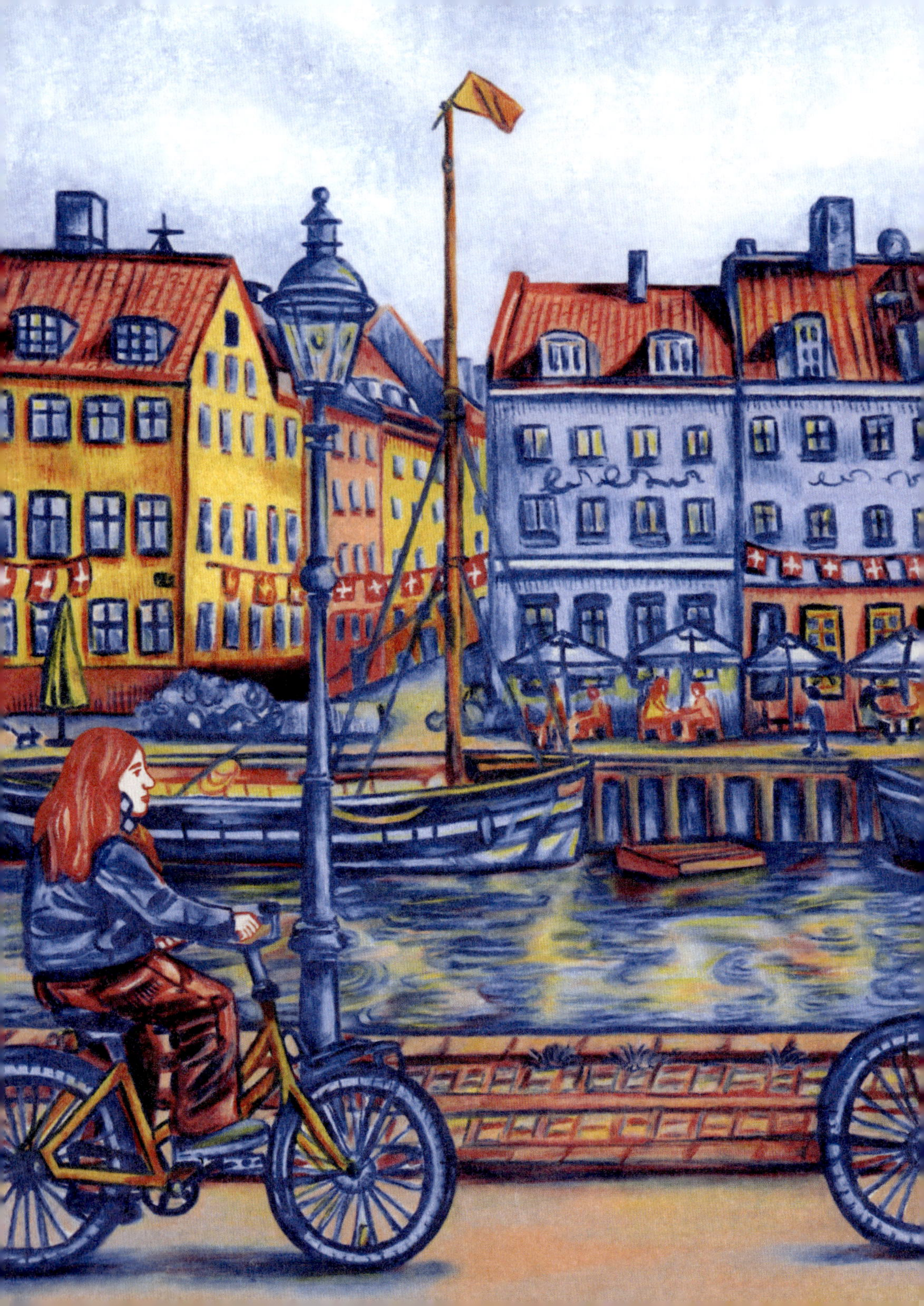

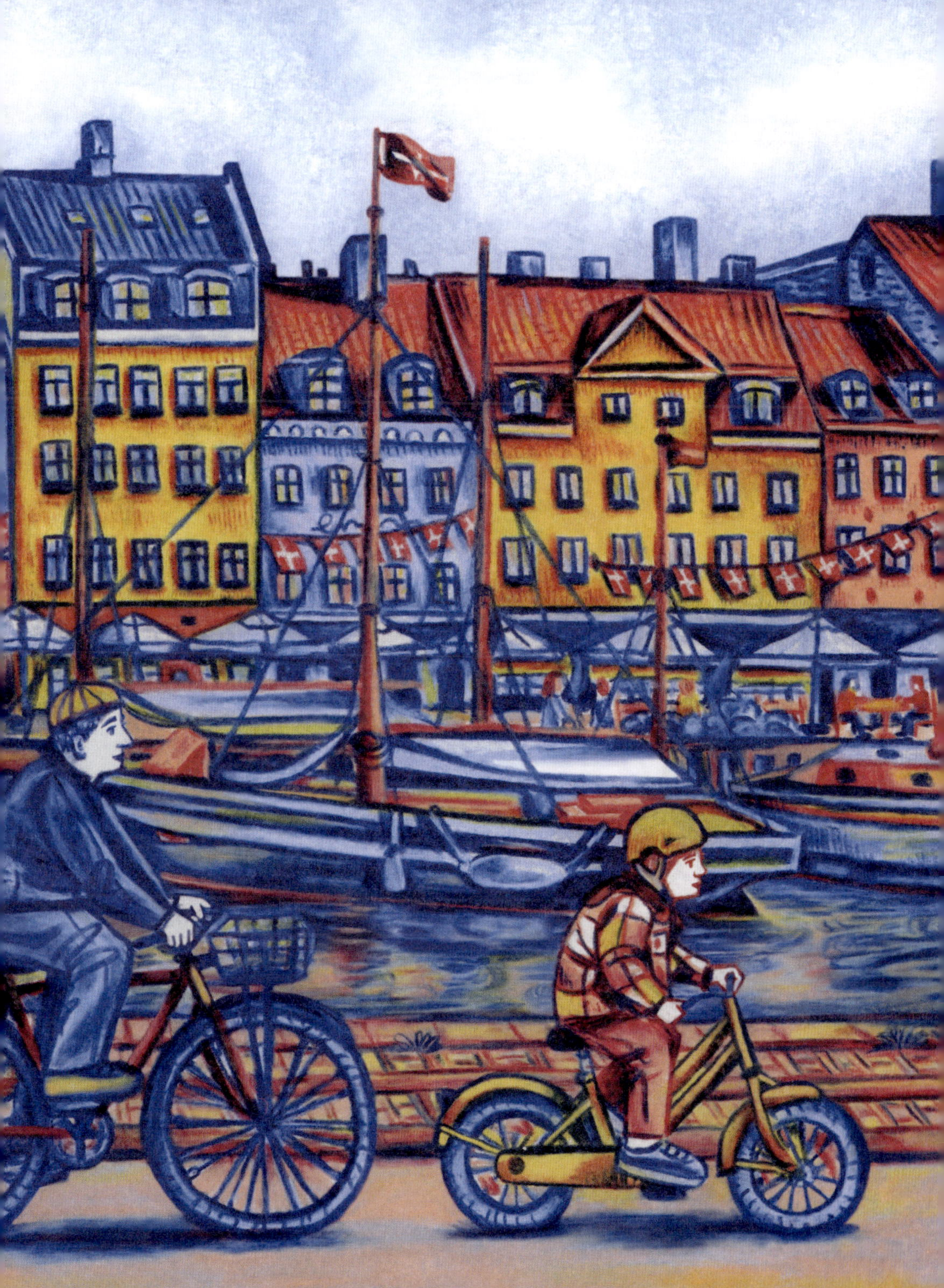

Vespas

Vespas always remind me of my time in Italy, especially a trip to Milan where I stayed with a local designer. His welcoming home was full of graphic design work and illustrated books – a true creative haven. Alongside his love for design, he was particularly fond of his old Vespa. I remember him proudly showing it to me on Google Maps, so excited that it still appears there, parked outside his home, even though he no longer owns it. This Vespa drawing is a reminder of that inspiring and memorable trip.

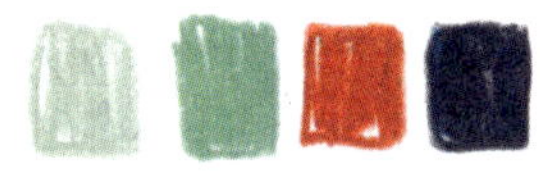

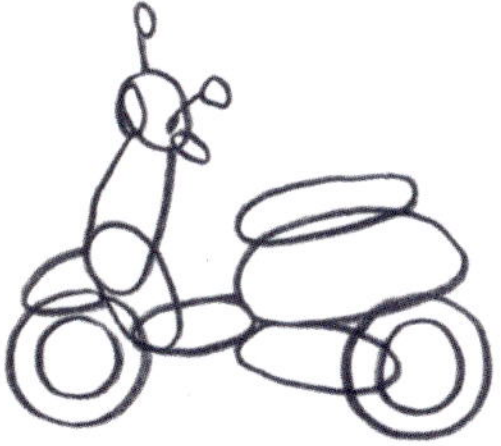

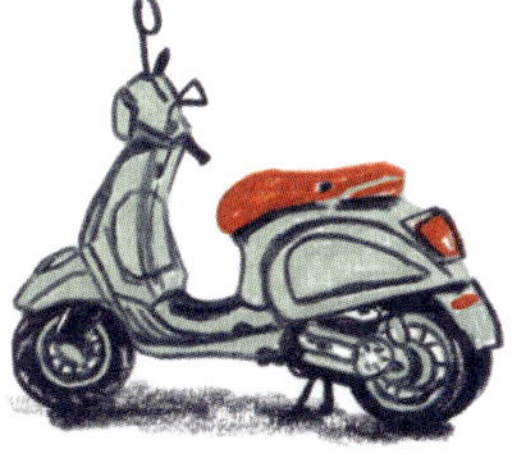

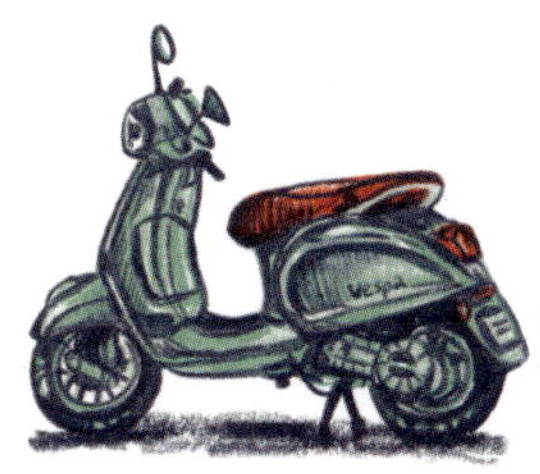

STEP 1

Sketch the basic shape. As this is an object with flowing lines, focus on fluid ovals and circles. If you are struggling with proportions, go back to the trick of using your pencil as a measuring tool (see page 53). For example, pick the wheel as your guide and see how many times it fits into the Vespa.

STEP 2

Next, use the side of the pencil to apply a light wash of the main color – here, I have covered most of the Vespa in mint green. For the red seat, I used stronger, more confident strokes with a steeper pencil angle to block in the shape. Then, outline the Vespa using charcoal gray. You can also suggest the shadow beneath the vehicle to help ground it; again, use the side of the pencil to apply broad, dark marks.

STEP 3

If you would like to develop the drawing further, introduce a darker green for shadows. Finish with a few shading lines in charcoal gray, following the direction of the shape of the Vespa. This will help to create depth in your drawing.

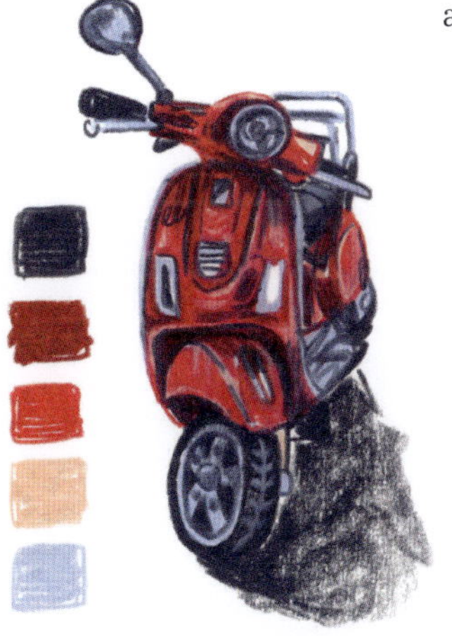

If you have a busy scene, and the Vespa is not a focal point, I suggest finishing on step two with just the background color and outline. This way it won't distract from your focal point. This is an example of a Vespa from the front, using a different color palette. I have limited it to two main hues – red and blue – and varied the tonal values within each. This approach creates a more harmonious palette and allows you to focus on highlights and shadows without introducing additional colors.

For motorcycles and electric scooters, I follow the same steps as with the Vespa. However, when drawing on location, I skip drawing the rough outline and begin by blocking out the surface area with my main color.

Cars

Cars are such a common sight in any city, so learning how to capture them will be a valuable addition to your illustration toolbox. In the following pages, I will take you through drawing cars, starting with an illustration for visual inspiration, then how to approach cars at an angle and finishing with a step-by-step guide for taxis.

To begin, I am sharing a fun drawing of a trio of cars I saw in Bologna, Italy, showing how to quickly bring vehicles to life in your sketches. For this style, I focus on strong, expressive marks, building up the shape with each color.

STEP 1

Start with a light-blue pencil using a steep angle and fast marks. Block out all the lightest areas and leave spaces for the shadows.

STEP 2

In the spaces, add a mid-blue in the same expressive style, while blending the gradient transitions between the blues.

STEP 3

Now bring in a light pink for the windows and a dark earthy orange for the car lights.

STEP 4

Finally, introduce dark-blue outlines, shading details and a shadow to ground the cars - keeping the marks rough to create a lively outcome.

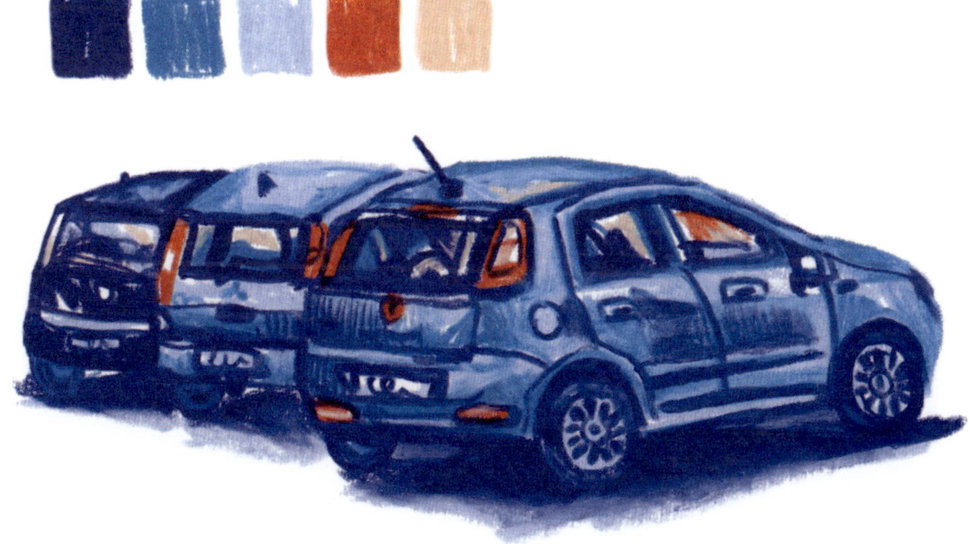

CARS AT AN ANGLE

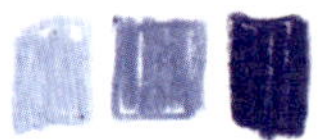

Achieving accurate proportions when drawing cars can be challenging, especially when faced with a car at an angle. Here is an example of how I would approach a car when drawing from a balcony, looking down on the subject at an angle.

I am using a monochromatic palette with a light, mid and dark blue. In each step, I introduce a darker tone to create depth in the drawing. For accurate angles, remember to use your pencil as a reference tool, bringing the lines from the scene down onto your paper (see page 53). The outline details and intense shadow make all the difference in this drawing, adding tonal contrast and context.

STEP 1

Start with the lightest blue to draw the outline of the car and lightly add a background color. Analyze how the angles change with perspective. Use guidelines along the sides and roof of the car to help you build an accurate structure. Remember that the front of the car is further away from you, so it will be narrower than the back of the car, which is closer to you.

To check proportions, you can add a vanishing point slightly in front of the car (see page 47). Draw lines from the car sides and roof toward this point - if the lines don't meet here, change them to correct the angles.

STEP 2

Now introduce the mid-blue tone. Define the main lines of the car and block in the shadow areas across the body, leaving spaces where the light blue comes through for highlights.

STEP 3

The final step is to add your darkest blue for shading details, creating depth through tonal contrast. Add parallel shading lines, in the direction of the car shape, for shadow areas. Underneath the car add a strong shadow in fast and expressive marks. For a smoother car body, use the light-blue pencil in circular motions to blend any gradients.

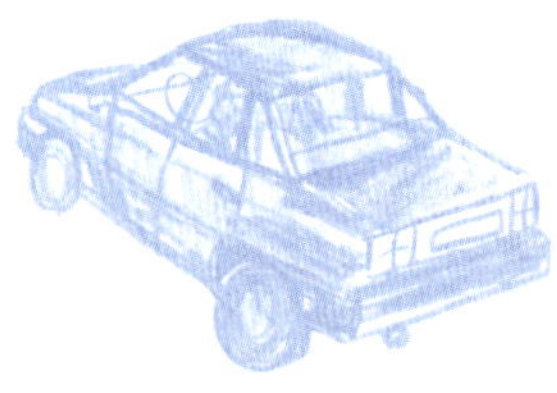

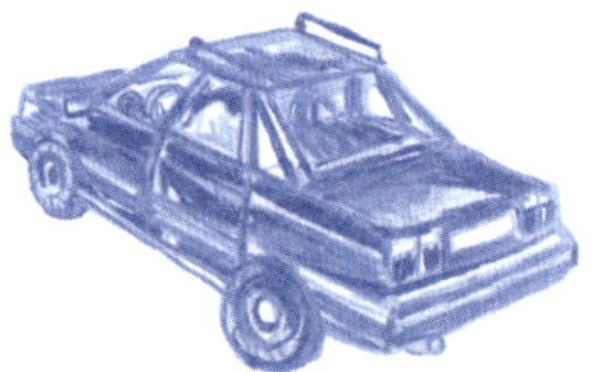

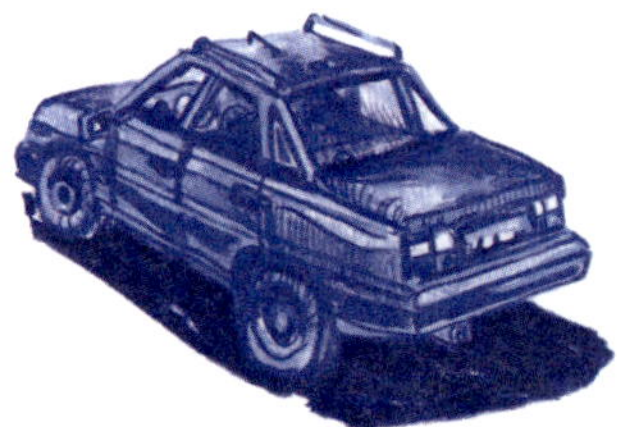

TAXIS

New York is home to one of the most iconic vehicles - the yellow taxi. These cabs are deeply associated with the energy of the city.

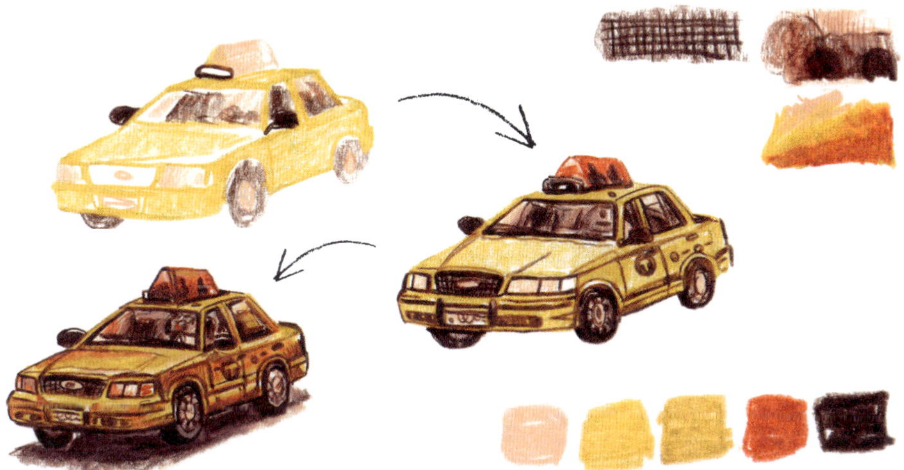

STEP 1

Start by blocking out the main colors for each section. As always, use the side of the pencil to fill in these areas, leaving white spaces for the highlights. For the window, use a soft pink and dark brown - pink for warm reflections and dark brown to suggest the interior seats.

STEP 2

Now add outlines and your mid-tones. Introduce a yellow ocher for the shadows on the body of the car and keep in mind the direction of the light. Then, use dark brown to outline the taxi details and define the structure.

STEP 3

Next, bring in a warm earthy orange for the dark shadows on the car and add subtle touches of this orange across the windows. Use your pink in circular motions to help blend for warmth and cohesion. To blend the gradients across the car body, use a lighter yellow.

STEP 4

Finally, add a few shading marks in dark brown, following the shape of the car. To ground the taxi, continue with this brown and the side of the pencil to add the shadows underneath. Blend in the pink to soften the edges.

Buses *and* Trams

As someone living in London, England, one of the first images that comes to mind when thinking of this vibrant city is the iconic red double-decker bus – a splash of color weaving its way through the city's streets.

Here, we will break down how to capture this iconic vehicle – starting with blocking out the main colors, then adding simple outlines and details. You will see how much of a difference basic lines can make to grounding the illustration and bringing it to life.

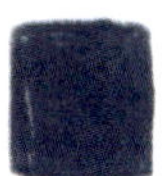

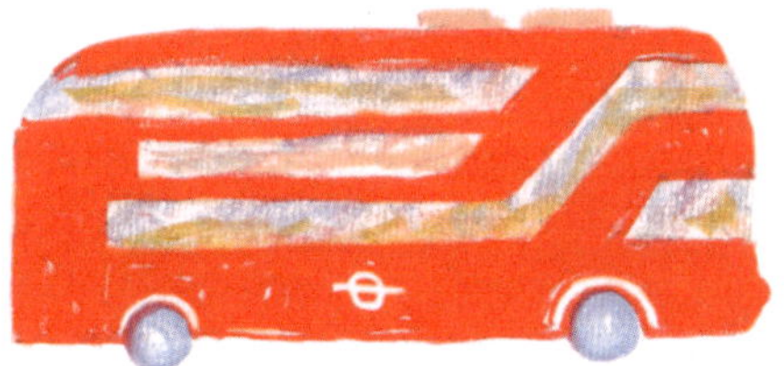

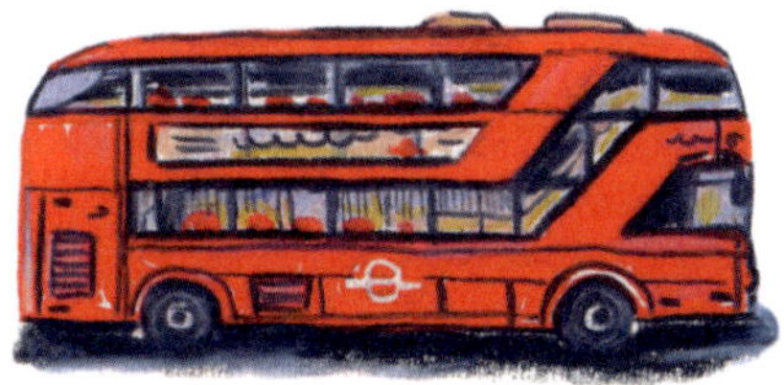

STEP 1

Rather than drawing the bus outline, start by focusing on adding a base color to block out the vehicle shape. For this, begin with a bright scarlet pencil to draw the main structure of the bus. Use strong marks with a steep pencil angle to confidently color in the main red form - leaving white gaps for the windows and logo.

STEP 2

Now focus on the window colors. Start with sky blue, using the side of your pencil and light pressure to softly color in the window sections. Layer this blue background with expressive side strokes in yellow ocher and soft pink to suggest reflections across the glass, making it look more realistic. Then use the sky blue to draw the suggestion of the wheels.

STEP 3

Finally, add outlines and details in charcoal gray. Outline the windows and the main structural lines of the bus - such as the panels across the body, squiggles for the advertising text, and the wheel details.

For the windows, start by using the scarlet color to draw seats. Then bring back the sky blue with a stronger pressure to more confidently color in the windows, leaving sections of the yellow and pink to come through. Layer this up with charcoal gray to add reflection lines. Use the side of the pencil to create streaky horizontal shadow marks for the darker areas of the window and draw vertical shading for lighter shadows.

To ground the drawing, add a shadow underneath the bus. Draw with the side of the pencil in charcoal gray to roughly block out the shadow shape, focusing on creating textural marks. To produce a gradient and softer shadow edges, layer sky blue on top and blend in circular motions.

TRAMS

I grew up in the countryside so only saw trams while on holiday, but they have since become one of my favorite modes of transport. I love to see how they are integrated into the design of the city. It's also a pleasure to travel in them and enjoy a sightseeing tour. The design of trams is very similar to that of trains, so you can use this approach for both subjects.

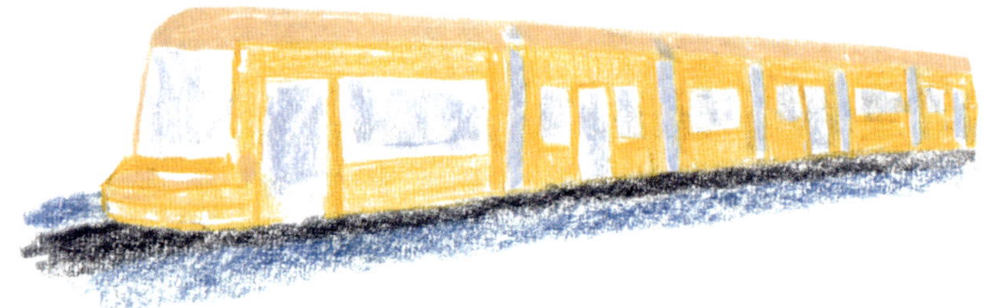

STEP 1

Use the side of the pencil to create the reference shape - sunflower yellow for the body of the tram, buttery yellow for the roof and a slight wash of light blue across the windows. This becomes your foundation to build on top of.

Remember to think about perspective and how the tram dimensions will change with distance. Each section of the tram will get smaller as it recedes. To work out the angles and shape, you can add a vanishing point on the right side of the page, in a central position just beyond the end of the tram (see page 47.) Draw the front of the tram and then draw a line from the top of the vehicle and one from the bottom, meeting at this vanishing point. This will create a triangle shape and be your reference lines for the shape and perspective of the subject.

STEP 2

Now you are confident with the shape, you can add marks with more pressure. Fully block out the sunflower yellow areas of the tram using a steeper angle - use the lightest yellow for subtle highlights along the tram.

For the windows, combine three blues. Keep a light blue for the highlights and then create a gradient with dusty blue and charcoal gray.

STEP 3

Time for blending and outlines. To form the window texture, use light blue to blend the gradients, then add highlights with subtle bright yellow touches. You will need to apply a lot of pressure to get the yellow to stand out. For extra details, draw a few shading swirls and lines across the glass in darker blue. The light blue can also be used across the roof to draw soft shadows.

STEP 4

To finish off, use charcoal gray to outline the tram, define its details and introduce a few shading lines at the front. For the shadows and pavement, blend your blue tones to create a gradient: start with dark charcoal gray near the tram, transition into mid-blue and softly blend in the light blue toward the edges.

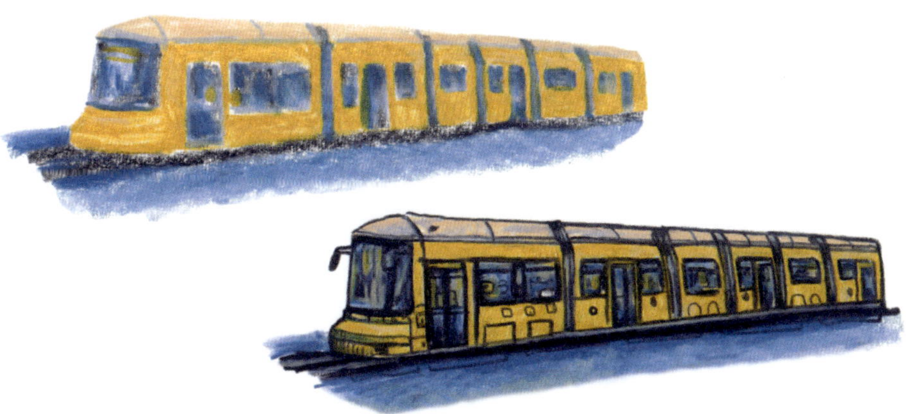

You might also enjoy sketching from inside a moving vehicle. There is something poetic about this narrative. On longer journeys, I often end up drawing, either capturing the scene outside or the interior of the vehicle - showing a snapshot of everyday life in that city.

When it comes to drawing moving scenery, the goal is to suggest the environment rather than capture every detail. One exercise you could try is to create a continuous line drawing: place your pencil on the paper and follow the main skyline or outlines of what you pass - buildings, trees, rooftops - without lifting your hand. When you get to the end of the page, continue the line beneath, creating a flowing path that traces your journey.

If you would rather work with colors or tone, try using loose, gestural marks. Use the side of your pencil to block in rough shapes you see in the surrounding environment. Focus on using color and shapes in an abstract way to imply the environment. Add a few quick diagonal strokes for details and creating textures. Deliberately leave unfinished areas and negative space to help evoke the sense of the scenery rushing past.

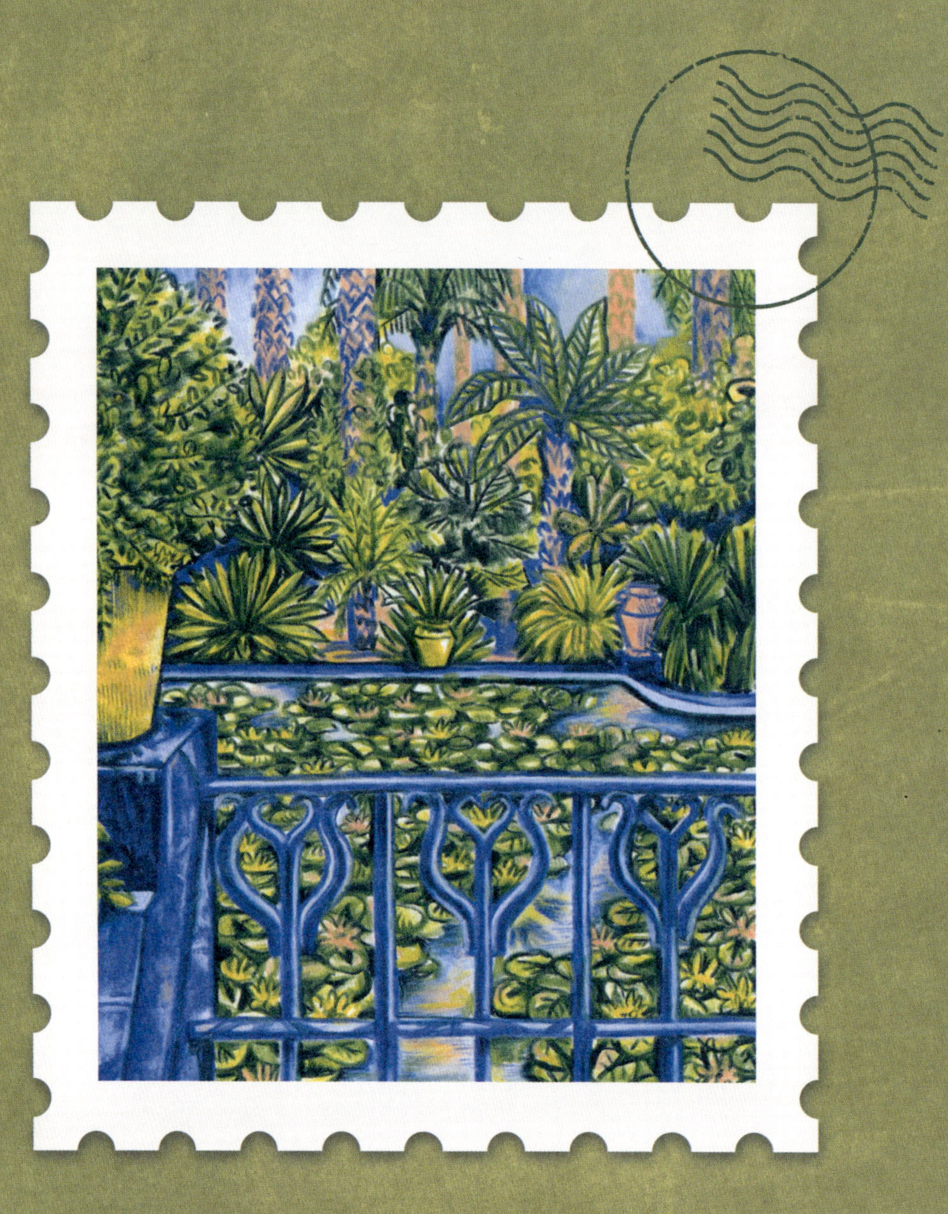

CHAPTER SIX

Nature *in the* City

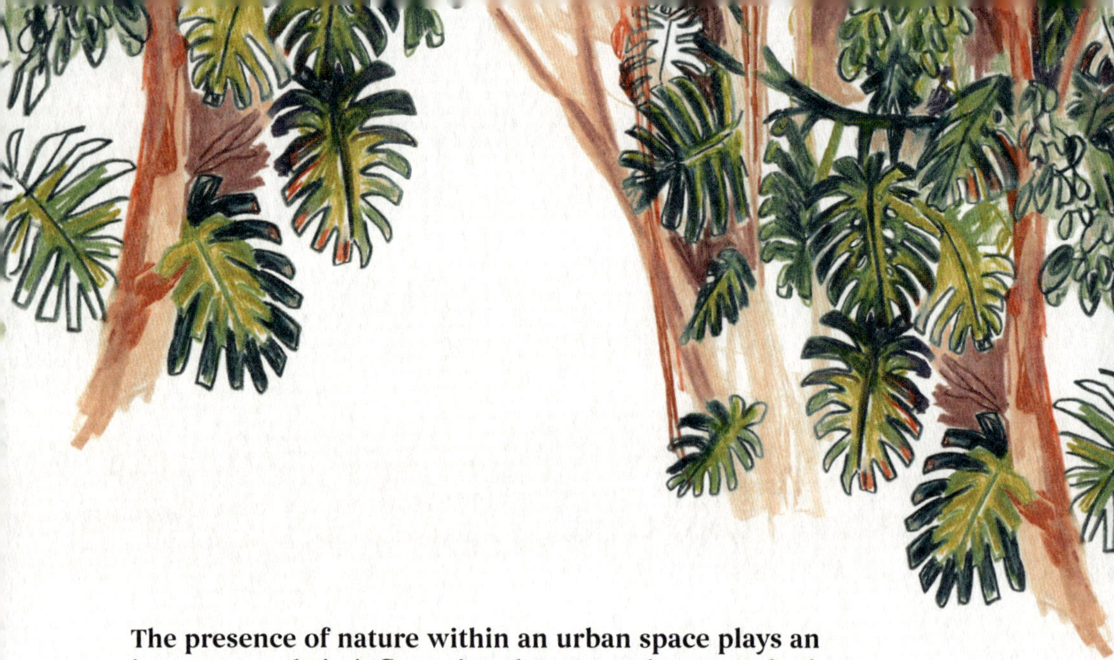

The presence of nature within an urban space plays an important role in influencing the atmosphere, aesthetics and our response to the city. Nature is calming and grounding, introducing fluidity against the geometric man-made structures.

When traveling, it is always interesting to see how each city integrates greenery. whether this is balconies in Milan sprawling with plants, beautiful parks and open spaces in London, or trees growing throughout the outdoor eateries in Kuala Lumpur.

In this chapter I will take you through different natural elements you are likely to see during your city walks, from trees and potted plants to rivers and grass. When exploring nature, I want you to focus on three key topics: texture, layers and lines of motion.

Texture
Natural subjects are full of interesting textures - perfect for exploring more expressive ways of using your pencil.

Layers
To create depth and a variety of different textures, you need to start soft and light and slowly build up the layers.

Lines of motion
Nature follows flowing lines. You should make sure you are always drawing in the direction of motion of your subject.

SHAPES

Before starting full-colored illustrations, it is great to strengthen your visual language with confident line drawings. This will help you recognize the main shapes in nature.

For this warm-up exercise, you need to be in a natural environment, or you can use plant reference photos. Just use a single-colored pencil or graphite pencil to draw the outline of the leaves and plant shapes, as if creating a coloring sheet.

Focusing on the outline will allow you to look for the overall shape, without worrying about colors and shading. This exercise is great for getting inspiration for shapes you can utilize later.

You can even integrate these line sketches into your drawings. I often like to contrast a busy architectural scene with the outline of nature. This creates a juxtaposition of the man-made and natural and introduces negative space to let the detailed areas breathe.

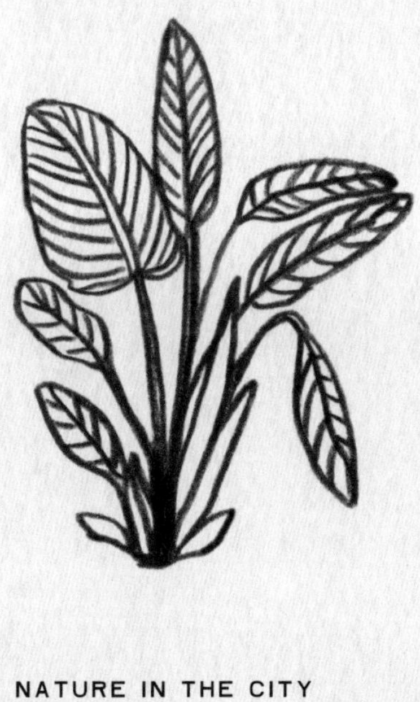

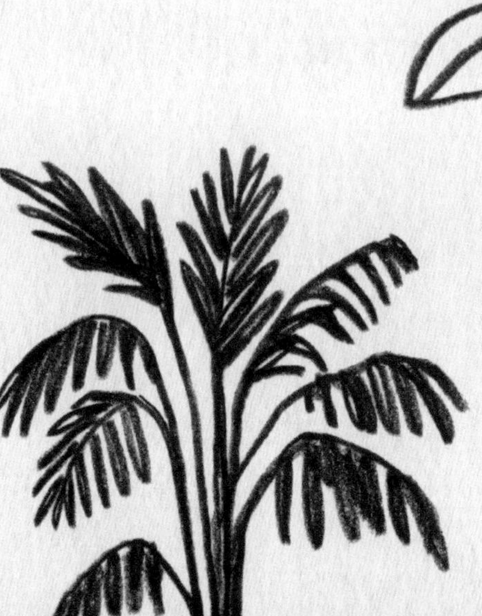

Trees

Trees are one of the most common natural subjects you will find in a city. Each city will have its own varieties, giving context to the location, climate and season.

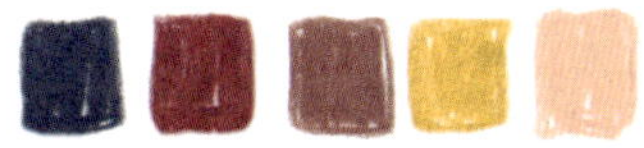

BARK

Trees are filled with a variety of shapes, patterns and textures, especially in the bark. When drawing this beautiful surface, think flowing, playful lines, viewing the bark textures as a pattern.

STEP 1

To build up the bark you need light layers. Start with soft pink and dusty mauve to create the background, introducing the mauve in areas of shadows. Remember to always draw in the direction of the growth of the bark. You want to keep the marks 'brushy' to create the bark texture, while following the curves of the trunk to build the impression of a three-dimensional form.

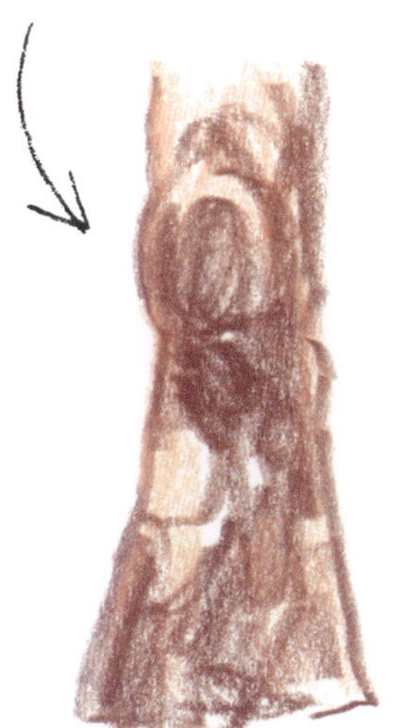

STEP 2

Using a deep plum red, shade the darker shadow areas. Layer charcoal gray in energetic and playful marks to suggest the textural details.

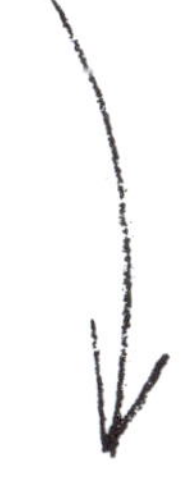

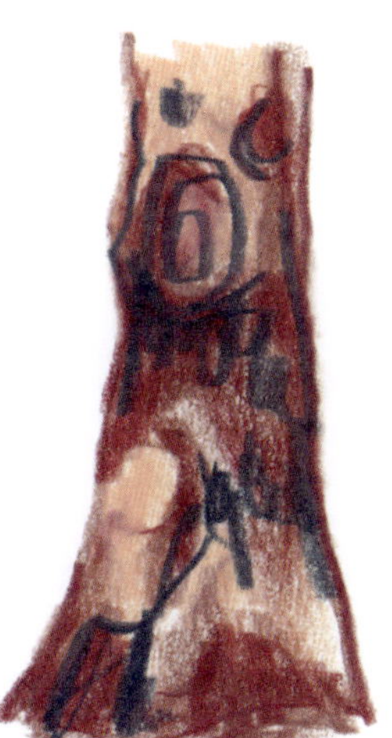

STEP 3

Now blend the colors with soft pink and bring in yellow highlights. The final layer involves expressive mark-making in charcoal gray. Have fun with the different curving lines you can create, following the curves of the tree roots and the circles of the bark.

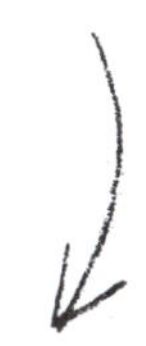

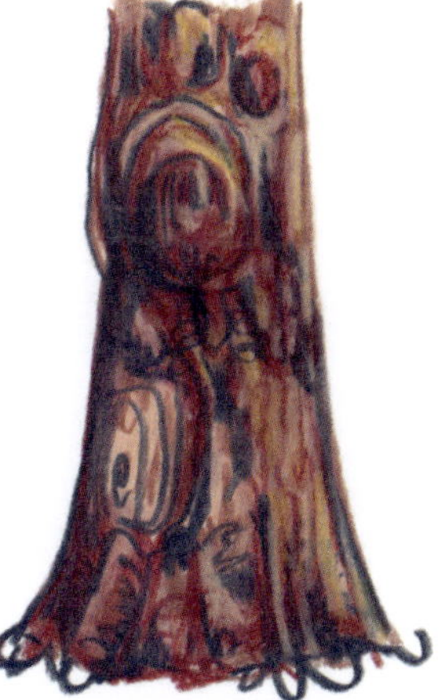

VALENCIA ORANGE TREES

With Valencia, Spain, being known as the 'Orange City', you are sure to be delighted by the beauty and sweetness of the abundant orange trees when walking along the city streets. Since visiting as a child, these streets full of oranges have stuck in my mind.

STEP 1

To form the lovely bushy leaf texture, start with a mossy green, using the side of your pencil in circular motions. View your pencil like a brush as you paint the tree background. Remember to maintain a soft pressure, as you will be building up the layers afterward. Use dark brown and the side of the pencil to draw the rough tree trunk and branches.

STEP 2

Focus on strong intuitive marks as you layer up the green, building up the tonal values by applying more pressure with each stroke. Continue using the side of your pencil in broad circular marks and let your pencil guide you through the motions. When deciding what marks to make, use the leaf shape as a reference. Are they spiky, broad, thin or flowing?

At this stage you are working on the mid-tones, so you can also add rough circular shapes for the oranges and some more definitive leaf shapes.

STEP 3

Now move on to the darker tones and textural details. Use the mossy green at a steep angle with lots of pressure to fully shade in some leaf shapes. Then play with areas of squiggles and swirls to connect everything together.

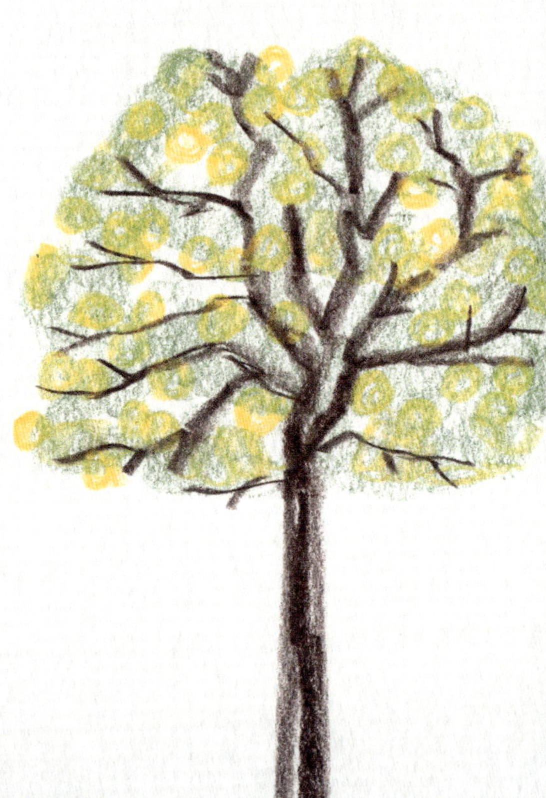

Layer up a dark forest green to draw a few leaf outlines – like the warm-up exercise on page 123. If you want more structure and tonal contrast, use dark brown to introduce another layer to the branches. Use this same brown to draw details in the oranges, with small circles for suggestions of the center and little curved shading marks for the skin texture. For the shadows between leaves, use your darkest green and brown to shade in these gaps.

STEP 4

The final touch is in the blending and highlights. If you would like a smoother appearance, use the lightest green to blend some of the tonal transitions. Finally, go in with touches of yellow to make the highlights pop.

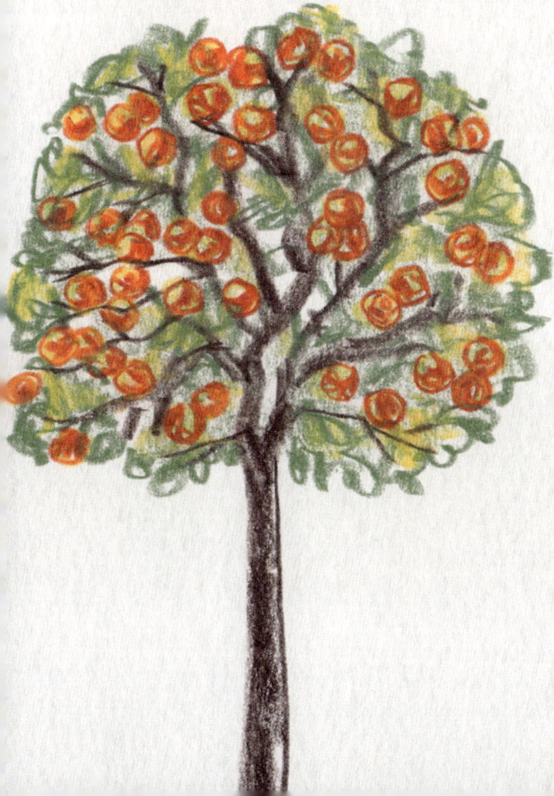

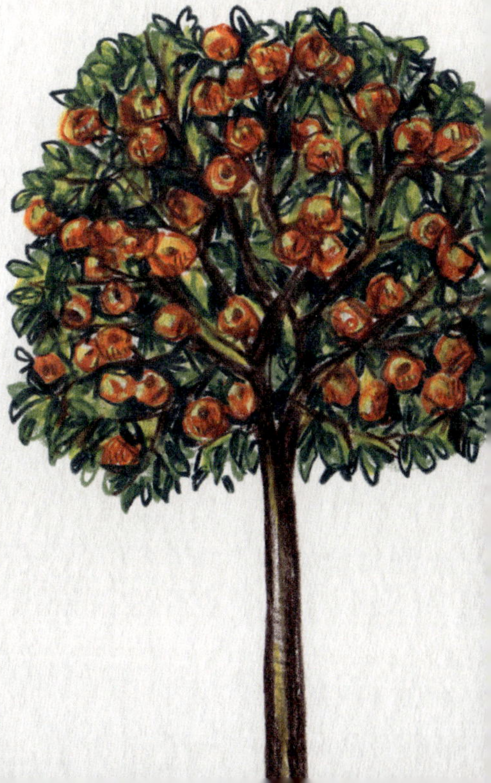

BUSHES

As the artist, you are in control of how you would like to portray the world. You don't have to follow the color palette you see in real life; instead, choose colors that best capture the atmosphere and essence of the location.

In this drawing, I opted for a harmonious monochromatic palette centered on blues to create a relaxed atmosphere. For monochromatic palettes, you need to ensure you have enough tonal contrast between your light, mid and dark colors.

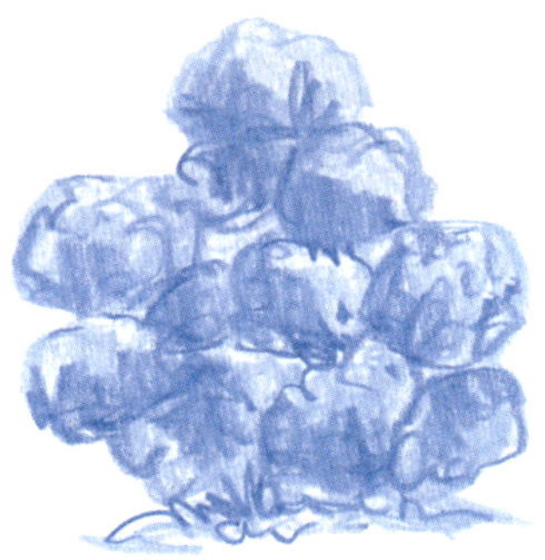

STEP 1

In light blue, draw the rough bush shape, applying side strokes in circular motions to mimic the texture. Introduce the mid-blue with slightly more pressure to help define the layers and form.

STEP 2

Next, use your darkest blue to draw leaf suggestions. Draw rapid marks with a steep pencil angle in circles and swirls to mirror the leaf patterns.

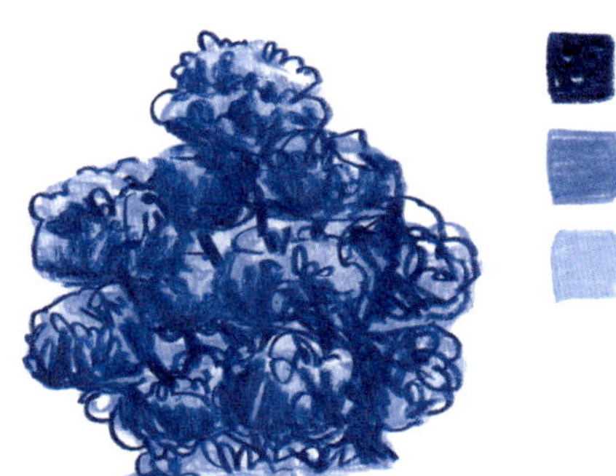

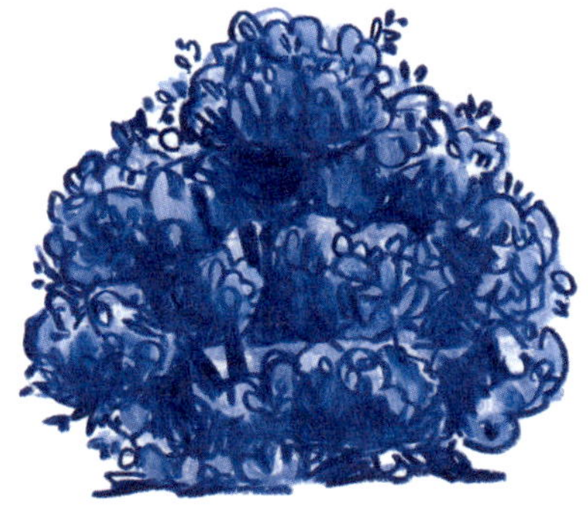

STEP 3

To create a smoother gradient, use light blue for blending tonal transitions. Then in dark blue, add a few small leaf shapes outside the border and swirly, energetic lines around the edges to build fluidity. To make sure the bush doesn't look like it is floating, draw the shadow underneath in dark blue with a few fast lines using the side of your pencil.

FLOWERING SHRUBS

While walking through the streets of Milan, Italy, you will see endless balconies covered in potted plants and blooming flowers, making the urban structures feel a little more natural.

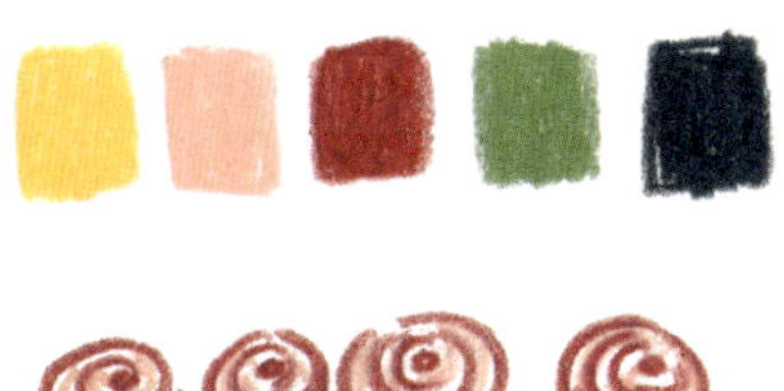

STEP 1

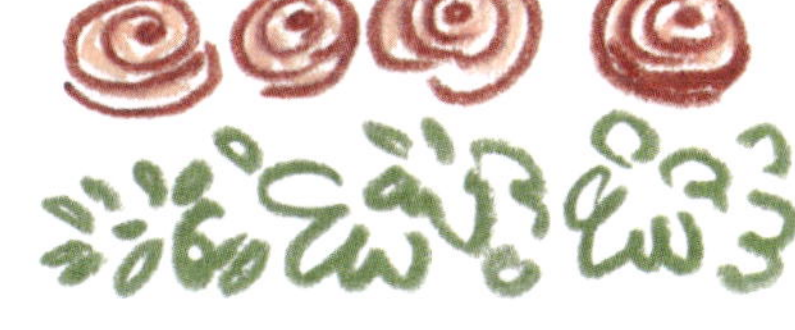

Start with a mossy green base, creating the main shape of the foliage. As usual, apply light pressure with the side of the pencil in circular motions. Add areas of golden yellow as your highlights where the light hits the bush.

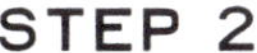

STEP 2

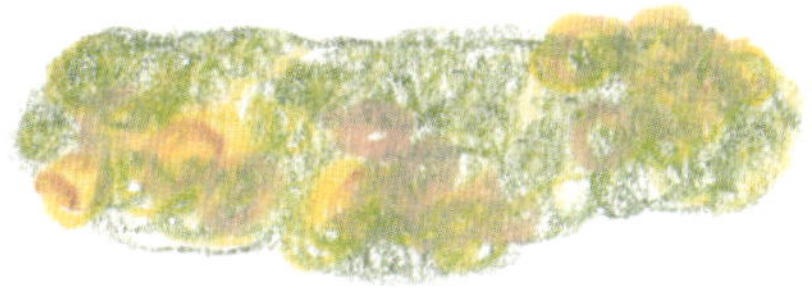

For the flowers, use a light pink, drawing with the side of the pencil in a spiral motion, as if you are following the lines of a cinnamon bun or a snail shell. Continue until the flower is the desired size. For the leaves, use the same playful swirls that you saw in the orange tree illustration, drawing inspiration from the leaf shapes.

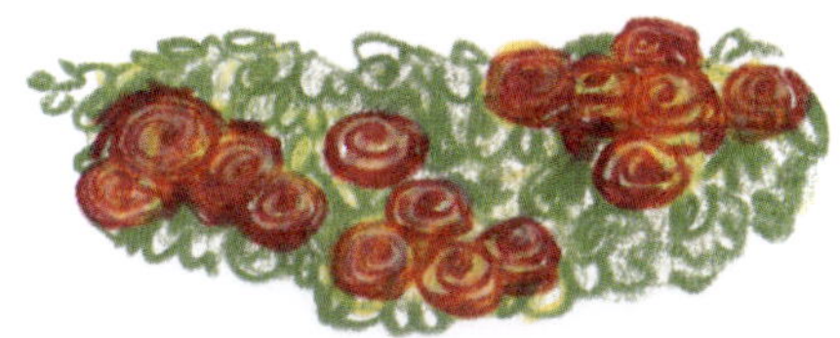

STEP 3

Repeat the same flowing leaf marks, but this time with a darker forest green. To create tonal contrast, bring yellow in for highlights across the leaves and flowers. If you want to make the flower shape more visible, outline the shape using dark green.

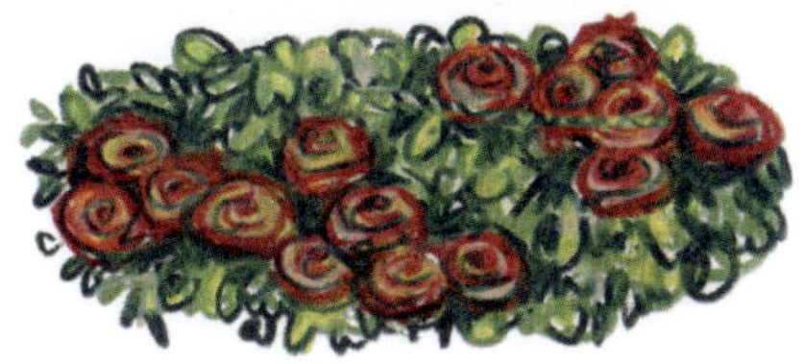

IVY

In many cities, you will see ivy or other crawling plants covering the walls of buildings and balconies. Drawing ivy follows a similar technique as for bushes and trees, focusing on contrast, layers and outlines.

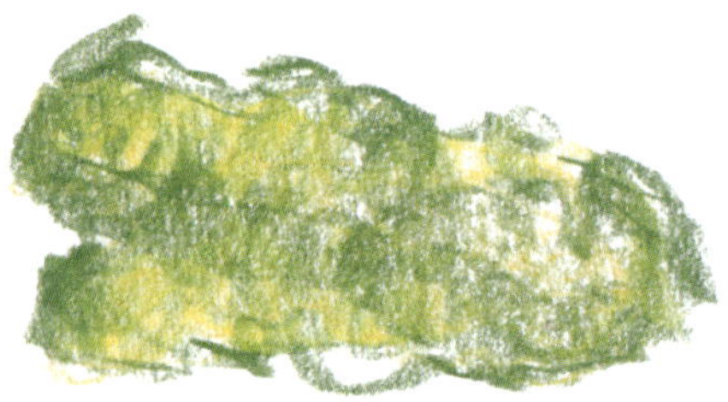

STEP 1

Start with a soft background in light green, with patches of yellow highlights.

STEP 2

Observing the shape of the leaves, draw leaf outlines across the background. Include overlapping leaves to produce a more natural look. Where there are shadows, you can completely block out these areas in green.

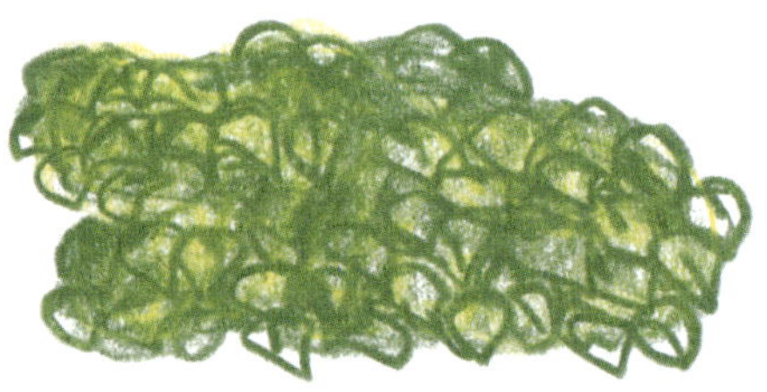

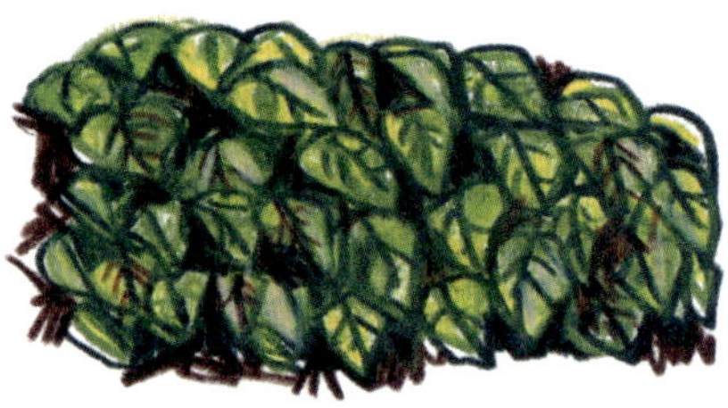

STEP 3

Finally, use darker green to go over the leaf outlines and shade the shadows in between some of the leaves. A warm dark brown is perfect to contrast the cool green background and define the darkest shadows and leaf patterns. For a final touch, use yellow to sharpen any highlights.

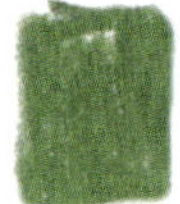
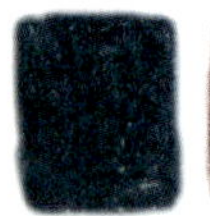

GRASS

In busy scenes, I typically use a single color for grass, varying the pressure for shadows and texture marks. These steps will teach you how to create this more detailed approach.

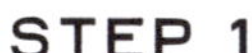

STEP 1

To replicate the bushy texture of grass, you need to vary your pencil pressure. Start with yellow ocher as the highlight color for the top of the grass and mossy green for the lower section, closer to the ground. I like to think of the grass in rows. This helps determine where each strand of grass grows and therefore how to draw the relevant marks.

STEP 2

Go on top with green ocher to blend the previous yellow and green transitions. Then start drawing the grass marks. Think about the direction of growth of the grass and be playful with a mixture of swirls and curved lines.

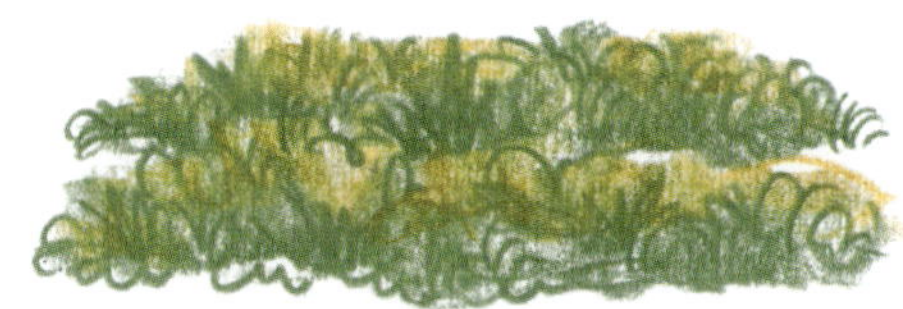

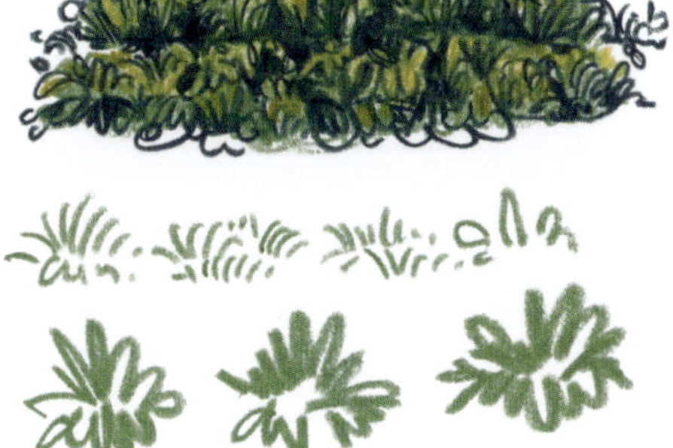

STEP 3

Layer dark green to create contrast and textural details. Again, be experimental with your mark-making. Take inspiration from the mark references on the left for how to approach these details.

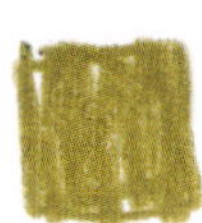

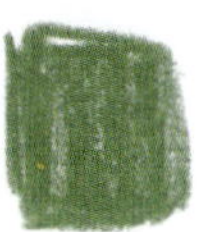

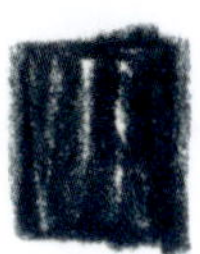

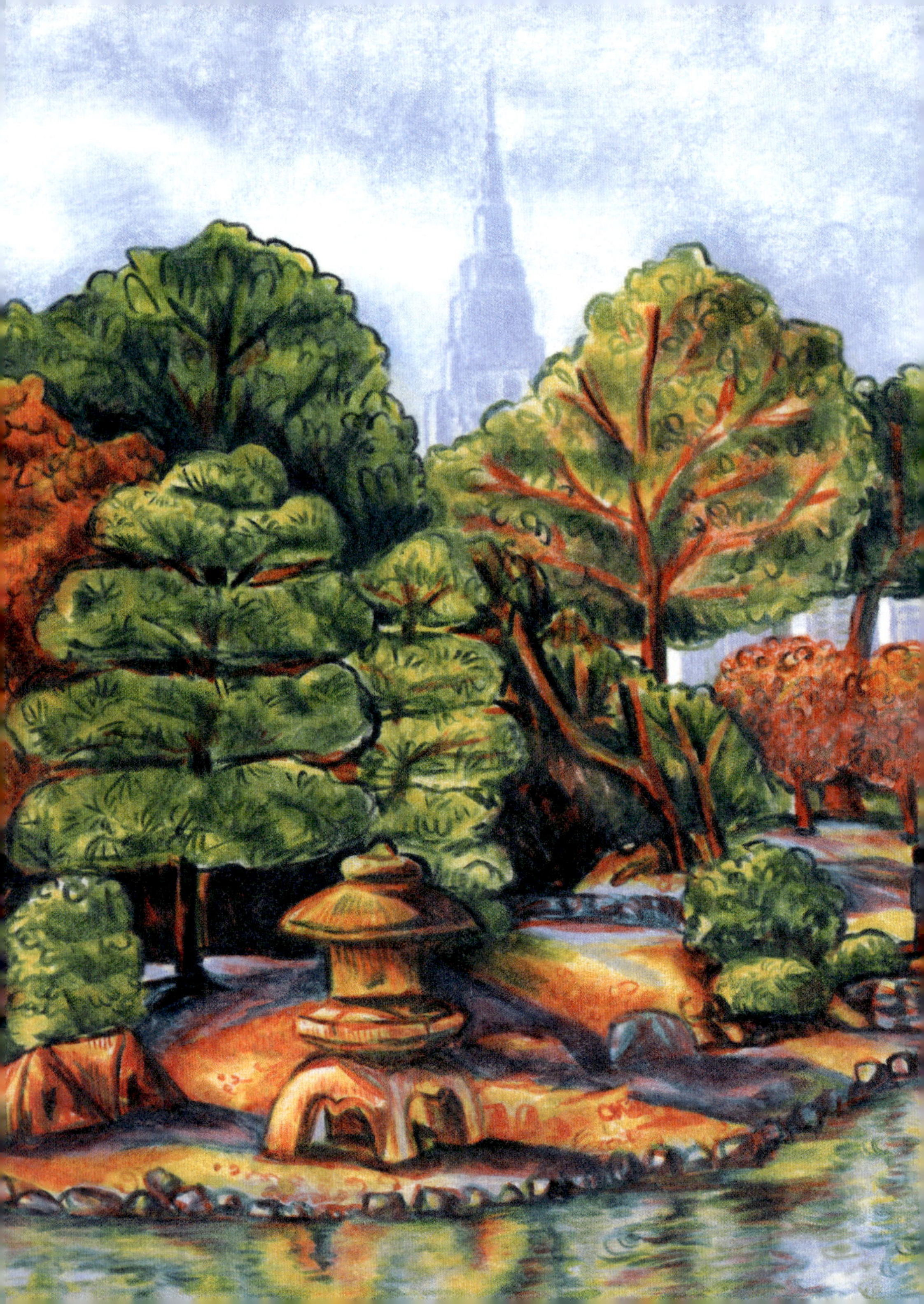

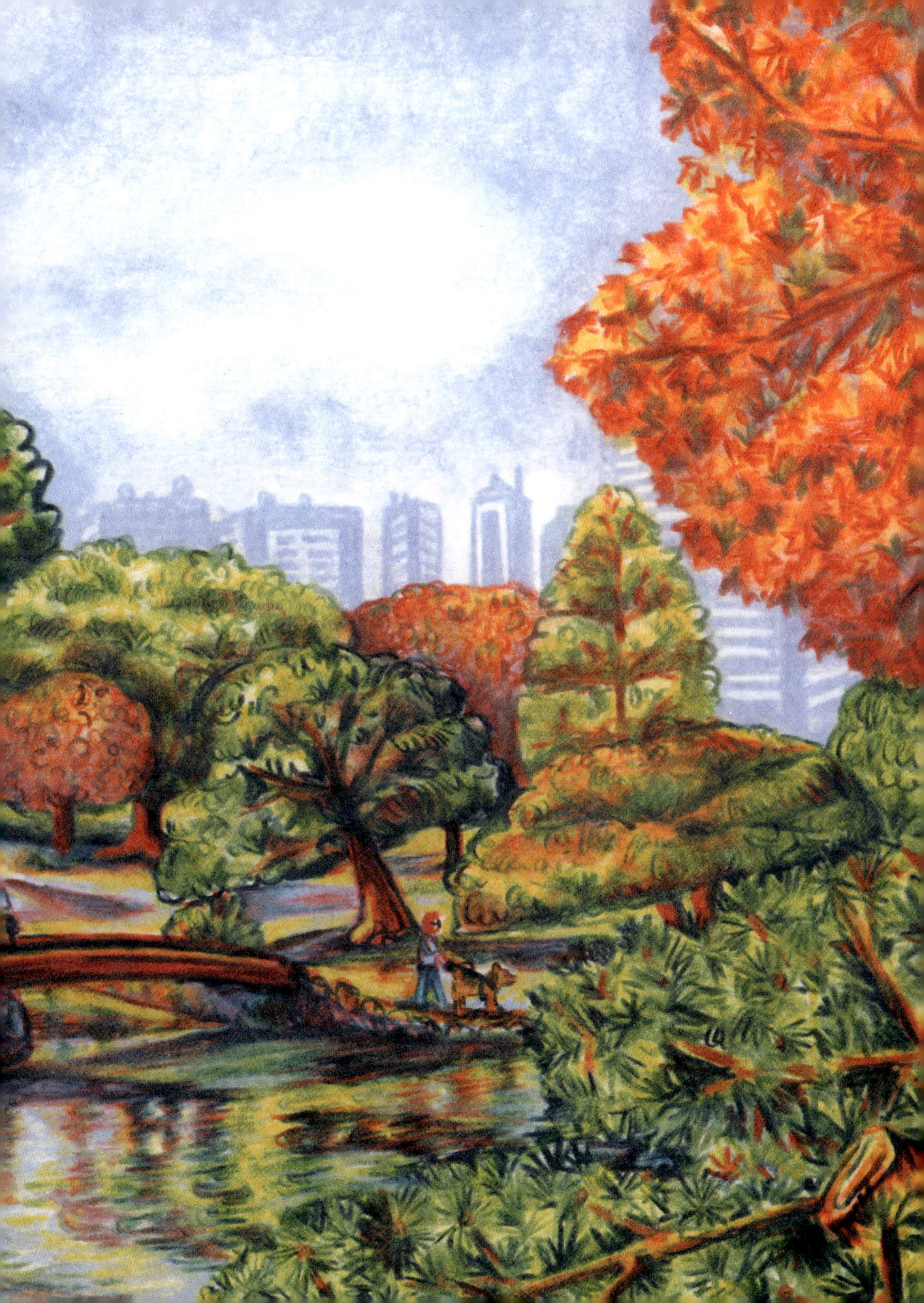

POTTED PLANTS

Potted plants are a lovely way of adding greenery in urban spaces, whether they are covering balconies, courtyards or cafés.

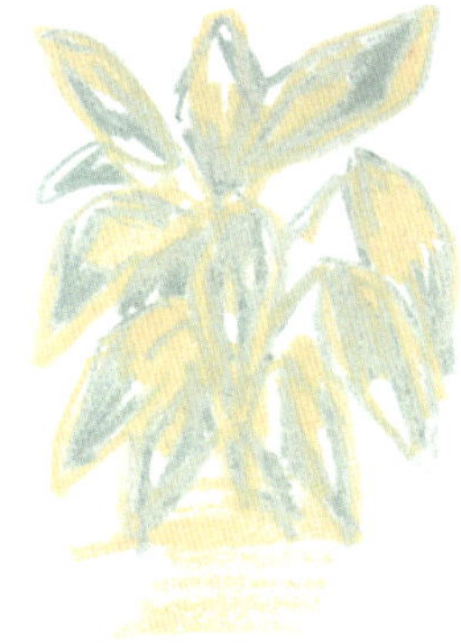

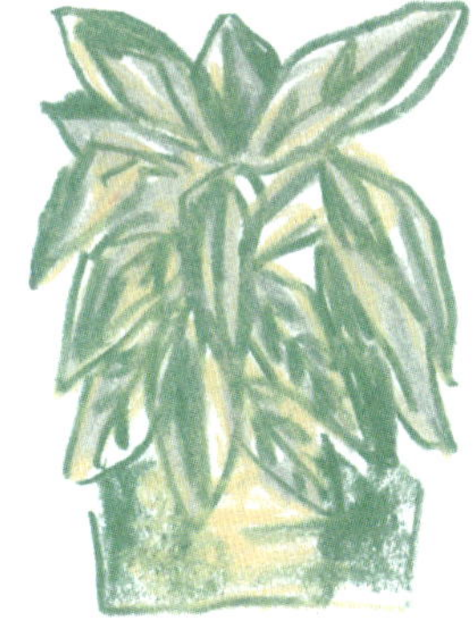

STEP 1

Start with your lightest color (pale yellow) to draw the highlights and block out the rough leaf shapes.

STEP 2

Now introduce mint green as the mid-tone for the leaves. Keep the marks very rough and angular to match the sharp shapes of the leaves.

STEP 3

Next, layer jade green for the leaf outlines and darker shadows across the surfaces. Use the side of the pencil, still in this green, to cover the shadowed edges of the plant pot.

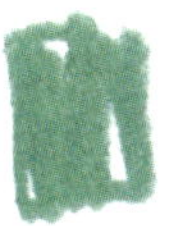

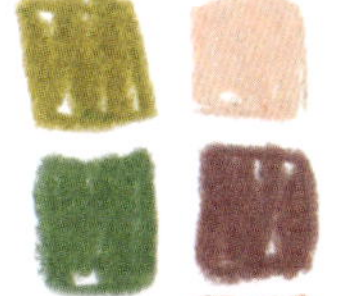

When you are drawing greenery and don't want to draw all the details behind the plant, you can experiment with a colorful background. Here you will see the difference it makes by using a warm orange, pink and purple against the green leaves to help the plant stand out, while creating a visually interesting backdrop.

To create this background wash, start with filling out the negative space in light pink using the side of the pencil. Slowly build this up with soft purple and finally warm orange, creating a gradient with the darkest area closest to the leaves.

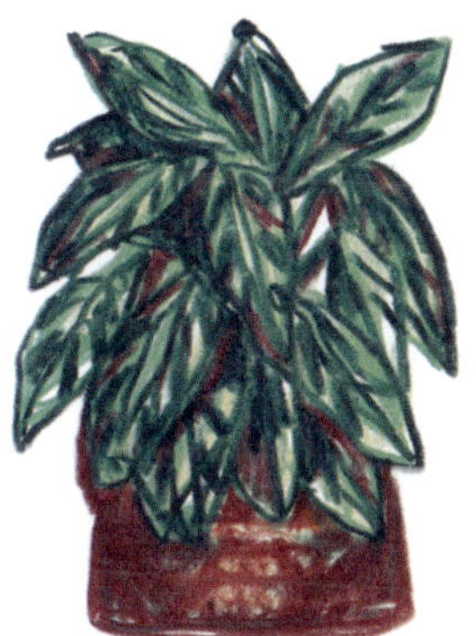

STEP 4

Now using dark green, define the outlines and leaf patterns and fill in the dark spaces in between the leaves. At the same time, use a deep-plum-red pencil to apply subtle hints of a warmer color along the shadows of the leaves and where they overlap. For the plant pot, draw in a sideways curving motion in the deep plum red to show the darker areas - particularly where the leaves go over the edges.

STEP 5

For the last touches, use pale yellow to add highlights along the center of the leaves and the circle pattern across the pot. Use dark green to draw shading marks across the sides of the plant pot and to redefine the gaps in between and under the leaves. This will help emphasize the tonal contrast and add depth.

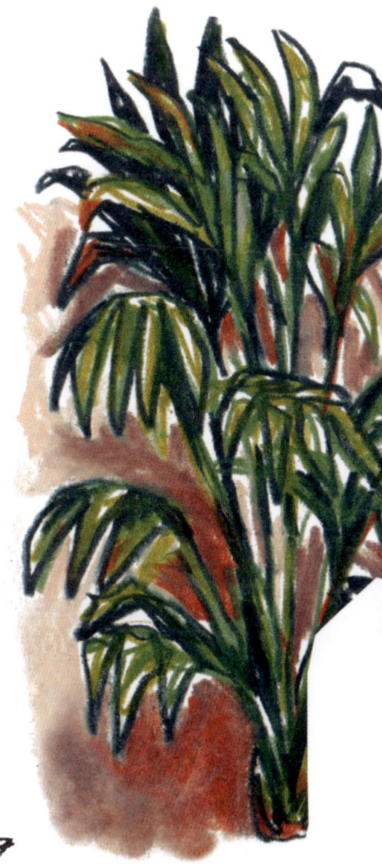

WATER

To replicate the fluidity of water with pencils, you need to look at the direction the water is flowing and make sure your marks continuously follow these lines of motion.

STEP 1

The colors you choose for water will be heavily influenced by the surrounding environment. Water is a reflective surface, so it mirrors the colors around it. If you are surrounded by trees along a river, you will see greens throughout the water. As this example is demonstrating water in a city location, I am using pinks, yellows and earthy tones to capture the surrounding building colors reflected across the water.

Start with your pencil wash in light blue, yellow ocher and soft pink. Imagine your pencils are like watercolors and use broad, light strokes to create the background, leaving white sections for highlights.

Add a brushy strip of light pink and yellow for suggestions of the building reflections. Follow a zigzagging curvy 'z' shape for these marks, rocking from side to side as you go down the page.

STEP 2

Go in to define the direction of the ripples. Continue with the rocking motion, now in a mid-blue. These marks will help create the impression of the ripples across the surface.

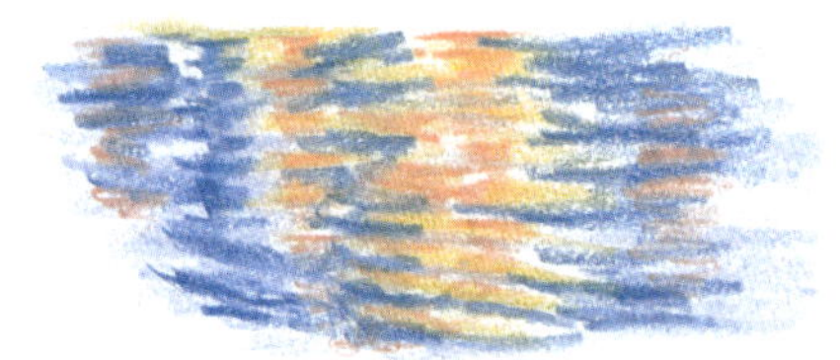

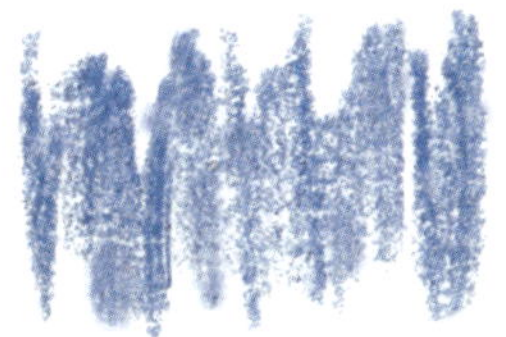

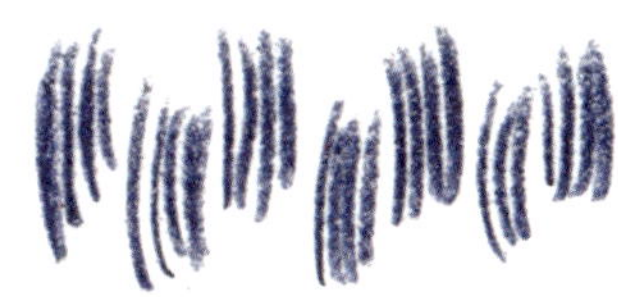

STEP 3

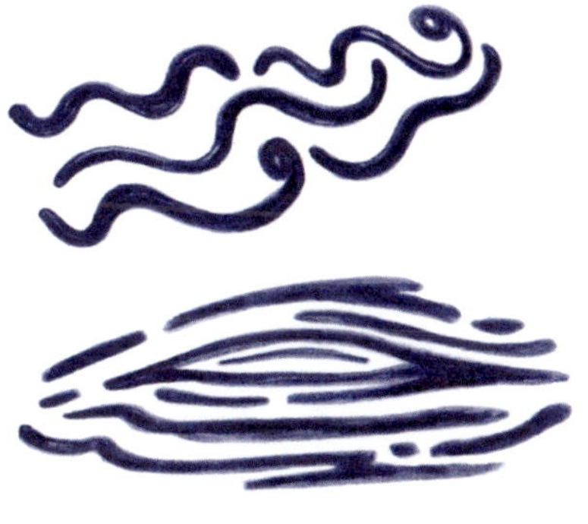

Now move on to blending the layers using your light blue. Apply a lot of pressure as you smooth the transitions between the light and dark areas.

You can also add extra ripple details in dark blue – draw curving swirls that guide you across the shimmering water. The final touch is to reintroduce the yellow and pink as stronger reflections.

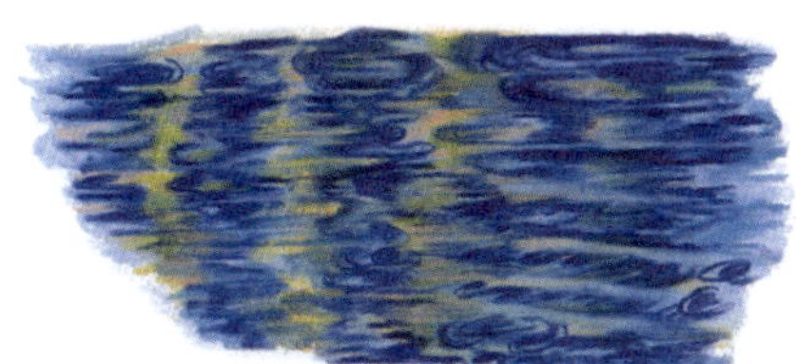

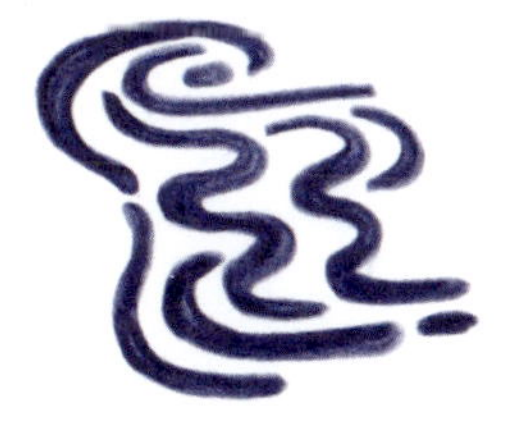

Drawing water can take some time. However, by building up these layers, playing with reflection colors and drawing lines in the direction of motion, you can create beautiful flowing surfaces with your pencils.

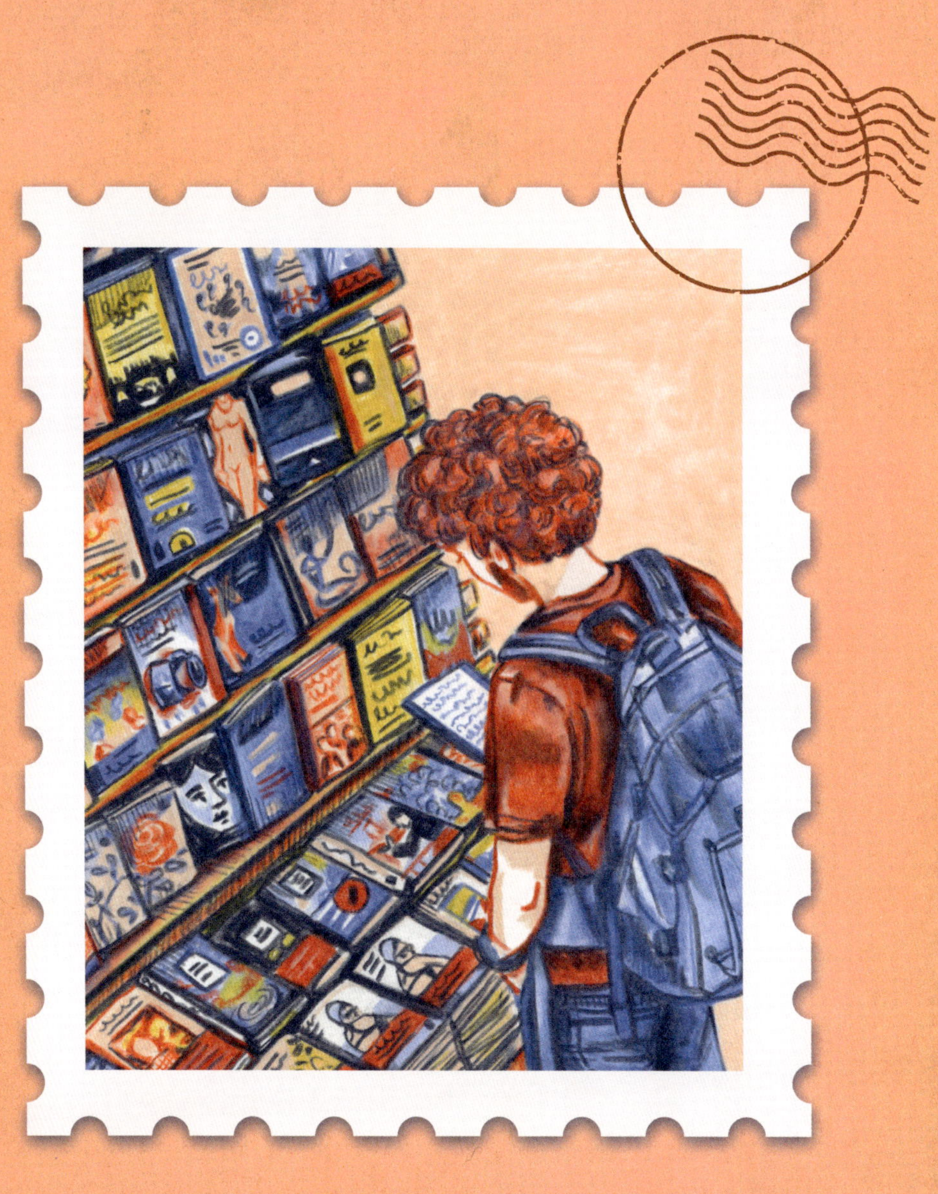

CHAPTER SEVEN

Everyday City Life

Now that you have explored drawing different city subjects, let's put these into practice with a couple of everyday scenes. Markets and cafés are two of my favorite places for location drawings, perfect for capturing the essence of a city and its people. They give you a glimpse into day-to-day life: the food eaten, the community and the architecture.

CAFÉS

Drawing in a café is great if you want to find a comfortable spot to get into drawing on location. You can sit in a relaxing environment while observing the world go by.

With a café scene, there are so many different narrative options. I typically lean toward sharing the life of the space: the interactions between customers and staff, the barista making a coffee or behind the scenes. A café is full of people and life, so I want to show this through the drawing and composition.

The drawing below is of one of the oldest cafés in Barcelona, Spain, Granja M. Viader. I wanted to make the customers look natural in the scene, so I spent some time observing their different activities, how they interacted with each other and the space. Were they drinking coffee, reading a newspaper or serving customers?

Cafés can be very busy locations, with lots of interior details and moving parts, so negative space is very important. This will be your breathing room within the design. For this drawing, the waiter is the focal point. To guide the viewer to this point, I have positioned

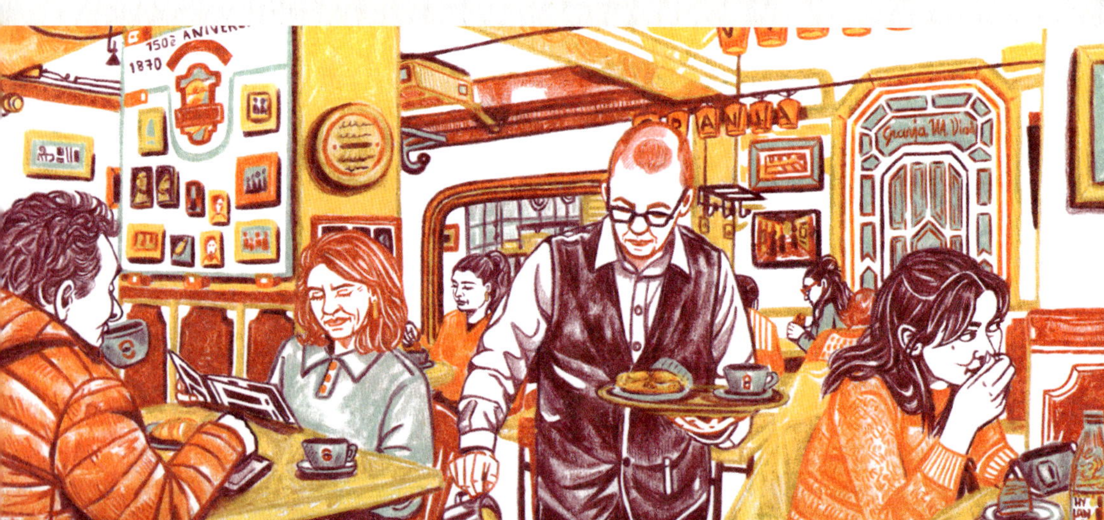

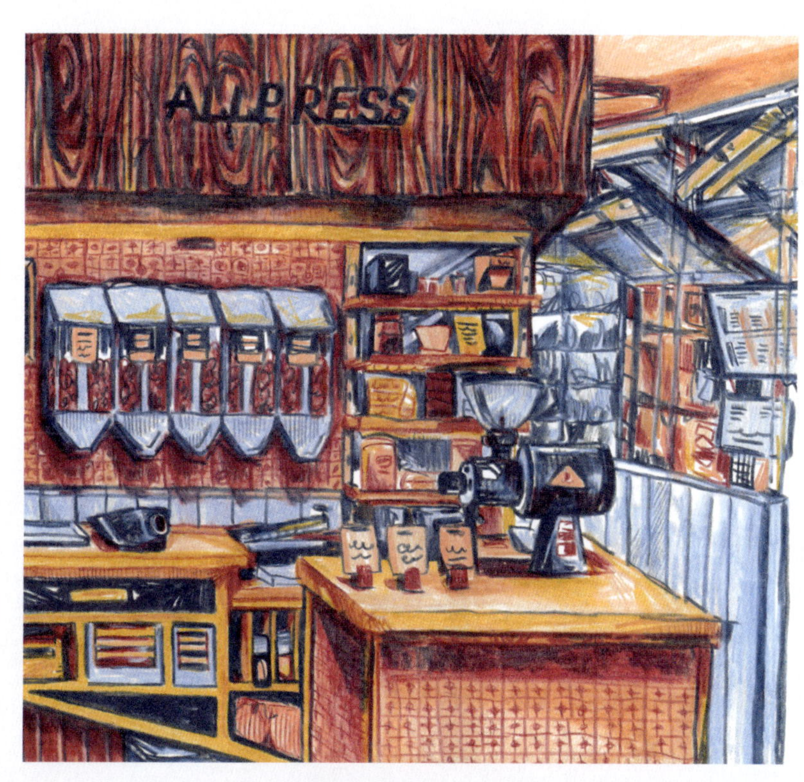

Allpress Roastery

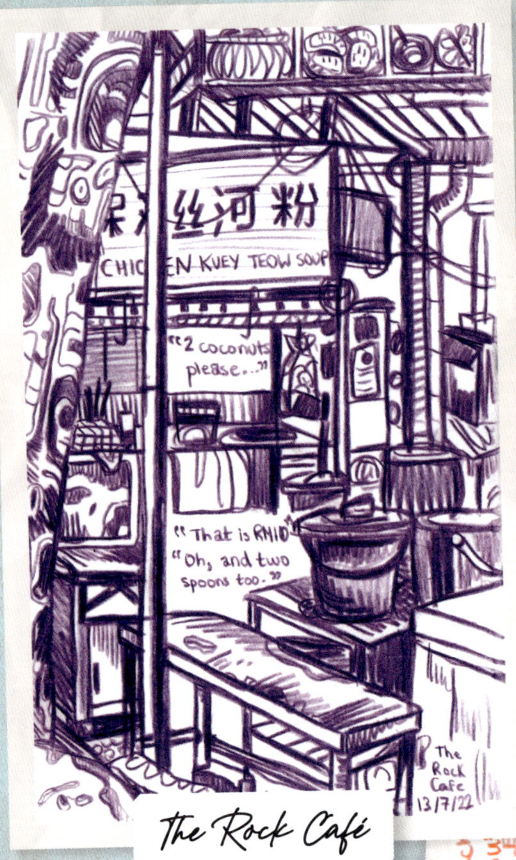

The Rock Café

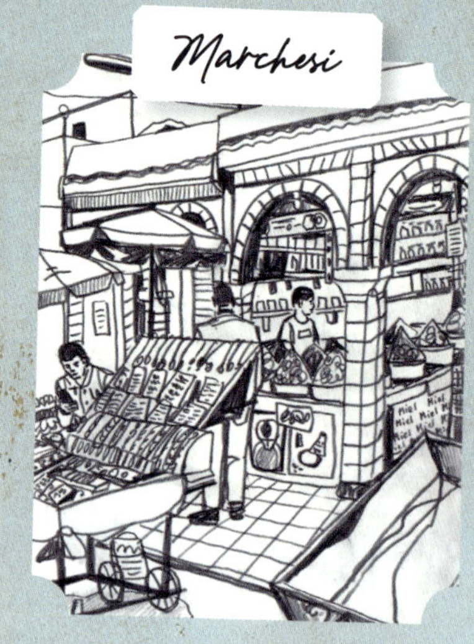
Marchesi

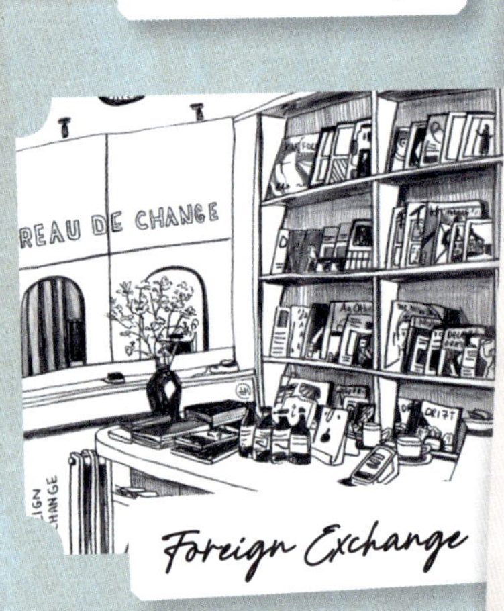

Foreign Exchange

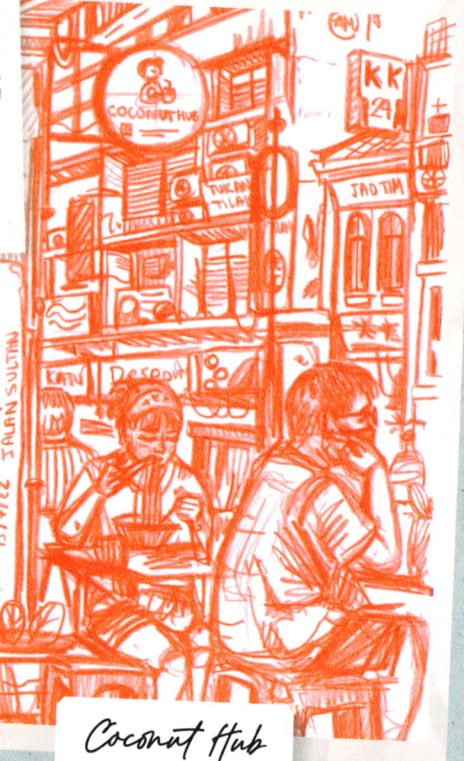

Coconut Hub

the waiter in the center third and used complementary colors, with the purple and surrounding yellow. This creates balance while the colors introduce contrast that grabs our attention.

Composition is very important in creating the narrative for a café scene. You could use the framing technique, mentioned at the beginning of the book (see pages 46–47), to draw the viewer to certain areas of the scene. In the drawing of my favorite courtyard bookstore café in Barcelona, featured on page 33, I have used the tree going across one of the three rows of my grid to create a balanced composition, while also framing the people below.

If drawing people is not on your agenda, then you could capture the interior design. Cafés are a haven of texture, with tiled walls, wooden surfaces and shiny coffee-making equipment.

The drawing on page 141, created at the lovely Allpress Roastery in London, England, is an example of how you can implement contrast between the foreground and background through changing your technique. I used tighter and more detailed mark-making for the focal point of the coffee counter, and faster, rougher marks for the more distant kitchen. The change in the tightness of the marks helps create the idea of perspective and depth in the drawing.

If you don't have much time to draw on location, then you can use a single graphite pencil, concentrating on the main lines and a few shading details. These graphite drawings help you quickly and confidently capture a scene – such as these examples opposite, inside the deli Marchesi in Milan and Foreign Exchange café in London.

If you would like to add another layer to your location drawing, you could introduce text. Whether this is an overheard conversation, thoughts about the space or your own narrative, think about ways you can include text within the composition. You could leave negative space or make the text part of the design itself.

Also opposite are two drawings I did of cafés in Malaysia when I began my journey into reportage illustration. During this trip, I loved including overheard conversations within the illustration, giving a greater insight into the scene.

BOTTLES AND GLASSES

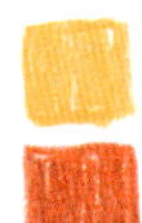
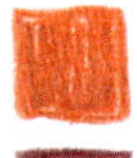
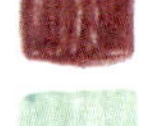

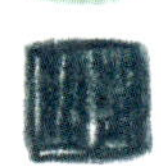

In many cafés I have visited in southern Europe, notably in Spain and Italy, I noticed a distinct charm in the way bottles are displayed. Since my time in Barcelona, glass bottles have become a favorite subject to draw due to the colors they add to the scene and how the light hits their surface.

Here you can see how the vibrant complementary colors add a pop of energy, making this subject a joy to draw.

STEP 1

Start with the bottle outline, playing with the shapes and heights. Use the main bottle color to outline the shape, adding the labels and top in a different color.

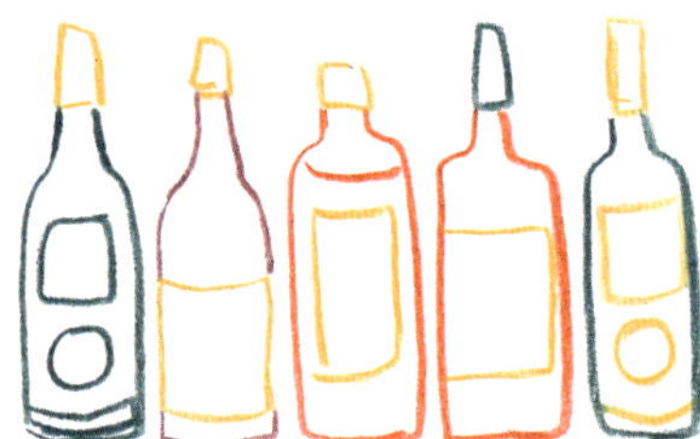

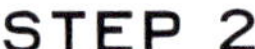

STEP 2

Now introduce the main body color. Draw with your pencil in a steep angle, applying lots of pressure and fast marks, to create the energetic appearance. Leave small gaps of white to form the reflective surface. Experiment with a combination of colors and how the placement influences the appearance and relationship between the colors.

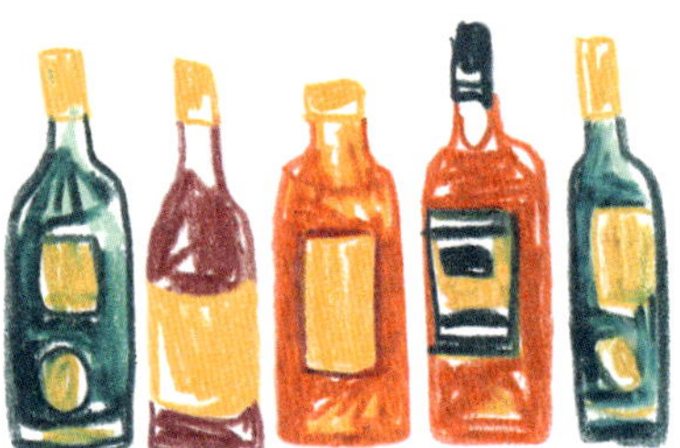

STEP 3

Time to add the details. We want to keep the design quite rough, so follow your intuition with the marks and blending. Play with blending darker and lighter tones to add the shadows to the bottles. Don't over blend, keep the pencil marks visible. The final touch is adding a few swirly lines for the suggestion of text on the labels.

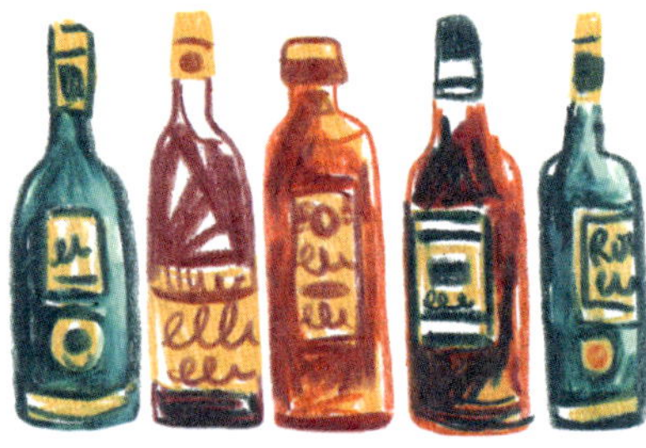

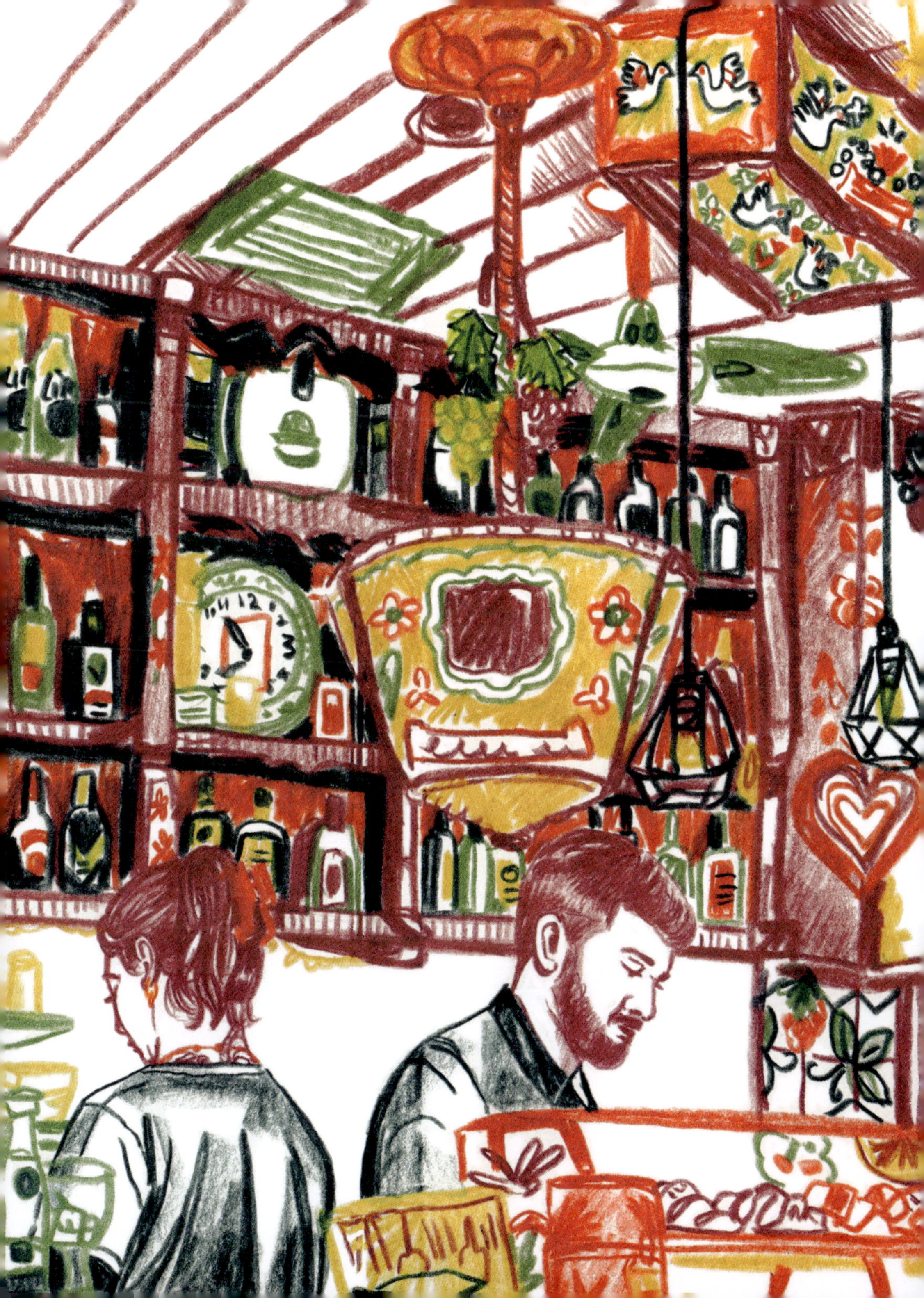

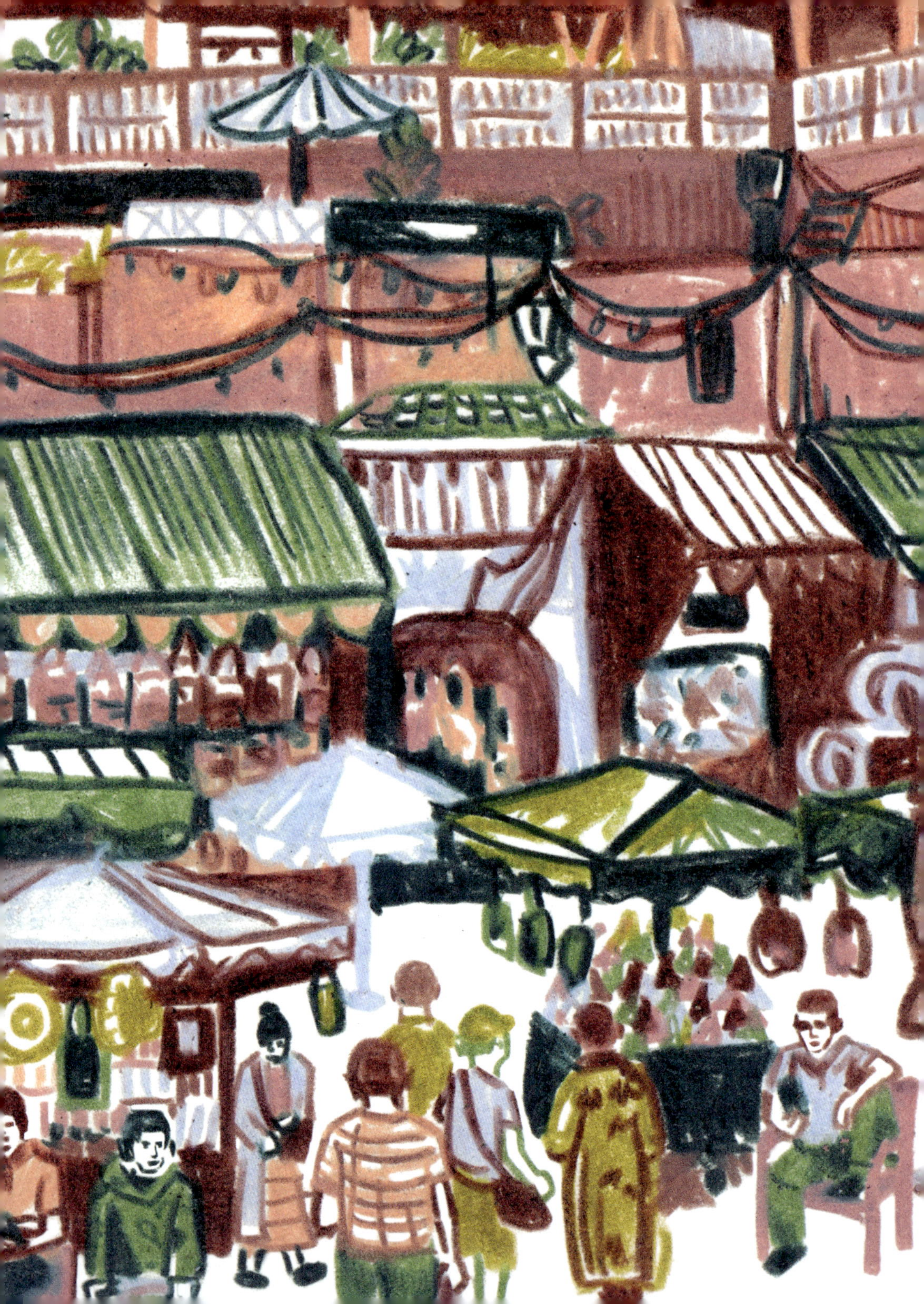

MARKET SCENES

Markets are locations full of activity, which can initially make them quite overwhelming drawing spots. However, when you build up your confidence, they are treasure troves of creative inspiration.

Here are a few examples of market drawings I have done on location across my travels. As I usually stand up when drawing in these places, with my sketchbook leaning against my arm, using a limited palette or a graphite pencil means I have fewer materials to hold and worry about.

When choosing the composition, you first need to decide the narrative. If I am focusing on stall owners or interactions with customers, then I will use a graphite pencil so I can quickly draw the moving figure. If I want to zoom out and show the whole scene, then colored pencils are my go-to for capturing the design and overall feeling of the space.

When working with busy and complex scenes like a market, it can be tricky to know where to start. If the drawing is capturing the whole market, then focus on the lines of the stalls and surrounding buildings to create the base of the drawing, and build up from there. If there is a repeated subject, such as these umbrellas in Marrakech, Morocco, then I like to start with this, as I can use the first umbrella drawing as a reference tool for working out the scale of the rest of the scene. I drew out all the umbrellas, working from the left to right, to ground the drawing before filling in the gaps with the extra details.

For drawing people in these locations, I keep to a simplified style. In this colorful drawing at Jemaa El-Fnaa Square in Marrakech, I blocked out the body of the figure in a main color then picked a new color for the outfit. Then I chose a single color to outline the clothing and add the patterns on top.

If you want the clothing outline to be more subtle, keep it monochromatic and just pick a darker shade for details. Or use a complementary color to make the clothing patterns stand out. Think about having a variation of the colors spread throughout the people, so you don't have a block of everyone wearing blue outfits and then green outfits. To make figures stand out, place colors with different tonal values next to each other. Remember, use a lighter tonal value to make an object appear distant and a darker one to bring it forward.

In this drawing I have split the scene into three, using the rule of thirds as a composition guide (see page 44). The lower third is for the people, the mid-ground is for the stalls and the top third is the building details. By having the darker greens in the foreground and softer purples and pinks in the background, it creates a sense of depth and perspective. This is a useful technique for busy market scenes.

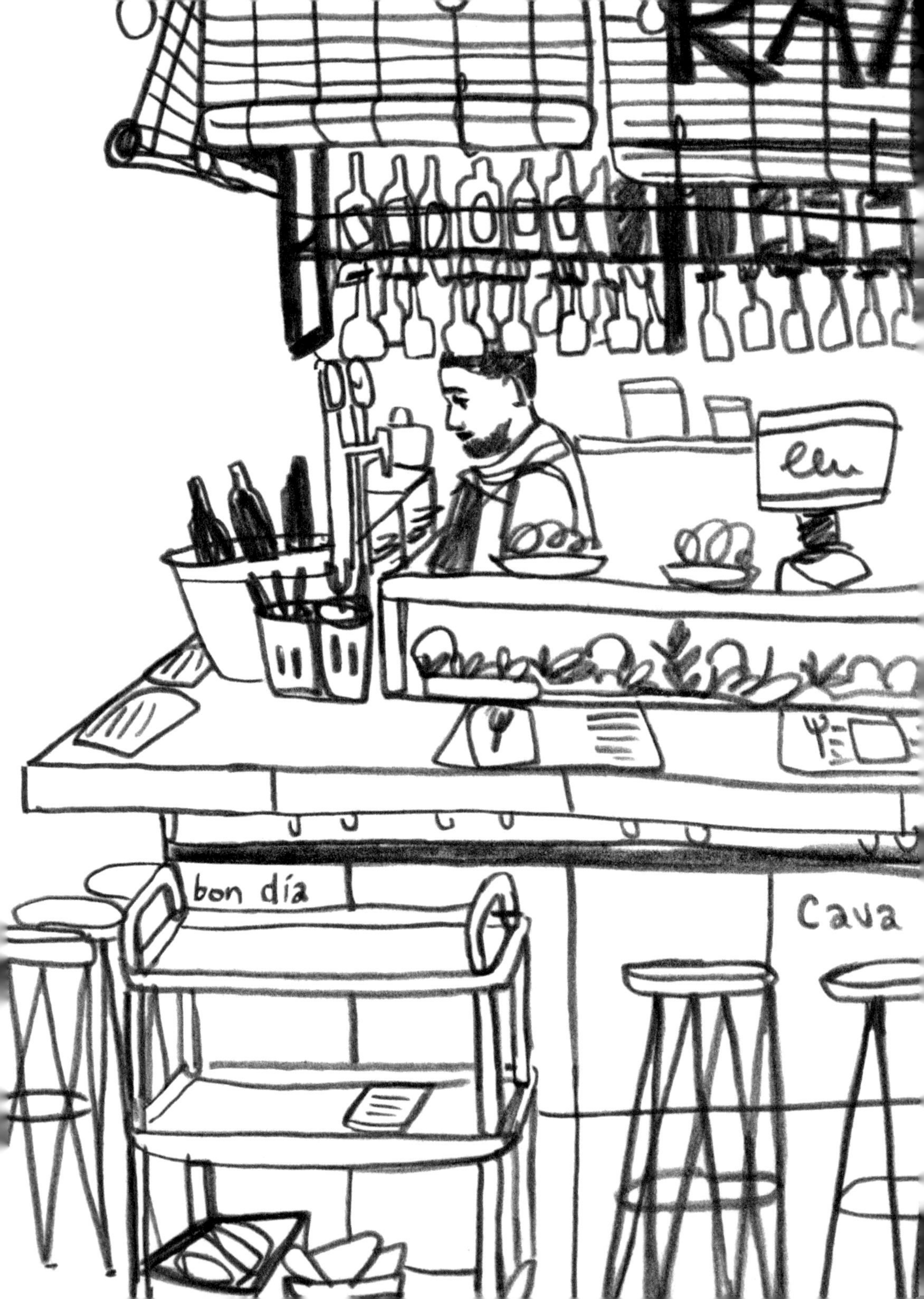
bon día
Cava

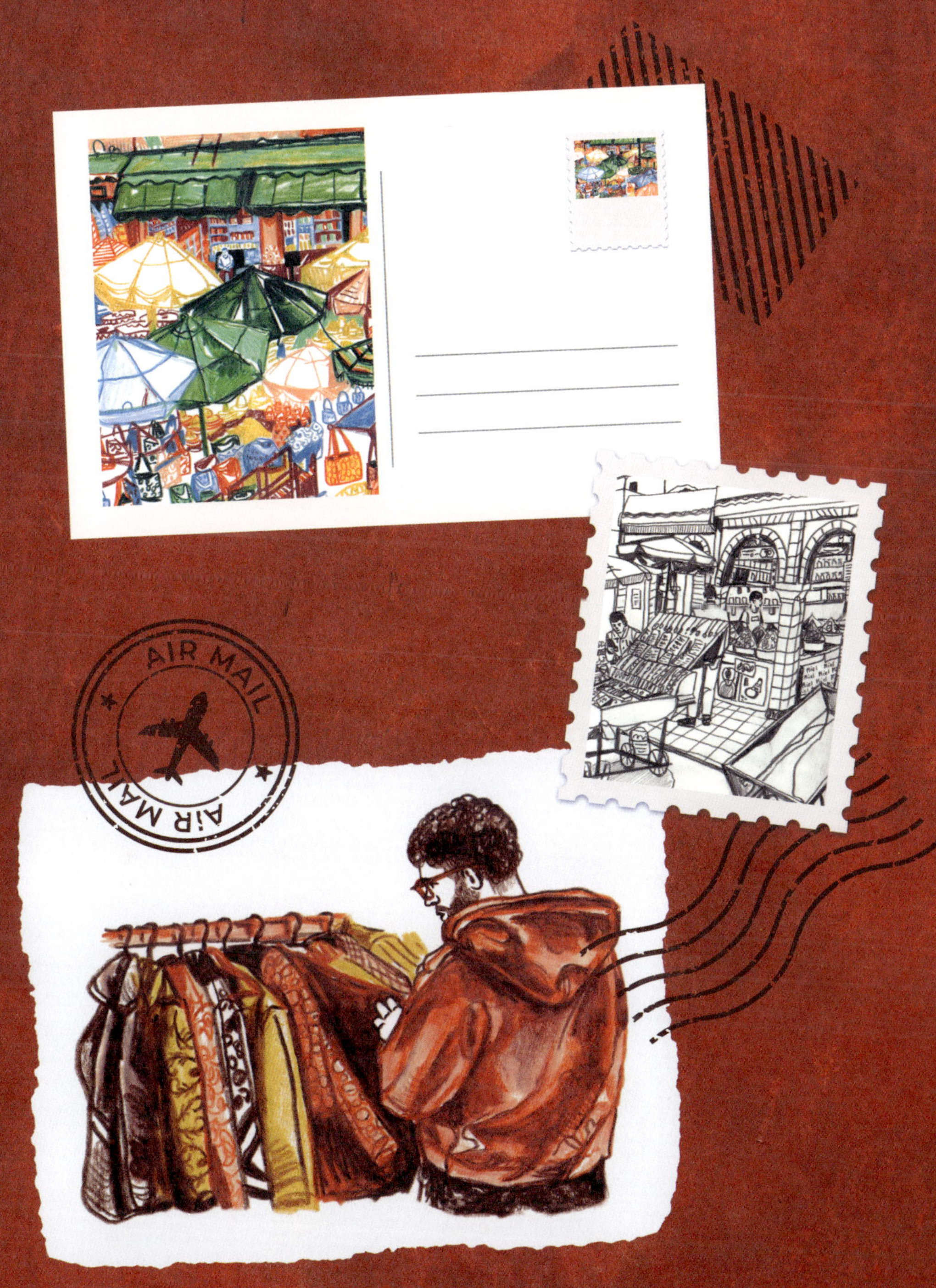
AIR MAIL
AIR MAIL

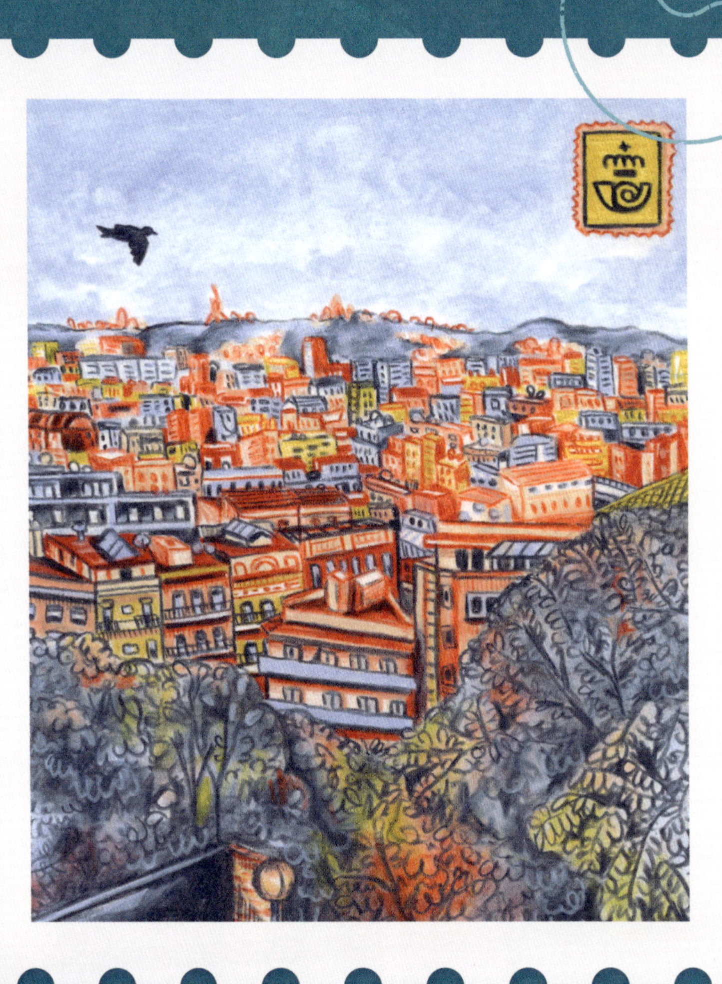

CHAPTER EIGHT

Other Ways *to* Sketch

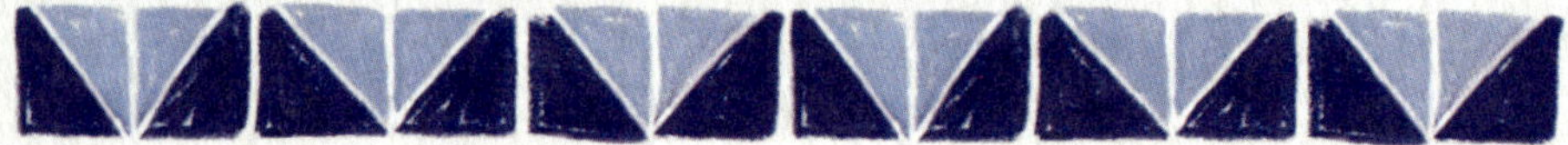

ILLUSTRATED TRAVEL POSTCARDS

A lovely idea for your next adventure is to create your own travel postcard.

You can start with some visual research for inspiration, looking through shops in the city that sell postcards and prints, or perhaps creating a mood board. This will help spark some ideas for compositions, subjects and text-to-image relationship.

For the subject, you could perhaps draw your favorite memory from the trip, an aesthetically pleasing location or place of cultural or historical interest. Every time you look at the postcard you will be transported straight back to the city and reminded of your time there. You could also make an extra one to post back home to someone special, creating a truly unique way of sharing your trip while capturing your memories.

Sending a postcard you have illustrated yourself feels a lot more meaningful, intentional and considered than sending a photo and text message. Art is very personal and takes time. If you choose to send your creation to someone, it shows how much you care.

If you are not traveling, don't worry, I have another option for you. For the design, you could research a favorite location of yours, somewhere on your travel list, or use photos from previous trips. Then you can start your own illustrated travel postcard series. Either create one every time you travel to a new location, or create a series on locations you would love to visit.

For this postcard, I wanted to capture a relaxing memory of one of the vibrant riads I stayed at in Marrakech. Here I have kept to a single scene, but you could play around with the composition through adding text, creating a collage of different city spots or playing with the border design. To hint back to the location, you could also create a border design inspired by tiles or patterns you came across.

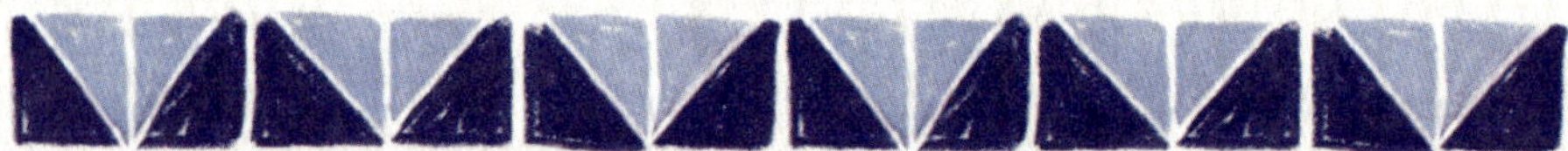

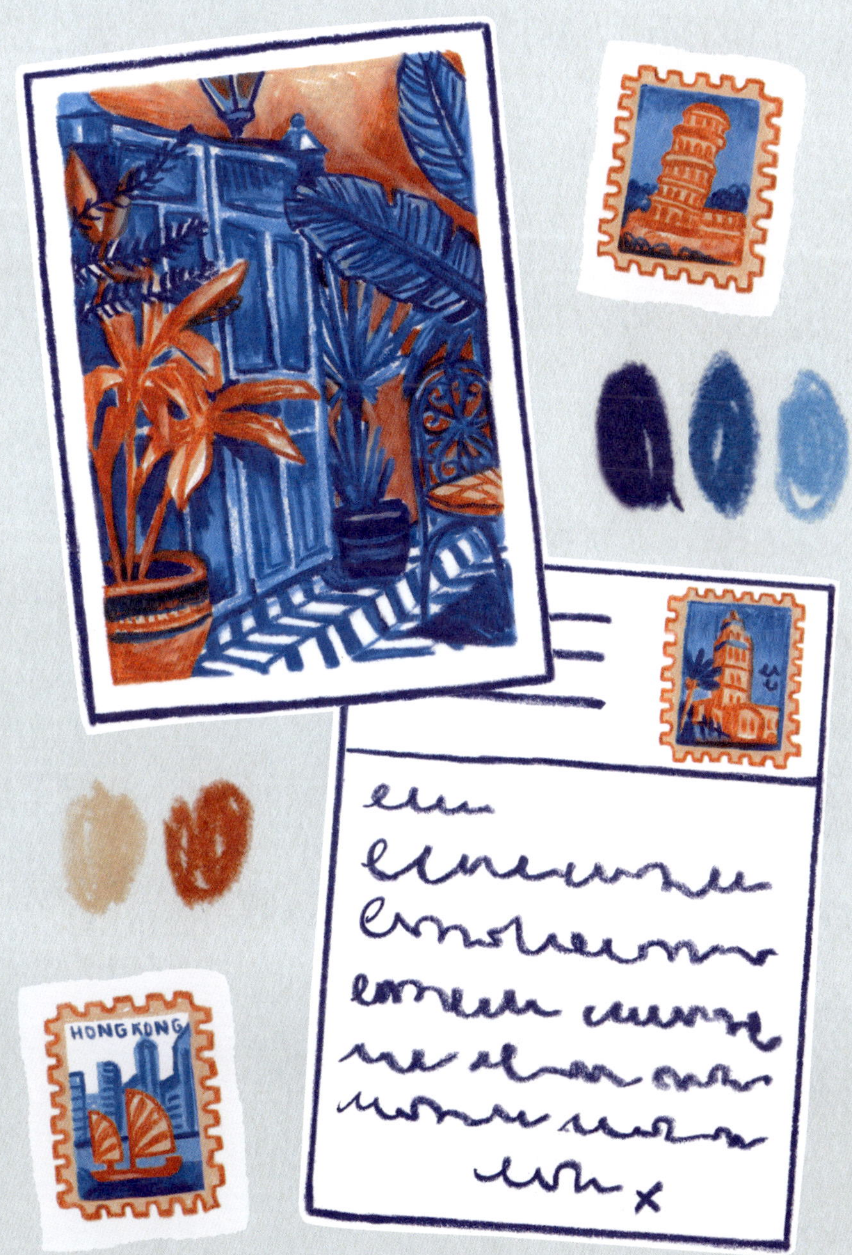
HONG KONG

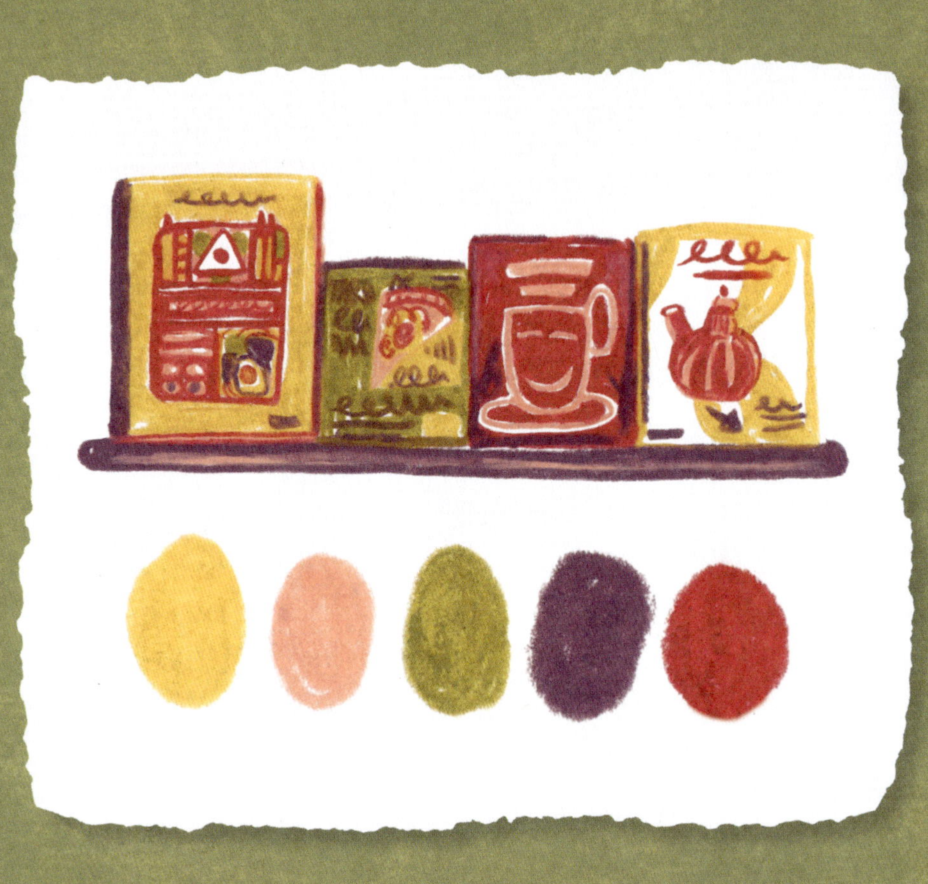

SKETCHING FROM PHOTOS, MAPS AND MAGAZINES

If you don't have any travel plans coming up, but love drawing and exploring, you can still create something beautiful.

You don't need to travel far - or at all - to find inspiring scenes to draw. Simply stepping outside and walking around your local area can provide a wealth of drawing opportunities.

Everyday settings such as your local café, bookstore or public transport can be just as rich with character as a faraway city. If you spend time drawing your local area, it encourages you to notice the beauty in the ordinary and strengthens your observational skills.

If you can't get outside, or you would like to draw a place you have never visited, there are plenty of other ways to find inspiration. Travel magazines, books, Google Maps and websites provide plenty of sources for reference images.

Do some research on a location that you are interested in or is special to you. Create a few illustrations that you believe best represent the city. Think about different parts of everyday life. What colors are prominent in that location? What is the weather like? What makes that city unique? These questions will help you decide the subject, composition and color palette.

Google Maps is a great source for images, allowing you to transport yourself to different cities without leaving your home. This makes it a perfect resource to draw places you have never visited.

Using magazine cut-outs, you could create a collaged scene, piecing together different images from the city to produce your own representation of the place.

If you are drawing from a reference photo, make sure to use the reference ethically. If you are sharing your work anywhere, include the source you used for the drawing. Or use the photo as a starting point, taking inspiration from the main aspects and then putting it into your own style.

When looking at a photo, whether online, from a book or one you have taken yourself, return to the key technique of viewing the scene in black and white. Start with a quick tonal study of the composition to identify where your colors should go. Then add the corresponding colors from your palette to the relevant tonal values in the scene.

When deciding the palette, swatch the most common colors from the reference images. Then pick two or three of these hues and add a different tonal value of two of these colors. Make sure to have a light, mid and dark tone to create depth. Remember to go back and ask yourself what you want to say with your work and use your color knowledge to pick a palette that best represents this narrative.

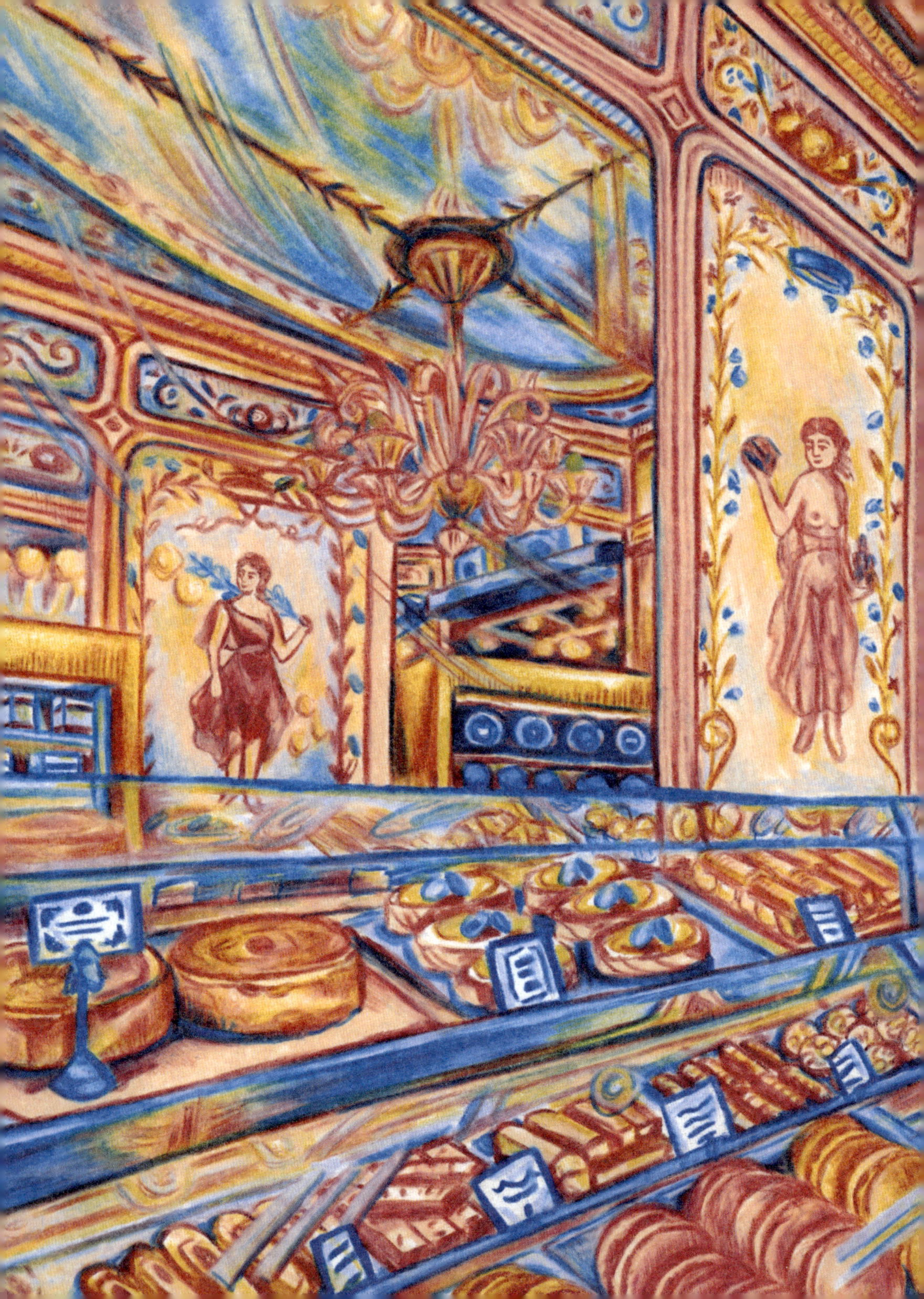

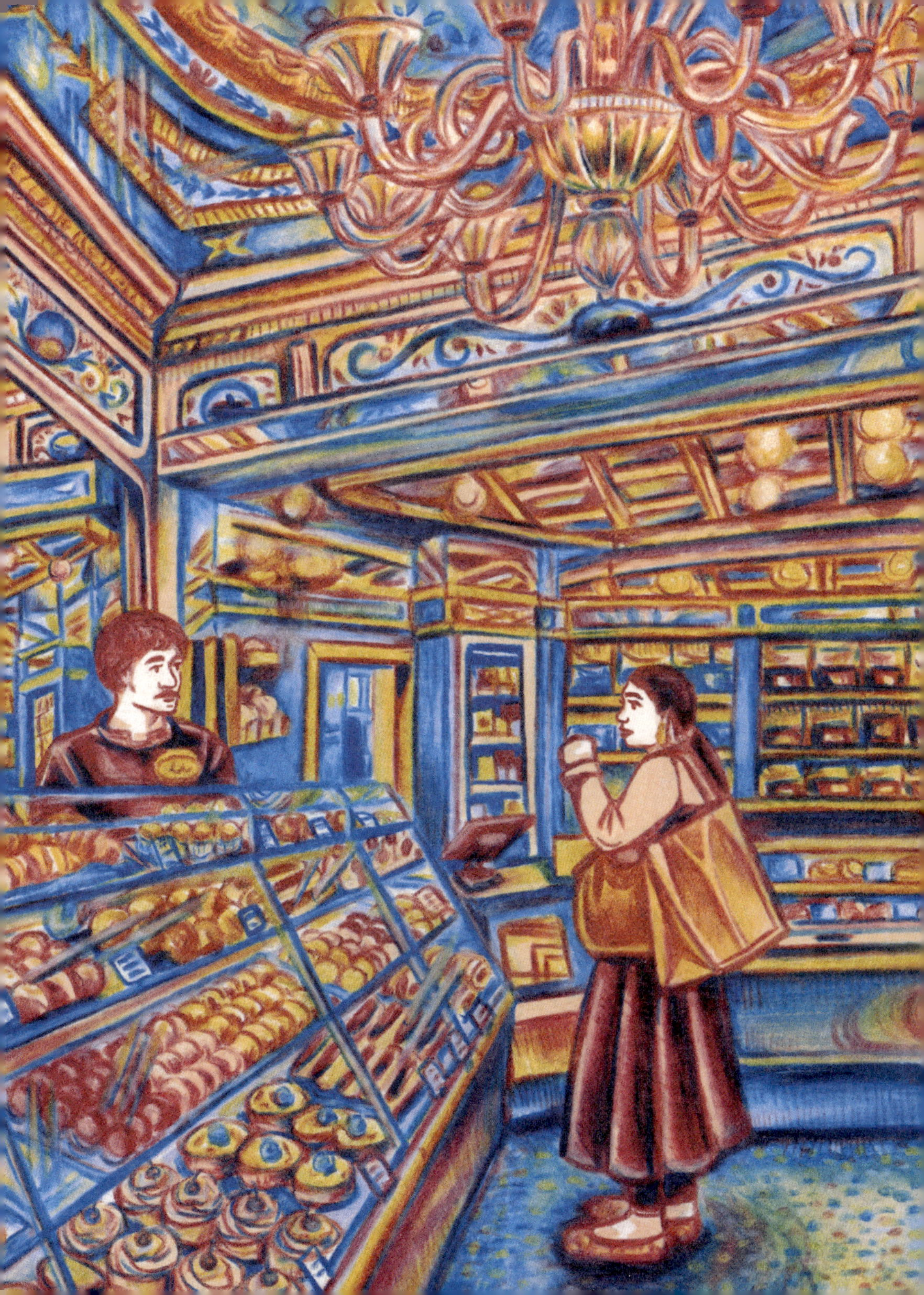

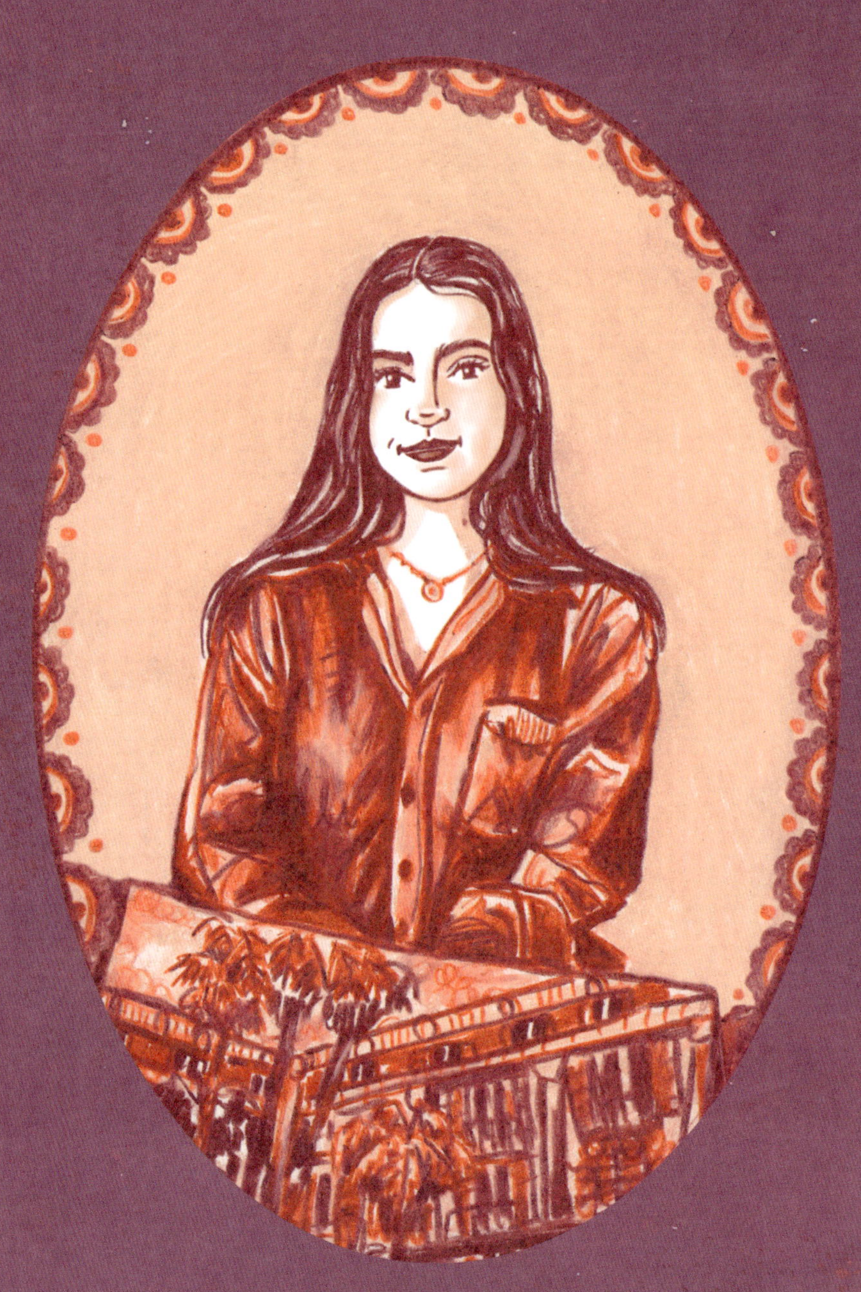

ABOUT THE AUTHOR

Hello, I'm Alice Mawdsley and I'm a traveling illustrator from the UK. My art studio is based in Hackney, London, but I spend a lot of my time living abroad. My work focuses on reportage illustration, exploring different cultures, everyday life and food. You will usually find me drawing on location, capturing real moments as they unfold – celebrating community and the similarities that connect us all.

Since graduating I have worked with charities and global clients on editorial, advertising, publishing, clothing and product illustration. The most fulfilling projects have been those involving a combination of writing, drawing, filming and interviewing. A favorite of mine was a six-month project with Syrian refugee families in Cornwall, England, sharing the stories, journeys and everyday life of the children. The illustrations enabled their voices to be heard while raising money for charity.

Most of my work is done in colored pencil on location, but when I have the opportunity, I love screen printing. I also enjoy spending my time learning new languages, doing Pilates, being in nature and trying coffee places.

ACKNOWLEDGMENTS

I would like to say a big thank you to all the special people who made this book possible. It is truly a product of my love and passion for illustration. Behind the scenes, I spent most of my time in and out of hospital. No matter where I was, this book was always the thing that kept my spark going.

I want to start by thanking the Penguin Random House team for reaching out to me with this delightful project. A huge thank you to Harriet and Issy who supported me throughout it all as well as the design team at Nic+Lou who brought the vision together.

Another thank you goes to my family who have not only enjoyed seeing the book come together but have also been there every step of the journey, cheering me on. An extra appreciation goes to my parents, for bringing me up to be a curious traveler. I am so grateful for our travels which have sparked my desire to explore and learn from others. Also, a huge thank you to Anass who has always believed in my work, stayed by my side and has watched me grow through the process.

Finally, I want to share my appreciation for all the beautiful souls I've met across my travels who inspired the content of this book. Each illustration is full of positive memories and the process has reminded me of the joy of drawing on location, how it connects us across cultures and reminds us of the beauty in everyday life. I am so grateful for all your support and I hope this book can be a source of inspiration for others to get out and be creative. I can't wait to bring more art into the world and share the power and positivity it can bring.

Quadrille, Penguin Random House UK, One Embassy Gardens, 8 Viaduct Gardens, London SW11 7BW

Quadrille Publishing Limited is part of the Penguin Random House group of companies whose addresses can be found at global.penguinrandomhouse.com

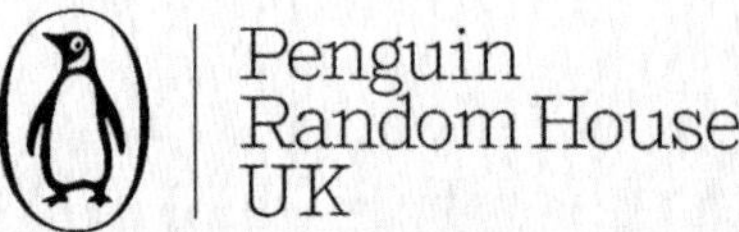

Published by Quadrille in 2026

www.penguin.co.uk

A CIP catalogue record for this book is available from the British Library

ISBN 978-1-83783-619-2
10 9 8 7 6 5 4 3 2 1

Managing Director, Publishing: Sarah Lavelle
Editorial Director: Harriet Butt
Commissioning Editor: Isabel Gonzalez-Prendergast
Assistant Editor: Harriet Thornley
Designer: Olivia Bush | Nic + Lou Studio
Production Manager: Sabeena Atchia
Production Controller: Sumayyah Waheed

Colour reproduction by F1 Colour Ltd

Printed in China by C&C Offset Printing Co., Ltd.

The authorized representative in the EEA is Penguin Random House Ireland, Morrison Chambers, 32 Nassau Street, Dublin D02 YH68

Penguin Random House is committed to a sustainable future for our business, our readers and our planet. This book is made from Forest Stewardship Council® certified paper.